SONNETS FOR MICHELANGELO

THE
OTHER VOICE
IN
EARLY MODERN
EUROPE

A Series Edited by Margaret L. King and Albert Rabil Jr.

RECENT BOOKS IN THE SERIES

Vittoria Colonna

SONNETS FOR
MICHELANGELO

A Bilingual Edition

ॐ

Edited and Translated by
Abigail Brundin

THE UNIVERSITY OF CHICAGO PRESS
Chicago & London

Vittoria Colonna, 1492–1547

Abigail Brundin is lecturer in the Italian Department, University of Cambridge, and Director of Studies in Modern Languages at St. Catharine's College.

The University of Chicago Press, Chicago 60637
The University of Chicago Press, Ltd., London
© 2005 by The University of Chicago
All rights reserved. Published 2005
Printed in the United States of America

14 13 12 11 10 09 08 07 06 05   1 2 3 4 5

ISBN: 0-226-11391-4 (cloth)
ISBN: 0-226-11392-2 (paper)

Library of Congress Cataloging-in-Publication Data

Colonna, Vittoria, 1492–1547.
[Poems. English & Italian. Selections]
Sonnets for Michelangelo : a bilingual edition / Vittoria Colonna ;
edited and translated by Abigail Brundin.
p. cm.—(The other voice in early modern Europe)
"Colonna's Sonnets for Michelangelo with English translations on facing pages."
Includes bibliographical references and index.
ISBN 0-226-11391-4 (cloth : alk. paper)—ISBN 0-226-11392-2 (pbk. : alk. paper)
1. Michelangelo Buonarroti, 1475–1564. I. Brundin, Abigail.
II. Title. III. Series.
PQ4620.A24 2005
851'.3—dc22
2004030001

CONTENTS

ACKNOWLEDGMENTS

My greatest debt of gratitude is owed to Virginia Cox, who first steered me in the direction of Colonna a number of years ago and has been a continued source of guidance and knowledge ever since. More specifically, she generously agreed to read far more than her fair share of drafts of poems, offering insights and suggestions that have added a great deal to this translation.

Warm thanks also to Letizia Panizza, who gave valuable feedback on an early draft of the introduction, to Philip Ford for reading a number of poems, and to my colleagues from the Italian Department at the University of Cambridge, who are always generous with their time and expertise. My thanks are also due to Al Rabil for expertly steering this project through to completion and for his great help in securing funding.

Thanks to John Palcewski, who sent me beautiful photographs of the Ischia altarpiece and who has generously agreed to their reproduction here.

I am grateful for funding from the National Endowment for the Humanities, which allowed me to complete this project in good time, and for the generosity of the fellowship of St. Catharine's College, Cambridge, which funded trips to the Roman archives. I would also like to thank the staff of the British Library, the Vatican Library, and the Cambridge University Library for their assistance.

Special thanks are of course owed to my family, especially Dan, Adelaide, and Saul (who arrived just in time to see this book go to press) and to Judy and Clark Brundin, to whom this volume is dedicated with love.

Abigail Brundin

NOTE ON THE TRANSLATION

The poetic texts referred to for translation in this edition are exclusively those of the Codice Vaticano Latino 11539, which in a number of cases differ, in spelling, word order, and sometimes content, from those included in Allan Bullock's 1982 complete edition of the sonnets. In all of the Italian sonnets, certain spelling anomalies have been eradicated, such as initial *h* and *t* in place of *z* (so *satia* has been changed to *sazia*, for example). Otherwise, spelling has been retained in its archaic forms. (This is not the case for Italian texts from the period derived from other sources that are quoted in the endnotes to the introduction: these have been cited as they appear in the sources given.) The punctuation of the Italian sonnets has been brought in line with modern standards and mirrors as far as possible the punctuation of the English translations, although in a few cases this did not prove possible. Accents employed in standard modern Italian have also been introduced into the Italian text of the poems throughout. Capitalization of initial letters in every line has been retained in the Italian text of the sonnets, in line with the presentation of the original manuscript and to preserve some of its flavor. The English translations, given their looser free verse structure, have not retained this format, but are simply capitalized in line with the norms of English grammar.

I have not attempted to reproduce the strict rhythmic and rhyme schemes of the original verses in translation for fear of detracting too much from their complex and often elusive meaning, so the translations are in free verse, although the fourteen-line sonnet structure has been maintained. The sonnets present a number of translation difficulties with regard to the "spare" quality of the original Italian, which in many cases needs to be expanded in English in order to clarify the sense (in particular, in instances where the endings of words in Italian offer clues to interpretation that English cannot provide). This leads in places to the necessary sacrifice of conciseness in translation in pursuit of clarity.

Allusions to reform concepts and doctrines have been clarified as far as possible in endnotes, as have references to Petrarch, Dante, and, where relevant, other likely sources. In particular, New Testament scriptural derivations have been traced wherever possible in order to point out the biblical tone of the whole work. The Douay-Rheims Version of the Catholic Bible has been consulted throughout for English translations of relevant passages. While this version is generally considered to be a less elegant English translation than the Protestant King James Bible, it is a translation directly from Saint Jerome's Latin Vulgate (declared authoritative for Catholics at the Council of Trent) and can therefore be considered to be theologically closer to Colonna's own position and beliefs. Proper names have been translated into English throughout, using what is deemed to be the most common form of the saint's name in English (for example, Mary Magdalene, Saint Francis). All translations of other works in Italian from the period are my own unless specified in the notes or bibliography.

THE OTHER VOICE IN
EARLY MODERN EUROPE:
INTRODUCTION TO THE SERIES

Margaret L. King and Albert Rabil Jr.

THE OLD VOICE AND THE OTHER VOICE

In western Europe and the United States, women are nearing equality in the professions, in business, and in politics. Most enjoy access to education, reproductive rights, and autonomy in financial affairs. Issues vital to women are on the public agenda: equal pay, child care, domestic abuse, breast cancer research, and curricular revision with an eye to the inclusion of women.

These recent achievements have their origins in things women (and some male supporters) said for the first time about six hundred years ago. Theirs is the "other voice," in contradistinction to the "first voice," the voice of the educated men who created Western culture. Coincident with a general reshaping of European culture in the period 1300–1700 (called the Renaissance or early modern period), questions of female equality and opportunity were raised that still resound and are still unresolved.

The other voice emerged against the backdrop of a three-thousand-year history of the derogation of women rooted in the civilizations related to Western culture: Hebrew, Greek, Roman, and Christian. Negative attitudes toward women inherited from these traditions pervaded the intellectual, medical, legal, religious, and social systems that developed during the European Middle Ages.

The following pages describe the traditional, overwhelmingly male views of women's nature inherited by early modern Europeans and the new tradition that the "other voice" called into being to begin to challenge reigning assumptions. This review should serve as a framework for understanding the texts published in the series the Other Voice in Early Modern Europe. Introductions specific to each text and author follow this essay in all the volumes of the series.

TRADITIONAL VIEWS OF WOMEN, 500 B.C.E.–1500 C.E.

Embedded in the philosophical and medical theories of the ancient Greeks were perceptions of the female as inferior to the male in both mind and body. Similarly, the structure of civil legislation inherited from the ancient Romans was biased against women, and the views on women developed by Christian thinkers out of the Hebrew Bible and the Christian New Testament were negative and disabling. Literary works composed in the vernacular of ordinary people, and widely recited or read, conveyed these negative assumptions. The social networks within which most women lived—those of the family and the institutions of the Roman Catholic Church—were shaped by this negative tradition and sharply limited the areas in which women might act in and upon the world.

GREEK PHILOSOPHY AND FEMALE NATURE. Greek biology assumed that women were inferior to men and defined them as merely childbearers and housekeepers. This view was authoritatively expressed in the works of the philosopher Aristotle.

Aristotle thought in dualities. He considered action superior to inaction, form (the inner design or structure of any object) superior to matter, completion to incompletion, possession to deprivation. In each of these dualities, he associated the male principle with the superior quality and the female with the inferior. "The male principle in nature," he argued, "is associated with active, formative and perfected characteristics, while the female is passive, material and deprived, desiring the male in order to become complete."[1] Men are always identified with virile qualities, such as judgment, courage, and stamina, and women with their opposites—irrationality, cowardice, and weakness.

The masculine principle was considered superior even in the womb. The man's semen, Aristotle believed, created the form of a new human creature, while the female body contributed only matter. (The existence of the ovum, and with it the other facts of human embryology, was not established until the seventeenth century.) Although the later Greek physician Galen believed there was a female component in generation, contributed by "female semen," the followers of both Aristotle and Galen saw the male role in human generation as more active and more important.

---

1. Aristotle, *Physics* 1.9.192a20–24, in *The Complete Works of Aristotle*, ed. Jonathan Barnes, rev. Oxford trans., 2 vols. (Princeton, 1984), 1:328.

In the Aristotelian view, the male principle sought always to reproduce itself. The creation of a female was always a mistake, therefore, resulting from an imperfect act of generation. Every female born was considered a "defective" or "mutilated" male (as Aristotle's terminology has variously been translated), a "monstrosity" of nature.[2]

For Greek theorists, the biology of males and females was the key to their psychology. The female was softer and more docile, more apt to be despondent, querulous, and deceitful. Being incomplete, moreover, she craved sexual fulfillment in intercourse with a male. The male was intellectual, active, and in control of his passions.

These psychological polarities derived from the theory that the universe consisted of four elements (earth, fire, air, and water), expressed in human bodies as four "humors" (black bile, yellow bile, blood, and phlegm) considered, respectively, dry, hot, damp, and cold and corresponding to mental states ("melancholic," "choleric," "sanguine," "phlegmatic"). In this scheme the male, sharing the principles of earth and fire, was dry and hot; the female, sharing the principles of air and water, was cold and damp.

Female psychology was further affected by her dominant organ, the uterus (womb), *hystera* in Greek. The passions generated by the womb made women lustful, deceitful, talkative, irrational, indeed—when these affects were in excess—"hysterical."

Aristotle's biology also had social and political consequences. If the male principle was superior and the female inferior, then in the household, as in the state, men should rule and women must be subordinate. That hierarchy did not rule out the companionship of husband and wife, whose cooperation was necessary for the welfare of children and the preservation of property. Such mutuality supported male preeminence.

Aristotle's teacher Plato suggested a different possibility: that men and women might possess the same virtues. The setting for this proposal is the imaginary and ideal Republic that Plato sketches in a dialogue of that name. Here, for a privileged elite capable of leading wisely, all distinctions of class and wealth dissolve, as, consequently, do those of gender. Without households or property, as Plato constructs his ideal society, there is no need for the subordination of women. Women may therefore be educated to the same level as men to assume leadership. Plato's Republic remained imaginary, however. In real societies, the subordination of women remained the norm and the prescription.

---

2. Aristotle, *Generation of Animals* 2.3.737a27–28, in *The Complete Works*, 1:1144.

The views of women inherited from the Greek philosophical tradition became the basis for medieval thought. In the thirteenth century, the supreme Scholastic philosopher Thomas Aquinas, among others, still echoed Aristotle's views of human reproduction, of male and female personalities, and of the preeminent male role in the social hierarchy.

ROMAN LAW AND THE FEMALE CONDITION. Roman law, like Greek philosophy, underlay medieval thought and shaped medieval society. The ancient belief that adult property-owning men should administer households and make decisions affecting the community at large is the very fulcrum of Roman law.

About 450 B.C.E., during Rome's republican era, the community's customary law was recorded (legendarily) on twelve tablets erected in the city's central forum. It was later elaborated by professional jurists whose activity increased in the imperial era, when much new legislation was passed, especially on issues affecting family and inheritance. This growing, changing body of laws was eventually codified in the *Corpus of Civil Law* under the direction of the emperor Justinian, generations after the empire ceased to be ruled from Rome. That *Corpus*, read and commented on by medieval scholars from the eleventh century on, inspired the legal systems of most of the cities and kingdoms of Europe.

Laws regarding dowries, divorce, and inheritance pertain primarily to women. Since those laws aimed to maintain and preserve property, the women concerned were those from the property-owning minority. Their subordination to male family members points to the even greater subordination of lower-class and slave women, about whom the laws speak little.

In the early republic, the *paterfamilias*, or "father of the family," possessed *patria potestas*, "paternal power." The term *pater*, "father," in both these cases does not necessarily mean biological father but denotes the head of a household. The father was the person who owned the household's property and, indeed, its human members. The *paterfamilias* had absolute power—including the power, rarely exercised, of life or death—over his wife, his children, and his slaves, as much as his cattle.

Male children could be "emancipated," an act that granted legal autonomy and the right to own property. Those over fourteen could be emancipated by a special grant from the father or automatically by their father's death. But females could never be emancipated; instead, they passed from the authority of their father to that of a husband or, if widowed or orphaned while still unmarried, to a guardian or tutor.

Marriage in its traditional form placed the woman under her husband's authority, or *manus*. He could divorce her on grounds of adultery, drinking wine, or stealing from the household, but she could not divorce him. She could neither possess property in her own right nor bequeath any to her children upon her death. When her husband died, the household property passed not to her but to his male heirs. And when her father died, she had no claim to any family inheritance, which was directed to her brothers or more remote male relatives. The effect of these laws was to exclude women from civil society, itself based on property ownership.

In the later republican and imperial periods, these rules were significantly modified. Women rarely married according to the traditional form. The practice of "free" marriage allowed a woman to remain under her father's authority, to possess property given her by her father (most frequently the "dowry," recoverable from the husband's household on his death), and to inherit from her father. She could also bequeath property to her own children and divorce her husband, just as he could divorce her.

Despite this greater freedom, women still suffered enormous disability under Roman law. Heirs could belong only to the father's side, never the mother's. Moreover, although she could bequeath her property to her children, she could not establish a line of succession in doing so. A woman was "the beginning and end of her own family," said the jurist Ulpian. Moreover, women could play no public role. They could not hold public office, represent anyone in a legal case, or even witness a will. Women had only a private existence and no public personality.

The dowry system, the guardian, women's limited ability to transmit wealth, and total political disability are all features of Roman law adopted by the medieval communities of western Europe, although modified according to local customary laws.

CHRISTIAN DOCTRINE AND WOMEN'S PLACE. The Hebrew Bible and the Christian New Testament authorized later writers to limit women to the realm of the family and to burden them with the guilt of original sin. The passages most fruitful for this purpose were the creation narratives in Genesis and sentences from the Epistles defining women's role within the Christian family and community.

Each of the first two chapters of Genesis contains a creation narrative. In the first "God created man in his own image, in the image of God he created him; male and female he created them" (Gn 1:27). In the second, God created Eve from Adam's rib (2:21–23). Christian theologians relied principally on Genesis 2 for their understanding of the relation between man and woman, interpreting the creation of Eve from Adam as proof of her subordination to him.

The creation story in Genesis 2 leads to that of the temptations in Genesis 3: of Eve by the wily serpent and of Adam by Eve. As read by Christian theologians from Tertullian to Thomas Aquinas, the narrative made Eve responsible for the Fall and its consequences. She instigated the act; she deceived her husband; she suffered the greater punishment. Her disobedience made it necessary for Jesus to be incarnated and to die on the cross. From the pulpit, moralists and preachers for centuries conveyed to women the guilt that they bore for original sin.

The Epistles offered advice to early Christians on building communities of the faithful. Among the matters to be regulated was the place of women. Paul offered views favorable to women in Galatians 3:28: "There is neither Jew nor Greek, there is neither slave nor free, there is neither male nor female; for you are all one in Christ Jesus." Paul also referred to women as his coworkers and placed them on a par with himself and his male coworkers (Phlm 4:2–3; Rom 16:1–3; 1 Cor 16:19). Elsewhere, Paul limited women's possibilities: "But I want you to understand that the head of every man is Christ, the head of a woman is her husband, and the head of Christ is God" (1 Cor 11:3).

Biblical passages by later writers (although attributed to Paul) enjoined women to forgo jewels, expensive clothes, and elaborate coiffures; and they forbade women to "teach or have authority over men," telling them to "learn in silence with all submissiveness" as is proper for one responsible for sin, consoling them, however, with the thought that they will be saved through childbearing (1 Tm 2:9–15). Other texts among the later Epistles defined women as the weaker sex and emphasized their subordination to their husbands (1 Pt 3:7; Col 3:18; Eph 5:22–23).

These passages from the New Testament became the arsenal employed by theologians of the early church to transmit negative attitudes toward women to medieval Christian culture—above all, Tertullian (*On the Apparel of Women*), Jerome (*Against Jovinian*), and Augustine (*The Literal Meaning of Genesis*).

THE IMAGE OF WOMEN IN MEDIEVAL LITERATURE. The philosophical, legal, and religious traditions born in antiquity formed the basis of the medieval intellectual synthesis wrought by trained thinkers, mostly clerics, writing in Latin and based largely in universities. The vernacular literary tradition that developed alongside the learned tradition also spoke about female nature and women's roles. Medieval stories, poems, and epics also portrayed women negatively—as lustful and deceitful—while praising good house-keepers and loyal wives as replicas of the Virgin Mary or the female saints and martyrs.

There is an exception in the movement of "courtly love" that evolved in southern France from the twelfth century. Courtly love was the erotic love between a nobleman and noblewoman, the latter usually superior in social rank. It was always adulterous. From the conventions of courtly love derive modern Western notions of romantic love. The tradition has had an impact disproportionate to its size, for it affected only a tiny elite, and very few women. The exaltation of the female lover probably does not reflect a higher evaluation of women or a step toward their sexual liberation. More likely it gives expression to the social and sexual tensions besetting the knightly class at a specific historical juncture.

The literary fashion of courtly love was on the wane by the thirteenth century, when the widely read *Romance of the Rose* was composed in French by two authors of significantly different dispositions. Guillaume de Lorris composed the initial four thousand verses about 1235, and Jean de Meun added about seventeen thousand verses—more than four times the original—about 1265.

The fragment composed by Guillaume de Lorris stands squarely in the tradition of courtly love. Here the poet, in a dream, is admitted into a walled garden where he finds a magic fountain in which a rosebush is reflected. He longs to pick one rose, but the thorns prevent his doing so, even as he is wounded by arrows from the god of love, whose commands he agrees to obey. The rest of this part of the poem recounts the poet's unsuccessful efforts to pluck the rose.

The longer part of the *Romance* by Jean de Meun also describes a dream. But here allegorical characters give long didactic speeches, providing a social satire on a variety of themes, some pertaining to women. Love is an anxious and tormented state, the poem explains: women are greedy and manipulative, marriage is miserable, beautiful women are lustful, ugly ones cease to please, and a chaste woman is as rare as a black swan.

Shortly after Jean de Meun completed *The Romance of the Rose*, Mathéolus penned his *Lamentations*, a long Latin diatribe against marriage translated into French about a century later. The *Lamentations* sum up medieval attitudes toward women and provoked the important response by Christine de Pizan in her *Book of the City of Ladies*.

In 1355, Giovanni Boccaccio wrote *Il Corbaccio*, another antifeminist manifesto, although ironically by an author whose other works pioneered new directions in Renaissance thought. The former husband of his lover appears to Boccaccio, condemning his unmoderated lust and detailing the defects of women. Boccaccio concedes at the end "how much men naturally surpass women in nobility" and is cured of his desires.[3]

WOMEN'S ROLES: THE FAMILY. The negative perceptions of women expressed in the intellectual tradition are also implicit in the actual roles that women played in European society. Assigned to subordinate positions in the household and the church, they were barred from significant participation in public life.

Medieval European households, like those in antiquity and in non-Western civilizations, were headed by males. It was the male serf (or peasant), feudal lord, town merchant, or citizen who was polled or taxed or succeeded to an inheritance or had any acknowledged public role, although his wife or widow could stand as a temporary surrogate. From about 1100, the position of property-holding males was further enhanced: inheritance was confined to the male, or agnate, line—with depressing consequences for women.

A wife never fully belonged to her husband's family, nor was she a daughter to her father's family. She left her father's house young to marry whomever her parents chose. Her dowry was managed by her husband, and at her death it normally passed to her children by him.

A married woman's life was occupied nearly constantly with cycles of pregnancy, childbearing, and lactation. Women bore children through all the years of their fertility, and many died in childbirth. They were also responsible for raising young children up to six or seven. In the propertied classes that responsibility was shared, since it was common for a wet nurse to take over breast-feeding and for servants to perform other chores.

Women trained their daughters in the household duties appropriate to their status, nearly always tasks associated with textiles: spinning, weaving, sewing, embroidering. Their sons were sent out of the house as apprentices or students, or their training was assumed by fathers in later childhood and adolescence. On the death of her husband, a woman's children became the responsibility of his family. She generally did not take "his" children with her to a new marriage or back to her father's house, except sometimes in the artisan classes.

Women also worked. Rural peasants performed farm chores, merchant wives often practiced their husbands' trades, the unmarried daughters of the

---

3. Giovanni Boccaccio, *The Corbaccio, or The Labyrinth of Love*, trans. and ed. Anthony K. Cassell, rev. ed. (Binghamton, NY, 1993), 71.

urban poor worked as servants or prostitutes. All wives produced or embellished textiles and did the housekeeping, while wealthy ones managed servants. These labors were unpaid or poorly paid but often contributed substantially to family wealth.

WOMEN'S ROLES: THE CHURCH. Membership in a household, whether a father's or a husband's, meant for women a lifelong subordination to others. In western Europe, the Roman Catholic Church offered an alternative to the career of wife and mother. A woman could enter a convent, parallel in function to the monasteries for men that evolved in the early Christian centuries.

In the convent, a woman pledged herself to a celibate life, lived according to strict community rules, and worshiped daily. Often the convent offered training in Latin, allowing some women to become considerable scholars and authors as well as scribes, artists, and musicians. For women who chose the conventual life, the benefits could be enormous, but for numerous others placed in convents by paternal choice, the life could be restrictive and burdensome.

The conventual life declined as an alternative for women as the modern age approached. Reformed monastic institutions resisted responsibility for related female orders. The church increasingly restricted female institutional life by insisting on closer male supervision.

Women often sought other options. Some joined the communities of laywomen that sprang up spontaneously in the thirteenth century in the urban zones of western Europe, especially in Flanders and Italy. Some joined the heretical movements that flourished in late medieval Christendom, whose anticlerical and often antifamily positions particularly appealed to women. In these communities, some women were acclaimed as "holy women" or "saints," whereas others often were condemned as frauds or heretics.

In all, although the options offered to women by the church were sometimes less than satisfactory, they were sometimes richly rewarding. After 1520, the convent remained an option only in Roman Catholic territories. Protestantism engendered an ideal of marriage as a heroic endeavor and appeared to place husband and wife on a more equal footing. Sermons and treatises, however, still called for female subordination and obedience.

THE OTHER VOICE, 1300–1700

When the modern era opened, European culture was so firmly structured by a framework of negative attitudes toward women that to dismantle it was a monumental labor. The process began as part of a larger cultural movement that entailed the critical reexamination of ideas inherited from the ancient and medieval past. The humanists launched that critical reexamination.

THE HUMANIST FOUNDATION. Originating in Italy in the fourteenth century, humanism quickly became the dominant intellectual movement in Europe. Spreading in the sixteenth century from Italy to the rest of Europe, it fueled the literary, scientific, and philosophical movements of the era and laid the basis for the eighteenth-century Enlightenment.

Humanists regarded the Scholastic philosophy of medieval universities as out of touch with the realities of urban life. They found in the rhetorical discourse of classical Rome a language adapted to civic life and public speech. They learned to read, speak, and write classical Latin and, eventually, classical Greek. They founded schools to teach others to do so, establishing the pattern for elementary and secondary education for the next three hundred years.

In the service of complex government bureaucracies, humanists employed their skills to write eloquent letters, deliver public orations, and formulate public policy. They developed new scripts for copying manuscripts and used the new printing press to disseminate texts, for which they created methods of critical editing.

Humanism was a movement led by males who accepted the evaluation of women in ancient texts and generally shared the misogynist perceptions of their culture. (Female humanists, as we will see, did not.) Yet humanism also opened the door to a reevaluation of the nature and capacity of women. By calling authors, texts, and ideas into question, it made possible the fundamental rereading of the whole intellectual tradition that was required in order to free women from cultural prejudice and social subordination.

A DIFFERENT CITY. The other voice first appeared when, after so many centuries, the accumulation of misogynist concepts evoked a response from a capable female defender: Christine de Pizan (1365–1431). Introducing her *Book of the City of Ladies* (1405), she described how she was affected by reading Mathéolus's *Lamentations:* "Just the sight of this book . . . made me wonder how it happened that so many different men . . . are so inclined to express both in speaking and in their treatises and writings so many wicked insults about women and their behavior."[4] These statements impelled her to

4. Christine de Pizan, *The Book of the City of Ladies*, trans. Earl Jeffrey Richards, foreword by Marina Warner (New York, 1982), 1.1.1, pp. 3–4.

detest herself "and the entire feminine sex, as though we were monstrosities in nature." [5]

The rest of *The Book of the City of Ladies* presents a justification of the female sex and a vision of an ideal community of women. A pioneer, she has received the message of female inferiority and rejected it. From the fourteenth to the seventeenth century, a huge body of literature accumulated that responded to the dominant tradition.

The result was a literary explosion consisting of works by both men and women, in Latin and in the vernaculars: works enumerating the achievements of notable women; works rebutting the main accusations made against women; works arguing for the equal education of men and women; works defining and redefining women's proper role in the family, at court, in public; works describing women's lives and experiences. Recent monographs and articles have begun to hint at the great range of this movement, involving probably several thousand titles. The protofeminism of these "other voices" constitutes a significant fraction of the literary product of the early modern era.

THE CATALOGS. About 1365, the same Boccaccio whose *Corbaccio* rehearses the usual charges against female nature wrote another work, *Concerning Famous Women*. A humanist treatise drawing on classical texts, it praised 106 notable women: ninety-eight of them from pagan Greek and Roman antiquity, one (Eve) from the Bible, and seven from the medieval religious and cultural tradition; his book helped make all readers aware of a sex normally condemned or forgotten. Boccaccio's outlook nevertheless was unfriendly to women, for it singled out for praise those women who possessed the traditional virtues of chastity, silence, and obedience. Women who were active in the public realm—for example, rulers and warriors—were depicted as usually being lascivious and as suffering terrible punishments for entering the masculine sphere. Women were his subject, but Boccaccio's standard remained male.

Christine de Pizan's *Book of the City of Ladies* contains a second catalog, one responding specifically to Boccaccio's. Whereas Boccaccio portrays female virtue as exceptional, she depicts it as universal. Many women in history were leaders, or remained chaste despite the lascivious approaches of men, or were visionaries and brave martyrs.

The work of Boccaccio inspired a series of catalogs of illustrious women of the biblical, classical, Christian, and local pasts, among them Filippo da

---

5. Ibid., 1.1.1–2, p. 5.

Bergamo's *Of Illustrious Women,* Pierre de Brantôme's *Lives of Illustrious Women,* Pierre Le Moyne's *Gallerie of Heroic Women,* and Pietro Paolo de Ribera's *Immortal Triumphs and Heroic Enterprises of 845 Women.* Whatever their embedded prejudices, these works drove home to the public the possibility of female excellence.

THE DEBATE. At the same time, many questions remained: Could a woman be virtuous? Could she perform noteworthy deeds? Was she even, strictly speaking, of the same human species as men? These questions were debated over four centuries, in French, German, Italian, Spanish, and English, by authors male and female, among Catholics, Protestants, and Jews, in ponderous volumes and breezy pamphlets. The whole literary genre has been called the *querelle des femmes,* the "woman question."

The opening volley of this battle occurred in the first years of the fifteenth century, in a literary debate sparked by Christine de Pizan. She exchanged letters critical of Jean de Meun's contribution to *The Romance of the Rose* with two French royal secretaries, Jean de Montreuil and Gontier Col. When the matter became public, Jean Gerson, one of Europe's leading theologians, supported de Pizan's arguments against de Meun, for the moment silencing the opposition.

The debate resurfaced repeatedly over the next two hundred years. *The Triumph of Women* (1438) by Juan Rodríguez de la Camara (or Juan Rodríguez del Padron) struck a new note by presenting arguments for the superiority of women to men. *The Champion of Women* (1440–42) by Martin Le Franc addresses once again the negative views of women presented in *The Romance of the Rose* and offers counterevidence of female virtue and achievement.

A cameo of the debate on women is included in *The Courtier,* one of the most widely read books of the era, published by the Italian Baldassare Castiglione in 1528 and immediately translated into other European vernaculars. *The Courtier* depicts a series of evenings at the court of the duke of Urbino in which many men and some women of the highest social stratum amuse themselves by discussing a range of literary and social issues. The "woman question" is a pervasive theme throughout, and the third of its four books is devoted entirely to that issue.

In a verbal duel, Gasparo Pallavicino and Giuliano de' Medici present the main claims of the two traditions. Gasparo argues the innate inferiority of women and their inclination to vice. Only in bearing children do they profit the world. Giuliano counters that women share the same spiritual and mental capacities as men and may excel in wisdom and action. Men and women are of the same essence: just as no stone can be more perfectly a stone than another, so no human being can be more perfectly human than others, whether male or female. It was an astonishing assertion, boldly made to an audience as large as all Europe.

THE TREATISES. Humanism provided the materials for a positive counterconcept to the misogyny embedded in Scholastic philosophy and law and inherited from the Greek, Roman, and Christian pasts. A series of humanist treatises on marriage and family, on education and deportment, and on the nature of women helped construct these new perspectives.

The works by Francesco Barbaro and Leon Battista Alberti—*On Marriage* (1415) and *On the Family* (1434–37)—far from defending female equality, reasserted women's responsibility for rearing children and managing the housekeeping while being obedient, chaste, and silent. Nevertheless, they served the cause of reexamining the issue of women's nature by placing domestic issues at the center of scholarly concern and reopening the pertinent classical texts. In addition, Barbaro emphasized the companionate nature of marriage and the importance of a wife's spiritual and mental qualities for the well-being of the family.

These themes reappear in later humanist works on marriage and the education of women by Juan Luis Vives and Erasmus. Both were moderately sympathetic to the condition of women without reaching beyond the usual masculine prescriptions for female behavior.

An outlook more favorable to women characterizes the nearly unknown work *In Praise of Women* (ca. 1487) by the Italian humanist Bartolommeo Goggio. In addition to providing a catalog of illustrious women, Goggio argued that male and female are the same in essence, but that women (reworking the Adam and Eve narrative from quite a new angle) are actually superior. In the same vein, the Italian humanist Mario Equicola asserted the spiritual equality of men and women in *On Women* (1501). In 1525, Galeazzo Flavio Capra (or Capella) published his work *On the Excellence and Dignity of Women*. This humanist tradition of treatises defending the worthiness of women culminates in the work of Henricus Cornelius Agrippa *On the Nobility and Preeminence of the Female Sex*. No work by a male humanist more succinctly or explicitly presents the case for female dignity.

THE WITCH BOOKS. While humanists grappled with the issues pertaining to women and family, other learned men turned their attention to what they perceived as a very great problem: witches. Witch-hunting manuals, explorations of the witch phenomenon, and even defenses of witches are not at first glance pertinent to the tradition of the other voice. But they do relate in this way: most accused witches were women. The hostility aroused by supposed witch activity is comparable to the hostility aroused by women. The evil deeds the victims of the hunt were charged with were exaggerations of the vices to which, many believed, all women were prone.

The connection between the witch accusation and the hatred of women is explicit in the notorious witch-hunting manual *The Hammer of Witches* (1486) by two Dominican inquisitors, Heinrich Krämer and Jacob Sprenger. Here the inconstancy, deceitfulness, and lustfulness traditionally associated with women are depicted in exaggerated form as the core features of witch behavior. These traits inclined women to make a bargain with the devil—sealed by sexual intercourse—by which they acquired unholy powers. Such bizarre claims, far from being rejected by rational men, were broadcast by intellectuals. The German Ulrich Molitur, the Frenchman Nicolas Rémy, and the Italian Stefano Guazzo all coolly informed the public of sinister orgies and midnight pacts with the devil. The celebrated French jurist, historian, and political philosopher Jean Bodin argued that because women were especially prone to diabolism, regular legal procedures could properly be suspended in order to try those accused of this "exceptional crime."

A few experts such as the physician Johann Weyer, a student of Agrippa's, raised their voices in protest. In 1563, he explained the witch phenomenon thus, without discarding belief in diabolism: the devil deluded foolish old women afflicted by melancholia, causing them to believe they had magical powers. Weyer's rational skepticism, which had good credibility in the community of the learned, worked to revise the conventional views of women and witchcraft.

WOMEN'S WORKS. To the many categories of works produced on the question of women's worth must be added nearly all works written by women. A woman writing was in herself a statement of women's claim to dignity.

Only a few women wrote anything before the dawn of the modern era, for three reasons. First, they rarely received the education that would enable them to write. Second, they were not admitted to the public roles—as administrator, bureaucrat, lawyer or notary, or university professor—in which they might gain knowledge of the kinds of things the literate public thought worth writing about. Third, the culture imposed silence on women, considering speaking out a form of unchastity. Given these conditions, it is remarkable that any women wrote. Those who did before the fourteenth century were almost always nuns or religious women whose isolation made their pronouncements more acceptable.

From the fourteenth century on, the volume of women's writings rose. Women continued to write devotional literature, although not always as cloistered nuns. They also wrote diaries, often intended as keepsakes for their children; books of advice to their sons and daughters; letters to family members and friends; and family memoirs, in a few cases elaborate enough to be considered histories.

A few women wrote works directly concerning the "woman question," and some of these, such as the humanists Isotta Nogarola, Cassandra Fedele, Laura Cereta, and Olympia Morata, were highly trained. A few were professional writers, living by the income of their pens; the very first among them was Christine de Pizan, noteworthy in this context as in so many others. In addition to *The Book of the City of Ladies* and her critiques of *The Romance of the Rose*, she wrote *The Treasure of the City of Ladies* (a guide to social decorum for women), an advice book for her son, much courtly verse, and a full-scale history of the reign of King Charles V of France.

WOMEN PATRONS. Women who did not themselves write but encouraged others to do so boosted the development of an alternative tradition. Highly placed women patrons supported authors, artists, musicians, poets, and learned men. Such patrons, drawn mostly from the Italian elites and the courts of northern Europe, figure disproportionately as the dedicatees of the important works of early feminism.

For a start, it might be noted that the catalogs of Boccaccio and Alvaro de Luna were dedicated to the Florentine noblewoman Andrea Acciaiuoli and to Doña María, first wife of King Juan II of Castile, while the French translation of Boccaccio's work was commissioned by Anne of Brittany, wife of King Charles VIII of France. The humanist treatises of Goggio, Equicola, Vives, and Agrippa were dedicated, respectively, to Eleanora of Aragon, wife of Ercole I d'Este, Duke of Ferrara; to Margherita Cantelma of Mantua; to Catherine of Aragon, wife of King Henry VIII of England; and to Margaret, Duchess of Austria and regent of the Netherlands. As late as 1696, Mary Astell's *Serious Proposal to the Ladies, for the Advancement of Their True and Greatest Interest* was dedicated to Princess Anne of Denmark.

These authors presumed that their efforts would be welcome to female patrons, or they may have written at the bidding of those patrons. Silent themselves, perhaps even unresponsive, these loftily placed women helped shape the tradition of the other voice.

THE ISSUES. The literary forms and patterns in which the tradition of the other voice presented itself have now been sketched. It remains to highlight the major issues around which this tradition crystallizes. In brief, there are four problems to which our authors return again and again, in plays and catalogs, in verse and letters, in treatises and dialogues, in every language:

the problem of chastity, the problem of power, the problem of speech, and the problem of knowledge. Of these the greatest, preconditioning the others, is the problem of chastity.

THE PROBLEM OF CHASTITY. In traditional European culture, as in those of antiquity and others around the globe, chastity was perceived as woman's quintessential virtue—in contrast to courage, or generosity, or leadership, or rationality, seen as virtues characteristic of men. Opponents of women charged them with insatiable lust. Women themselves and their defenders —without disputing the validity of the standard—responded that women were capable of chastity.

The requirement of chastity kept women at home, silenced them, isolated them, left them in ignorance. It was the source of all other impediments. Why was it so important to the society of men, of whom chastity was not required, and who more often than not considered it their right to violate the chastity of any woman they encountered?

Female chastity ensured the continuity of the male-headed household. If a man's wife was not chaste, he could not be sure of the legitimacy of his offspring. If they were not his and they acquired his property, it was not his household, but some other man's, that had endured. If his daughter was not chaste, she could not be transferred to another man's household as his wife, and he was dishonored.

The whole system of the integrity of the household and the transmission of property was bound up in female chastity. Such a requirement pertained only to property-owning classes, of course. Poor women could not expect to maintain their chastity, least of all if they were in contact with high-status men to whom all women but those of their own household were prey.

In Catholic Europe, the requirement of chastity was further buttressed by moral and religious imperatives. Original sin was inextricably linked with the sexual act. Virginity was seen as heroic virtue, far more impressive than, say, the avoidance of idleness or greed. Monasticism, the cultural institution that dominated medieval Europe for centuries, was grounded in the renunciation of the flesh. The Catholic reform of the eleventh century imposed a similar standard on all the clergy and a heightened awareness of sexual requirements on all the laity. Although men were asked to be chaste, female unchastity was much worse: it led to the devil, as Eve had led mankind to sin.

To such requirements, women and their defenders protested their innocence. Furthermore, following the example of holy women who had escaped the requirements of family and sought the religious life, some women began to conceive of female communities as alternatives both to family and to the cloister. Christine de Pizan's city of ladies was such a community. Moderata

Fonte and Mary Astell envisioned others. The luxurious salons of the French *précieuses* of the seventeenth century, or the comfortable English drawing rooms of the next, may have been born of the same impulse. Here women not only might escape, if briefly, the subordinate position that life in the family entailed but might also make claims to power, exercise their capacity for speech, and display their knowledge.

THE PROBLEM OF POWER. Women were excluded from power: the whole cultural tradition insisted on it. Only men were citizens, only men bore arms, only men could be chiefs or lords or kings. There were exceptions that did not disprove the rule, when wives or widows or mothers took the place of men, awaiting their return or the maturation of a male heir. A woman who attempted to rule in her own right was perceived as an anomaly, a monster, at once a deformed woman and an insufficient male, sexually confused and consequently unsafe.

The association of such images with women who held or sought power explains some otherwise odd features of early modern culture. Queen Elizabeth I of England, one of the few women to hold full regal authority in European history, played with such male/female images—positive ones, of course—in representing herself to her subjects. She was a prince, and manly, even though she was female. She was also (she claimed) virginal, a condition absolutely essential if she was to avoid the attacks of her opponents. Catherine de' Medici, who ruled France as widow and regent for her sons, also adopted such imagery in defining her position. She chose as one symbol the figure of Artemisia, an androgynous ancient warrior-heroine who combined a female persona with masculine powers.

Power in a woman, without such sexual imagery, seems to have been indigestible by the culture. A rare note was struck by the Englishman Sir Thomas Elyot in his *Defence of Good Women* (1540), justifying both women's participation in civic life and their prowess in arms. The old tune was sung by the Scots reformer John Knox in his *First Blast of the Trumpet against the Monstrous Regiment of Women* (1558); for him rule by women, defects in nature, was a hideous contradiction in terms.

The confused sexuality of the imagery of female potency was not reserved for rulers. Any woman who excelled was likely to be called an Amazon, recalling the self-mutilated warrior women of antiquity who repudiated all men, gave up their sons, and raised only their daughters. She was often said to have "exceeded her sex" or to have possessed "masculine virtue"— as the very fact of conspicuous excellence conferred masculinity even on the female subject. The catalogs of notable women often showed those female heroes dressed in armor, armed to the teeth, like men. Amazonian heroines romp through the epics of the age—Ariosto's *Orlando Furioso* (1532) and Spenser's *Faerie Queene* (1590–1609). Excellence in a woman was perceived as a claim for power, and power was reserved for the masculine realm. A woman who possessed either one was masculinized and lost title to her own female identity.

THE PROBLEM OF SPEECH. Just as power had a sexual dimension when it was claimed by women, so did speech. A good woman spoke little. Excessive speech was an indication of unchastity. By speech, women seduced men. Eve had lured Adam into sin by her speech. Accused witches were commonly accused of having spoken abusively, or irrationally, or simply too much. As enlightened a figure as Francesco Barbaro insisted on silence in a woman, which he linked to her perfect unanimity with her husband's will and her unblemished virtue (her chastity). Another Italian humanist, Leonardo Bruni, in advising a noblewoman on her studies, barred her not from speech but from public speaking. That was reserved for men.

Related to the problem of speech was that of costume—another, if silent, form of self-expression. Assigned the task of pleasing men as their primary occupation, elite women often tended toward elaborate costume, hairdressing, and the use of cosmetics. Clergy and secular moralists alike condemned these practices. The appropriate function of costume and adornment was to announce the status of a woman's husband or father. Any further indulgence in adornment was akin to unchastity.

THE PROBLEM OF KNOWLEDGE. When the Italian noblewoman Isotta Nogarola had begun to attain a reputation as a humanist, she was accused of incest—a telling instance of the association of learning in women with unchastity. That chilling association inclined any woman who was educated to deny that she was or to make exaggerated claims of heroic chastity.

If educated women were pursued with suspicions of sexual misconduct, women seeking an education faced an even more daunting obstacle: the assumption that women were by nature incapable of learning, that reasoning was a particularly masculine ability. Just as they proclaimed their chastity, women and their defenders insisted on their capacity for learning. The major work by a male writer on female education—that by Juan Luis Vives, *On the Education of a Christian Woman* (1523)—granted female capacity for intellection but still argued that a woman's whole education was to be shaped around the requirement of chastity and a future within the household. Female writers of the following generations—Marie de Gournay in France, Anna Maria van Schurman in Holland, and Mary Astell in England—began to envision other possibilities.

The pioneers of female education were the Italian women humanists who managed to attain a literacy in Latin and a knowledge of classical and

Christian literature equivalent to that of prominent men. Their works implicitly and explicitly raise questions about women's social roles, defining problems that beset women attempting to break out of the cultural limits that had bound them. Like Christine de Pizan, who achieved an advanced education through her father's tutoring and her own devices, their bold questioning makes clear the importance of training. Only when women were educated to the same standard as male leaders would they be able to raise that other voice and insist on their dignity as human beings morally, intellectually, and legally equal to men.

THE OTHER VOICE. The other voice, a voice of protest, was mostly female, but it was also male. It spoke in the vernaculars and in Latin, in treatises and dialogues, in plays and poetry, in letters and diaries, and in pamphlets. It battered at the wall of prejudice that encircled women and raised a banner announcing its claims. The female was equal (or even superior) to the male in essential nature—moral, spiritual, and intellectual. Women were capable of higher education, of holding positions of power and influence in the public realm, and of speaking and writing persuasively. The last bastion of masculine supremacy, centered on the notions of a woman's primary domestic responsibility and the requirement of female chastity, was not as yet assaulted—although visions of productive female communities as alternatives to the family indicated an awareness of the problem.

During the period 1300–1700, the other voice remained only a voice, and one only dimly heard. It did not result—yet—in an alteration of social patterns. Indeed, to this day they have not entirely been altered. Yet the call for justice issued as long as six centuries ago by those writing in the tradition of the other voice must be recognized as the source and origin of the mature feminist tradition and of the realignment of social institutions accomplished in the modern age.

We thank the volume editors in this series, who responded with many suggestions to an earlier draft of this introduction, making it a collaborative enterprise. Many of their suggestions and criticisms have resulted in revisions of this introduction, although we remain responsible for the final product.

PROJECTED TITLES IN THE SERIES

Isabella Andreini, *Mirtilla*, edited and translated by Laura Stortoni

Tullia d'Aragona, *Complete Poems and Letters*, edited and translated by Julia Hairston

Tullia d'Aragona, *The Wretch, Otherwise Known as Guerrino*, edited and translated by Julia Hairston and John McLucas

Francesco Barbaro et al., *On Marriage and the Family*, edited and translated by Margaret L. King

Laura Battiferra, *Selected Poetry, Prose, and Letters*, edited and translated by Victoria Kirkham

Francesco Buoninsegni and Arcangela Tarabotti, *Menippean Satire: "Against Feminine Extravagance" and "Antisatire,"* edited and translated by Elissa Weaver

Rosalba Carriera, *Letters, Diaries, and Art*, edited and translated by Catherine M. Sama

Madame du Chatelet, *Selected Works*, edited by Judith Zinsser

Vittoria Colonna, Chiara Matraini, and Lucrezia Marinella, *Marian Writings*, edited and translated by Susan Haskins

Princess Elizabeth of Bohemia, *Correspondence with Descartes*, edited and translated by Lisa Shapiro

Isabella d'Este, *Selected Letters*, edited and translated by Deanna Shemek

Fairy Tales by Seventeenth-Century French Women Writers, edited and translated by Lewis Seifert and Domna C. Stanton

Moderata Fonte, *Floridoro*, edited and translated by Valeria Finucci

Moderata Fonte and Lucrezia Marinella, *Religious Narratives*, edited and translated by Virginia Cox

Catharina Regina von Greiffenberg, *Meditations on the Life of Christ*, edited and translated by Lynne Tatlock

In Praise of Women: Italian Fifteenth-Century Defenses of Women, edited and translated by Daniel Bornstein

Louise Labé, *Complete Works*, edited and translated by Annie Finch and Deborah Baker

Lucrezia Marinella, *L'Enrico, or Byzantium Conquered*, edited and translated by Virginia Cox

Lucrezia Marinella, *Happy Arcadia*, edited and translated by Susan Haskins and Letizia Panizza

Chiara Matraini, *Selected Poetry and Prose*, edited and translated by Elaine MacLachlan

Alessandro Piccolomini, *Rethinking Marriage in Sixteenth-Century Italy*, edited and translated by Letizia Panizza

Christine de Pizan, *Life of Charles V*, edited and translated by Nadia Margolis

Christine de Pizan, *The Long Road of Learning*, edited and translated by Andrea Tarnowski

Madeleine and Catherine des Roches, *Selected Letters, Dialogues, and Poems*, edited and translated by Anne Larsen

Oliva Sabuco, *The New Philosophy: True Medicine*, edited and translated by Gianna Pomata

Margherita Sarrocchi, *La Scanderbeide*, edited and translated by Rinaldina Russell

Justine Siegemund, *The Court Midwife of the Electorate of Brandenburg* (1690), edited and translated by Lynne Tatlock

Gabrielle Suchon, *"On Philosophy" and "On Morality,"* edited and translated by Domna Stanton with Rebecca Wilkin

Sara Copio Sullam, *Sara Copio Sullam: Jewish Poet and Intellectual in Early Seventeenth-Century Venice*, edited and translated by Don Harrán

Arcangela Tarabotti, *Convent Life as Inferno: A Report*, introduction and notes by Francesca Medioli, translated by Letizia Panizza

Laura Terracina, *Works*, edited and translated by Michael Sherberg

Katharina Schütz Zell, *Selected Writings*, edited and translated by Elsie McKee

Figure 1 Michelangelo Buonarroti's sketch of the *Pietà* (date?), a gift drawn for Colonna around the same time she gave him the manuscript of the sonnets. Photograph courtesy Isabella Stewart Gardner Museum.

VOLUME EDITOR'S INTRODUCTION

> Sceglieronne una; e sceglierolla tale,
> che superato avrà l'invidia in modo,
> che nessun'altra potrà avere a male,
> se l'altre taccio, e se lei sola lodo.
> Quest'una ha non pur sé fatta immortale
> col dolce stil di che il meglior non odo;
> ma può qualunque di cui parli o scriva,
> trar del sepolcro, e far ch'eterno viva.
> —Ludovico Ariosto, *Orlando furioso* 37.16 [1]

THE OTHER VOICE

Ludovico Ariosto's famous tribute to Vittoria Colonna in the third edition of his Renaissance best seller, the *Orlando furioso* (1532), bears testament to the widespread admiration of her work already enjoyed by the poet in the early 1530s, and this despite the fact that an edition of her verses had yet to appear in print.[2] Unable, Ariosto maintains, to devote space to the numerous women writers who deserve praise, he will single out one, but one who is so worthy that none of those omitted will feel angered. In this way the author indicates both that the phenomenon of women writing is increasingly common in this period and that Colonna is generally considered to be the best of her generation.[3] In addition, Ariosto's specific praise of Colonna is twofold: he makes mention of her sweet poetic style, but also of her admi-

---

1. I will choose one and she whom I will name / No envious disdain or scorn will stir. / No other women will be put to shame / If I omit them all and praise but her. / Not only has she won immortal fame / With her sweet style—no sweeter do I hear; / To him of whom she speaks or writes, she gives / New life: awakened from the tomb, he lives. Ludovico Ariosto, *Orlando furioso* (*The Frenzy of Orlando*), trans. Barbara Reynolds (Harmondsworth: Penguin Books, 1975), 2: 383.

2. For full details of all sixteenth-century editions of Colonna's works (the first published in 1538), see Alan Bullock's comprehensive list in Colonna, *Rime* (Rome: Laterza, 1982), 258–80.

3. For a more detailed discussion of this passage, see Virginia Cox, "Women Writers and the Canon in Sixteenth-Century Italy: The Case of Vittoria Colonna," in *Strong Voices, Weak History? Medieval and Renaissance Women in Their Literary Canons: England, France, Italy*, ed. Pamela J. Benson and Victoria Kirkham (Ann Arbor: University of Michigan Press, 2004); and Nucio Ordine, "Vittoria Colonna nell'*Orlando Furioso*," *Studi e problemi di critica testuale* 42 (1991): 55–92.

rable ability to confer immortality upon her dead husband, Francesco D'Ava-
los (1490?–1525), who is the subject of her early amorous sonnets.

The moral and "wifely" element of Ariosto's praise of Colonna is signifi-
cant, playing as it does into a public image of the poet that she seems her-
self to have consciously fostered, that of a devoted *univira* mourning her dead
consort and dedicating all she does, including her writing, to his memory.[4]
Through a public insistence on her widow's role, the female writer's act of
transgression in venturing into the public literary arena is tempered by the
implicit control of a male authority, although in this case an altogether de-
funct one. We may suspect that the particular nature of Ariosto's praise of
Colonna (he goes on to compare her to a number of exemplary widows from
classical antiquity who remained devoted to their lost consorts) derives in
part from his own insecurities, or those of his age, about the challenge posed
by women writers. In the Marganorre episode recounted in the rest of canto
37 of the *Furioso*, for example, there appears to be implicit a warning about
the dangers of a female desire for revenge for long-term male tyranny.[5]
Nonetheless, in Colonna's case the poet's personal collusion in the dissemi-
nation of this chaste and devoted image is undeniable.[6]

It is perhaps on this level, and without underestimating her very con-
siderable literary talents, which will be dealt with separately, that Vittoria
Colonna's striking success as the most published and widely admired woman
writer of the sixteenth century in Italy should first be considered: that is, her
great skill at manipulating and disseminating the "correct" public image that
would aid, rather than hinder, her literary aspirations and at finding a wholly
successful means of tailoring those aspirations to fit the image. And it is
thanks in particular to this skill that her legacy, an acceptable model for lit-
erary production by secular women, could be handed down to successive
women writers well into the following century, writers who adopted her
model and openly cited her example in their own works.[7]

---

4. The *univira*, the once-married woman who never remarries after her husband's death, was
widely admired by the Romans and was considered to have attained the second purest state for
a woman (the first being perpetual virginity). See Judith Evans Grubbs, *Women and the Law in the
Roman Empire: A Sourcebook on Marriage, Divorce and Widowhood* (London: Routledge, 2002).

5. See Cox, "Women Writers and the Canon in Sixteenth-Century Italy."

6. On Colonna's careful melding of persona and literary production, see Giovanna Rabitti,
"Lyric Poetry, 1500–1650," trans. Abigail Brundin, in *A History of Women's Writing in Italy*, ed.
Letizia Panizza and Sharon Wood, 37–51 (Cambridge: Cambridge University Press, 2000),
at 37–38.

7. For Colonna's influence on a number of later women writers in Italy, see Rabitti "Lyric
Poetry, 1500–1650"; see also the entries in Rinaldina Russell, ed., *Italian Women Writers: A Bio-
Bibliographical Sourcebook* (London: Greenwood, 1994) for Isabella Adreini, Tullia d'Aragona,

Colonna's published literary output consisted in the main of sonnets in the Petrarchan vein (although she also wrote a smaller number of prose works). Thus her oeuvre was part of the well-established courtly genre of Petrarchism, based on an imitation of the vernacular poetic model found in Petrarch's *Rime sparse*, which celebrated an idealized love for an unattainable other, and concerned also with the correct usage of the vernacular language in accordance with the guidelines elucidated most influentially by Pietro Bembo (1470–1547) in the *Prose della volgar lingua* (1525).[8] Colonna may have been wise in electing to insert herself into such a popular literary tradition where the introduction of a new female voice would be less remarkable, but her reworking of the genre to suit the needs of her own particular position was entirely unprecedented. Where Petrarch bemoans an unreciprocated love for a mythical female whom he never possesses, but who rather evades him constantly, Colonna, as befits a respectable and aristocratic woman, celebrates the memory of a love that has not only been reciprocated but also legitimated through marriage. Her personal circumstances provided the necessary context of loss required by the Petrarchan format, in her husband's frequent extended absences from home and eventual death in battle, and it seems to be no accident that her fame as a poet began to grow exponentially after the death of D'Avalos in 1525.[9] As an apparently autobiographical genre, Petrarchan poetry establishes an intimate relationship between writer

---

Laura Battiferri Ammannati, Lucrezia Marinella, Chiara Matraini, Isabella di Morra, Gaspara Stampa, and Laura Terracina, among others.

8. On the phenomenon of Petrarchism generally, see Klaus Hempfer, "Per una definizione del Petrarchismo," in *Dynamique d'une expansion culturelle: Pétrarque en Europe XIVe–XXe siècle; Actes du XXVIe congrès international du CEFI, Turin et Chambéry, 11–15 décembre 1995, ed. Pierre Blanc, 23–52, Bibliothèque Franco Simone, 30 (Paris: Honoré Champion, 2001); Roland Greene, Post-Petrarchism: Origins and Innovations of Western Lyric Sequence (Princeton: Princeton University Press, 1991); Thomas Greene, The Light in Troy: Imitation and Discovery in Renaissance Poetry (New Haven: Yale University Press), 1982; Amedeo Quondam, Il naso di Laura: Lingua e poesia lirica nella tradizione del Classicismo (Ferrara: Panini, 1991). Pietro Bembo's work is "Delle Prose di M. Pietro Bembo nelle quali si ragiona della volgar lingua," in Opere in volgare, ed. M. Marti, 269–447 (Florence: Sansoni, 1961).

9. The connection between freedom from marriage and domestic duties and literary productivity has been well established. See, for example, Virginia Cox, "The Single Self: Feminist Thought and the Marriage Market in Early Modern Venice," Renaissance Quarterly 48 (1995): 513–81. Most notably, two other women writers of the early modern period in Italy, Lucrezia Marinella (1571–1653) and Laura Terracina (1519–ca. 1577), married late in life and were therefore able to benefit from the educational possibilities and relative freedom of the paternal home for extended periods. See Russell, Italian Women Writers, 234–42, 423–30. Veronica Gambara (1485–1550) was, like Colonna, widowed early in life. See Russell, Italian Women Writers, 145–53. Gaspara Stampa (1523?–54) remained unmarried (which has led later critics to assume she was a courtesan). See Fiora A. Bassanese, Gaspara Stampa (Boston: Twayne, 1982). Veronica Franco (ca. 1546–91) used her position as a courtesan, outside the norms of social respectabil-

and work (although it would be misleading to assume that this relationship is not at all times carefully controlled and presented by the poet), so that Colonna's deeply mournful and devoted verses contributed directly to the acceptance of her public image of unassailable piety and virtue, which was essential to her success as a writer.

In accordance with the dictates of such an image, Colonna's poetry insists in particular on the nonnegotiable, eternal quality of her devotion to D'Avalos, so that she will not begin to entertain thoughts of a new love or marriage after his death: "Nor do I fear a new fire, for the heat / of my first flame extinguished all others." [10] The focus on constancy, fidelity, and chastity can be considered perhaps the most crucial aspect of the female poet's literary self-presentation, as it negates and diffuses one of the most damaging misogynistic accusations of the period, that is, in line with Aristotelian principles, that women are by nature inconstant and voracious in their appetites. The archmisogynist of Castiglione's *Cortegiano* (1528), Gasparo Pallavicino, expresses this opinion in particularly robust terms (designed, one suspects, to ridicule him as much as damage the women he accuses) in book 3 of the dialogue, when he highlights the natural licentiousness of women: "For they, due to the stupidity of their sex, are far more governed by appetite than men are, and if sometimes they abstain from satisfying their desires, they do so out of a sense of shame and not through any lack of appetite." [11] The figure who mourns in Colonna's verses, in contrast to this negative image, embodies an entirely sublimated love, and unlike Petrarch, whose love impedes his access to grace, her love is the primary vehicle for arriving at divine fulfillment through the ennobling and purifying effect that the memory of the beloved has upon the poet's heart and soul.

The amorous and sorrowful context established by her verses in memory of D'Avalos, however, was only the very beginning of Colonna's poetic journey, and it is in her later, mature spiritual sonnets that the originality and startling beauty of her lyric voice become clearly apparent. [12] Through

---

ity, to legitimize her literary pursuits. See Margaret Rosenthal, *The Honest Courtesan: Veronica Franco, Citizen and Writer in Sixteenth-Century Venice* (Chicago: University of Chicago Press, 1992).

10. "Né temo novo caldo, ché 'l vigore / del primo foco mio tutt'altri estinse." See "Di così nobil fiamma Amor mi cinse," in Colonna, *Rime* (1982), 6.

11. "Le quali, per la imbecillità del sesso, sono molto più inclinate agli appetiti che gli omini, e se talor si astengono dal satisfare ai suoi desidèri, lo fanno per vergogna, non perché la volontà non sia loro prontissima." Baldassare Castiglione, *Il libro del cortegiano*, ed. Ettore Bonora (Milan: Mursia, 1988), 3.39.245.

12. Colonna's poetry is generally divided into three types (based on the manner in which the earliest sixteenth-century editions of her poetry were presented): early amorous sonnets (*rime amorose*), lauding the memory of her husband; more mature spiritual sonnets (*rime spirituali*) in which the subject of the verses is now Christ, although he retains many of the attributes of the

a process of neo-Platonic ascension, the poet's deceased husband is trans-
formed into the figure of Christ, and she now celebrates a potential future
union with a heavenly consort rather than longing anymore for the defunct
union with her earthly one. Unlike Petrarch, who aspires in his *canzoniere* to
be released from the prison of his earthly life and love, although the reader
senses he will never ultimately break free, Colonna in her later poems boldly
casts off the shackles of earthly ties and turns to celebrate a wholly divine
bond. And although this celebration is tempered by constant references to
her own unworthiness, the lowliness of her verses, and the doubtful out-
come of her aspirations toward a union with Christ, we sense beneath these
necessary disclaimers a joyful certainty in her status as an elected soul who
will one day join her divine "husband" in heaven. The optimism and self-
assertive nature of this poetic position is highly unusual, both in the context
of the Petrarchan genre and in the context of works authored by women.

Given the care and skill with which she presented herself and her work
to the sixteenth-century reading public, it is perhaps unsurprising that the
literary model developed and embodied by Vittoria Colonna—of pious and
devoted widowhood and poetry turned to the worthy cause of extolling an-
other's virtues—proved so enduring and continued to influence the strate-
gies of women writers in Italy into the seventeenth century. This is not to
say that all later women writers in Italy chose to compose sonnets in the
Petrarchan vein. In the latter half of the sixteenth century we find instead
works across a compelling range of genres being authored by women, in-
cluding chivalric romance (Tullia D'Aragona, Moderata Fonte), pastoral
drama (Isabella Andreini, Maddalena Campiglia), and polemical treatises
(Lucrezia Marinella). What these later writers inherited from Colonna was
not her specific literary approach (although some followed this closely, most
notably Chiara Matraini),[13] but rather her model for legitimate literary ex-
pression by secular women and her successful founding of a canon of female
voices that she herself headed. We can clearly assume a direct connection
between the huge success of her format for female literary production and
the enormous increase in the number of published women writers in Italy
during the sixteenth and early seventeenth centuries.[14]

---

earlier hero; and epistolary sonnets (*rime epistolari*) addressed to specific and identifiable con-
temporaries.

13. See Luciana Borsetto, "Narciso ed Eco. Figura e scrittura nella lirica femminile del Cinque-
cento: Esemplificazioni ed appunti," in *Nel cerchio della luna: Figure di donna in alcuni testi del XVI secolo*,
ed. Marina Zancan, 171–233 (Venice: Marsilio 1983); and Giovanna Rabitti, "Linee per il ri-
tratto di Chiara Matraini," *Studi e problemi di critica testuale* 22 (1981): 141–65, and "La metafora e
l'esistenza nella poesia di Chiara Matraini," *Studi e problemi di critica testuale* 27 (1983): 109–45.

14. Axel Erdmann records 201 published women writers in Italy during the sixteenth century,

A BRIEF BIOGRAPHY: VITTORIA COLONNA, 1490–1547

The information regarding Vittoria Colonna's life remains frustratingly sparse and incomplete, despite the poet's great fame in her own age. In attempting to piece together a biography, the writer becomes immediately aware that a satisfactory quantity of sixteenth-century sources is lacking and that much unsubstantiated received knowledge seems to have been circulated during the past three centuries, the origins of which are impossible to trace. In addition, a tendency toward unquestioningly autobiographical readings of Colonna's poetry has further muddied an already unclear picture, as has often been the fate of women writers.[15]

All sources do seem to agree, however, that the poet was born at Marino outside Rome in 1490, or some say 1492, into a highly aristocratic family, the second child of Fabrizio Colonna and Agnese di Montefeltro, daughter of the Duke of Urbino.[16] At a very young age she was betrothed to Francesco Ferrante D'Avalos, the future Marquis of Pescara, in what was without doubt a political maneuver, designed to forge an alliance between the powerful Colonna family and Ferdinand, king of Naples, and thereby seal the Roman family's loyalty to the Spanish throne. The marriage between Colonna and D'Avalos was celebrated in 1509 on the island of Ischia off the coast of Naples, after which the couple moved to a villa in the mountains overlooking the city.[17] Here they spent two years together before D'Avalos left home, in 1511, on the first of the military campaigns against the French,

---

compared with only thirty in France in the same period. See Axel Erdmann, *My Gracious Silence: Women in the Mirror of Sixteenth-Century Printing in Western Europe* (Luzern: Gilhofer and Rauschberg, 1999), 201–23.

15. For a striking example of this tendency, see Francesco Galdi, *Vittoria Colonna dal lato della neuro-psicopatologia* (Portici: Spedalieri, 1898). Galdi performed a psychoanalytic reading of Colonna's poems in order to diagnose her various neurotic illnesses.

16. The most recent source for biographical information on Colonna is Silvia Ferino-Pagden, ed., "Persönlichkeit und Leben," in *Vittoria Colonna: Dichterin und Muse Michelangelos* (Vienna: Skira, 1997), 19–147. See also (in alphabetical order) Colonna, *Carteggio,* ed. Ermanno Ferrero and Giuseppe Müller, 2d ed. (Turin: Ermanno Loescher, 1892); *Dizionario biografico degli italiani* (Rome: Istituto dell'Enciclopedia Italiana, 1982), 27: 448–57 (hereafter *DBI*); Jerrold, *Vittoria Colonna, Her Friends and Her Times* (New York: Freeport, 1906); Alfredo Reumont, *Vittoria Colonna: Vita, fede e poesia nel secolo decimosesto,* trans. Giuseppe Müller and Ermanno Ferrero (Turin: Ermanno Loescher, 1883); H. Roscoe, *Vittoria Colonna: Her Life and Poems* (London: MacMillan, 1868); and Suzanne Therault, *Un cénacle humaniste de la Renaissance autour de Vittoria Colonna châtelaine d'Ischia* (Paris: Didier; and Florence: Sansoni Antiquariato, 1968).

17. Some sources maintain that the Colonna family had been in residence on Ischia since 1501, when a dispute with Pope Alexander VI brought about the confiscation of their lands around Rome. See, for example, *DBI,* 27: 450.

which were to occupy him for the rest of his life. While her husband's almost continual absence from the marital home from this point may not suggest to us the happiest of marriages (and the couple remained childless, a fact alluded to in her poetry[18]), his warlike persona and growing reputation for heroism did allow Colonna to employ D'Avalos as a useful literary subject from her very earliest verses, emphasizing his courage, valor, and virtue and eventually, in her later spiritual poetry, fusing the earthly captain with Christ, the captain of the Christian battle for faith.[19]

While D'Avalos was away fighting, Colonna moved back to the court on Ischia, presided over by her aunt by marriage, Costanza D'Avalos (1460– 1541), herself a highly learned woman. It is probably during this period that the young woman's interest in poetry was first aroused, through contact with the many Neapolitan literary figures who frequented the court (among them the famed poet Iacopo Sannazaro [1455/6–1530]) and through access to the court library, which was substantially increased during her lifetime by her aunt Costanza.[20] It appears to be significant that so many of the young Colonna's formative years were spent in this environment of courtly erudition from which the principal male protagonists were absent, allowing space for a singular degree of female autonomy. A fascinating early altarpiece from Ischia, executed by an unknown Neapolitan artist in the first decades of the sixteenth century in the church of San Francesco or Sant'Antonio di Padova, depicts Colonna and her aunt kneeling beneath the Madonna of Mercy, who offers her breast to the infant Christ.[21] Colonna is in sumptuous secular dress, the only known extant depiction of her before her widowhood, and holding a book in one hand; Costanza is dressed in a widow's weeds.[22] The positioning of the two women side by side beneath the Madonna suggests a relationship of parity and their shared role as "first lady" at the court in the absence of their men folk. Presumably they are praying to Mary for the pro-

18. See "Quando Morte fra noi disciolse il nodo," in Colonna, *Rime* (1982), 18, lines 9–11: "Sterili i corpi fur, l'alme feconde; / il suo valor qui col mio nome unito/mi fan pur madre di sua chiara prole."

19. Paolo Giovio's contemporary biography of D'Avalos highlights his reputation in his day as a great military hero. See Paolo Giovio, *Le vite del gran Capitano e del Marchese di Pescara*, trans. Ludovico Domenichi (Bari: Laterza, 1931).

20. On the library on Ischia, see Ferino-Pagden, *Vittoria Colonna*, 67–76.

21. For further information on this altarpiece, see Ferino-Pagden, *Vittoria Colonna*, 135–56; Paola Giusti and Pierluigi Leone de Castris, *Pittura del Cinquecento a Napoli* (Naples: Electa, 1988), 1:74 and 84; and Giuliano Briganti, ed., *La Pittura in Italia: Il Cinquecento* (Naples: Electa, 1988), 2: 475.

22. For information on other portraits of Colonna, see Ferino-Pagden, *Vittoria Colonna*, 109–20.

tection of the male members of their family, away in battle, while the women remain at home in control of the domestic, diplomatic, and literary affairs that court life entailed. This implied assertion of female autonomy is furthered by the inclusion, in other panels of the polyptich altarpiece, of a number of other female saints and martyrs, namely, Catherine of Alexandria, Mary Magdalene, Saint Clare and Saint Lucy, clutching books and quills that emphasize their learning and erudition.[23] The assertive female slant of the whole work, and Colonna's prominent position within it, is striking.

Although none of Colonna's own poetry survives from this early period apart from a single poetic "Epistola" addressed to her husband, who had been imprisoned by the French in 1512, documentary sources indicate that she was already gaining a reputation for her poetry and her piety among other Neapolitan writers, who lauded in particular her chaste and devoted love for her husband and her nobility of soul.[24] It appears likely, therefore, that Colonna's earliest verses were already enjoying a significant manuscript circulation at this time, certainly in and around Naples if not further afield.

In 1520, Colonna was in Rome, where she had an audience with Pope Leo X who had recently awarded a cardinalship to her cousin Pompeo. It has been asserted that it was on the occasion of this audience that she also met Baldassare Castiglione (1478–1529) and Pietro Bembo, both of whom were in Rome as papal secretaries.[25] Colonna's father died in this year, her mother two years later in 1522. After a period in which it seems that she moved back and forth between Naples and her family's estates around Rome, she returned south to Ischia again in the spring of 1525. This was the year of the fateful battle of Pavia, during which Colonna's husband D'Avalos was wounded, although at the time he did not believe his injuries to be serious. By the end of that year, however, he sent word to his wife from Milan that he was gravely ill. As Colonna journeyed north to reach him, a message reached her in Viterbo that D'Avalos had died in Milan, leaving the

23. Further information on these female saints can be found in Agnes B. C. Dunbar, *A Dictionary of Saintly Women* (London: George Bell and Sons, 1904); James Hall, *Dictionary of Subjects and Symbols in Art*, rev. ed. (London: John Murray, 1984); and Lucy Menzies, *The Saints in Italy* (London: Medici Society, 1924).

24. On Colonna's Neapolitan context, see Mirella Scala, "Encomi e dediche nelle prime realzioni culturali di Vittoria Colonna," *Periodico della società storica comense* 54 (1990), 95–112; and Therault, *Un cénacle humaniste*. Colonna's poetic "Epistola" is reprinted in Colonna, *Rime* (1982), 53–56, and excerpts are translated in Laura Anna Stortoni, *Women Poets of the Italian Renaissance: Courtly Ladies and Courtesans*, trans. Laura Anna Stortoni and Mary Prentice Lillie (New York: Italica Press, 1997), 67.

25. See *DBI*, 27: 448.

Figure 2 Anonymous Neapolitan artist's altarpiece fresco *Madonna of Mercy* (second decade of
the sixteenth century, detail), Church of San Francesco or Sant'Antonio di Padova, from
the Island of Ischia, showing Colonna on the bottom right holding a book and her aunt by
marriage, Costanza d'Avalos, on the left. Photograph courtesy John Palcewski.

poet widowed and independently wealthy at the relatively young age of thirty-five.[26]

Colonna now made her way to Rome, where she retreated into the convent of San Silvestro in Capite. When she expressed the desire, early in 1526, to remain in San Silvestro and take up the contemplative life of the cloth, both her brother Ascanio and Pope Clement VII strongly objected. The pope even went as far as forbidding the nuns of the convent from allowing her to take her vows, should she request to do so.[27] It is probably the case that the desire to keep Colonna out of a convent was motivated by the value placed on her "remarriageability," which could be a useful political tool both for her family and for the pope. Despite pressure that may have been brought to bear on her, however, she never considered remarrying and instead turned her widowed status to the service of her poetry, as the references to marital devotion in the amorous sonnets clearly illustrate.[28]

The year following her husband's death was one of serious political turmoil in Rome, and the Colonna name was closely linked to the struggles that took place. On September 20, 1526, an attack on Rome was carried out by imperial troops, members of the Colonna family among their number: Vittoria was at this point taken out of the city by her brother Ascanio to the safety of the family seat at Marino. Despite her family's antipapal stance, however, she was able to preserve good relations with Pope Clement VII and later took on the role of intermediary between her family and the papal court when tensions reached a head in 1540.[29] It may be that as a woman, precisely by virtue of her relative political insignificance, she was able to maintain a greater degree of autonomy from family policy: certainly this is a clear illustration of the proximity she had to the great seats of power of her age, both papal and imperial. Rather than returning to Rome, as the turmoil showed no sign of abating, Colonna then left Marino and headed south for Naples and then Ischia, so she was not involved in the terrible events of the infamous and brutal Sack of Rome by imperial troops in May 1527.[30]

26. Some sources maintain that D'Avalos was in fact poisoned by conspirators acting on behalf of Pope Clement VII. See Ferino-Pagden, *Vittoria Colonna,* 19–21.

27. See Reumont, *Vittoria Colonna,* 88.

28. See Colonna, *Rime* (1982), 6, cited above on page 4.

29. On the events of the "Guerra del sale" of 1540, a struggle between the pope and the Colonna, see Reumont, *Vittoria Colonna,* 91; and Domenico Tordi, "Vittoria Colonna in Orvieto durante la Guerra del sale," *Bolletino della Società Umbra di Storia Patria* 1 (1895), 473–533. Colonna tried to negotiate for a peaceful resolution to the conflict with the pope through a number of intermediaries, but primarily through her long-standing correspondent Cardinal Giberti. See, for example, Colonna, *Carteggio,* 46–47.

30. For a contemporary account of the sack of Rome, see Luigi Giucciardini, *The Sack of Rome,* ed. and trans. James H. McGregor (New York: Italica Press, 1993).

During the late 1520s and early 1530s, while she was resident on Ischia once again, Colonna's poetry began to enjoy a wider scribal circulation throughout Italy, and her renown as a poet of chaste and devoted love for the memory of her husband began to be firmly established in the public imagination, as Ariosto's laudatory verses cited earlier clearly illustrate.[31] In addition, Pietro Bembo, the undisputed grandmaster of the Petrarchan style in which Colonna wrote, was first sent a copy of a sonnet by her in 1530, to which he responded in the most glowing terms: "I have received the sonnet by the Marchioness of Pescara . . . It truly is beautiful, ingenious and serious such as one would not expect from a woman: it has far surpassed my expectations."[32] From this point a regular exchange of verses and opinions was established between the two poets, which was to endure until their deaths in 1547. It was also during this period that Colonna became closely associated with Bernardino Ochino (1487–1564), the Capuchin preacher who fled Italy under suspicion of heresy in 1542 and whose evangelical and mystical style of preaching is thought to have had a profound effect on her literary style as well as her religious beliefs.[33]

An outbreak of plague in Naples in 1531 may have forced Colonna to leave the south by the following year. Certainly she was in Rome again by 1536, where she was visited by Emperor Charles V during his stay in that city. Like the pope, Charles from the first appears to have recognized Colonna's importance as an intermediary between his own representatives and the papal court, as is demonstrated by the letters between them that are still extant.[34] It was also at this time that Colonna first met Reginald Pole (1500–

31. On the way in which Ariosto first came to possess verses by Colonna, see Tobia Toscano, "Due 'allievi' di Vittoria Colonna: Luigi Tansillo e Alfonso d'Avalos," *Critica letteraria* 16 (1988): 739–73.

32. "Ebbi il sonetto della Marchesa di Pescara . . . Di vero egli è bello e ingenioso e grave più che da donna non pare sia richiesto: ha superato la espettation mia d'assai." For a discussion of the letter from Bembo to Carlo Gualteruzzi in which this comment is made, see Carlo Dionisotti, "Appunti sul Bembo e su Vittoria Colonna," in *Miscellanea Augusto Campana,* ed. Rino Avensani et al., 257–86 (Padua: Antenore, 1981), at 261–63; and Giovanna Rabitti, "Vittoria Colonna, Bembo e Firenze: Un caso di ricezione e qualche postilla," *Studi e problemi di critica testuale* 44 (1992): 127–55, at 147–49.

33. On Ochino's relationship with Colonna, see Carl Benrath, *Bernardino Ochino of Siena: A Contribution towards the History of the Reformation* (London: James Nisbet, 1876); and Gigliola Fragnito, "Appunti e documenti: Gli 'Spirituali' e la fuga di Bernardino Ochino," *Rivista storica italiana* 84 (1972): 777–813. The term "evangelical" is intended here in the sense in which it was defined by Delio Cantimori, to describe the particular characteristics of the Italian reform movement in the period before the Council of Trent. See Delio Cantimori, *Eretici italiani del Cinquecento e altri scritti,* ed. Adriano Prosperi (Turin: Einaudi, 1992), 565–604; and Paolo Simoncelli, *Evangelismo italiano del Cinquecento: Questione religiosa e nicodemismo politico* (Rome: Istituto storico italiano per l'età moderna e contemporanea, 1979), vii–xxxii.

34. Colonna, *Carteggio,* 27–31; 44–46; 56–57; 167–68; 227–29; 326–27.

1558), an English cardinal residing in Rome, and the two began what was to become an intense friendship.[35] In 1537, Colonna traveled from Rome to Ferrara, where she was hosted by Renée de France, wife of Duke Ercole II d'Este and infamous for her sympathy for the Reformation and her habit of sheltering French religious exiles (including Jean Calvin) at the Ferrarese court.[36] From Ferrara, her plan seems to have been to travel to Venice, make a pilgrimage to the tomb of Mary Magdalene in France, and then journey on to the Holy Land.[37] But ill health, or else familial and papal pressure, prevented this epic journey from taking place, and in early 1538 Colonna departed instead for Lucca, where she hoped that the waters would have a beneficial effect on her health.

In late 1538 or early 1539 Colonna returned to San Silvestro in Rome, where she remained for a couple of years and where it seems that she either met Michelangelo for the first time or an earlier friendship with him began to flourish. She moved briefly to Orvieto in 1541, when tensions between her brother Ascanio and Pope Paul III were becoming unbearable, and then to the convent of Santa Caterina in Viterbo in October of that year, to be near her friend Pole. Finally, in late 1544, in very poor health, Colonna returned to Rome where she settled in the convent of Sant'Anna de' Funari and remained there until her death in February 1547, the same year as her poetic mentor Bembo.[38]

Despite her wealth, her status, and her fame, Vittoria Colonna's later life may seem a somewhat unsettled and lonely one to the eyes of a modern observer. The years of her marriage, when she remained on Ischia in the company of her aunt Costanza, appear to offer the only period of relative stability in an existence otherwise marked by constant relocations and upheavals. Judging by the frequency with which she returned south after 1525, Colonna's relationship with the family of her late husband remained strong, no doubt aided substantially by her refusal to remarry, but the latter years of her widowhood seem to have offered her no fixed base, as she shifted from her brother's home to the various convents that housed her as a secular guest. It

35. On Reginald Pole, see Dermot Fenlon, *Heresy and Obedience in Tridentine Italy: Cardinal Pole and the Counter Reformation* (Cambridge: Cambridge University Press, 1972); and Thomas F. Mayer, *Reginald Pole: Prince and Prophet* (Cambridge: Cambridge University Press), 2000.

36. On the reform activities of Renée de France, see Charmarie Jenkins-Blaisdell, "Renée de France between Reform and Counter-Reform," *Archive for Reformation History* 63 (1972), 196–226.

37. A letter from Pope Paul III (Colonna, *Carteggio*, 131–32) makes mention of this plan. Mary Magdalene seems to have been a potent figure for Colonna and appears frequently in her poetry and prose.

38. The last period of Colonna's life is documented in Reumont, *Vittoria Colonna*, 220–25.

is interesting to ponder whether the relative freedom conferred by the poet's early widowhood and financial independence also brought with it undeniable disadvantages as she entered middle age, an unmarried and childless woman who had no direct claim on the land or houses belonging to her own family or that of her dead husband.³⁹ When she died, Colonna was heralded as the undisputed matriarch of Italian Petrarchism, yet her great fame and literary success are perhaps not well reflected in the solitary and secluded manner in which she ended her life.

REFORM SPIRITUALITY

During the late 1520s and early 1530s, when she was once again resident on Ischia and frequenting Neapolitan society, Colonna came into contact with a number of individuals who were to have a profound impact on her thinking and on her subsequent literary production. This was the group of aristocrats in the circle of a Spaniard residing in Naples named Juan de Valdés (1509?–41), who had left Spain to avoid the attentions of the Inquisition on charges of Lutheranism. A number of figures who were to become prominent in the movement for religious reform within Italy (men such as Marcantonio Flaminio [1498–1550], Pier Paolo Vergerio the younger [1498–1565], Pietro Vermigli [1500–62], and Pietro Carnesecchi [1508–67], as well as the Capuchin General Bernardino Ochino mentioned earlier, who was particularly close to Colonna) first came together to discuss their reform spirituality and began to elucidate their ideas more clearly under the guidance of Valdés; and Colonna too, whether or not she knew Valdés personally, moved in these circles and found herself exposed to the new and radical religious ideas under discussion.⁴⁰

Valdés's strikingly simple theology was centered on the Bible as the only source for spiritual understanding and illumination, bypassing the church fathers and institutions and advocating instead the individual's task of "divine consideration," which would set alight his faith like a fire within him.⁴¹

---

39. On inheritance laws as they related to women in the early modern period, see Samuel K. Cohn, Jr., *Women in the Streets: Essays on Sex and Power in Renaissance Italy* (Baltimore: Johns Hopkins University Press, 1996).

40. It has generally been accepted that Colonna knew Valdés and was one of his acolytes; but Massimo Firpo, "Vittoria Colonna, Giovanni Morone e gli 'spirituali,'" *Rivista di storia e letteratura religiosa* 24 (1988): 211–61 at 212, maintains that she could never have met him and rather absorbed his influence via contact with other individuals such as Ochino.

41. On Valdés's theology, which was essentially Lutheran in character, see Salvatore Caponetto, *The Protestant Reformation in Sixteenth-Century Italy*, trans. Anne C. Tedeschi and John Tedeschi, Six-

Clearly, such a view constitutes a direct challenge to the authority of the church to act as an intermediary between the individual Christian and God, exchanging his currency of prayer, attendance at mass, confession, good works, and even hard cash in the form of donations and purchase of indulgences for eventual salvation of his own soul or that of a loved one. According to Valdés and others who thought like him, including northern European reformers like Luther, this entire institutional apparatus was unnecessary and a hindrance to the Christian's capacity to arrive at a direct and loving bond with God.[42] It is only a short step from this position to an acceptance of the Lutheran doctrine of *sola fide*, or justification by faith without good works, the "watchword and touchstone of the Reformation."[43] This doctrine teaches, through a reading of Saint Paul via Saint Augustine, that man can do nothing by his own power to change his fate: he is either saved (justified) or lost only through the power of God's love and the working of his own faith. Good works, prayer, fasting, indulgences, and all the apparatus of Catholicism are therefore meaningless (although a man of faith will live a good life nonetheless, because of the fire that burns within him), and all that matters is abandoning oneself to the word of God contained in the gospels.

It must be borne in mind that, at the time in the early 1530s when Colonna was first exposed to Valdés's ideas and to the Lutheran doctrine of justification by faith, the Council of Trent had not yet been convened and a clear line between heresy and orthodoxy was yet to be drawn.[44] Luther had arrived at *sola fide* through his own reading of the gospels and the writings of Saint Augustine (most crucially Romans 3:28, from whence he claimed the authority for the addition of the crucial word "alone" to the doctrine of justification by faith[45]); in other words, the doctrine was considered to be clearly contained within some of the central texts of Catholicism and thus justifiable

---

teenth Century Essays and Studies, 43 (Kirksville, MO: Thomas Jefferson University Press, 1999), 63–94; E. Cione, *Juan de Valdés: La sua vita e il suo pensiero religioso*, 2d ed. (Naples: F. Fiorentino, 1963); José Nieto, *Juan de Valdés and the Origins of the Spanish and Italian Reformation* (Geneva: Droz, 1970); and Frederic C. Church, *Italian Reformers, 1534–1564* (New York: Columbia University Press, 1932), 50–78.

42. On the notion of the Reformation as a quarrel about such issues, see Natalie Zemon Davis, "Gifts and Bribes in Sixteenth-Century France," Iredell Lecture delivered at Lancaster University, Feb. 14, 1995.

43. G. R. Elton, *Reformation Europe, 1517–1559*, 2d ed. (Oxford: Blackwell, 1999), 2.

44. On the Council of Trent, which was called by Pope Paul III with the task of defining the true Roman Catholic religion and active from 1545, see Elton, *Reformation Europe*, 135–37.

45. See Michael Mullett, *The Catholic Reformation* (London: Routledge, 1999), 42–43.

as an appropriate response to scripture. It is for this reason that we find individuals at the heart of the Catholic establishment, including members of the College of Cardinals, drawn to *sola fide*, and many believed in the early decades of the sixteenth century that a compromise between the pope and groups of reformers could be achieved.[46] Thus we should not necessarily assume that Vittoria Colonna was aware of treating potentially heretical material in Naples in the 1530s when she first encountered these new ideas, and in fact it is quite possible that she arrived at a belief in *sola fide* via a quite orthodox and non-Lutheran route, through Augustine, for example, or through contact with the Neapolitan Accademia Pontaniana in which such concepts were discussed in a literary context.[47]

Whatever its genesis, the influence of *sola fide* began to make itself felt in Colonna's literary output from this period, and its particular effect on her Petrarchan lyric sequence is highly significant. The implications of such a doctrine for the individual Christian are of course immense, as she is handed the responsibility for developing a pure faith through a direct relationship with Christ and his gospels and is effectively unshackled from the labyrinthine and often mystifying authority of the earthly church. In Colonna's increasingly spiritual poetry we find the intimate and loving relationship with D'Avalos superseded by an equally intimate and loving relationship with Christ, expressed in a sensuous and mystical language that reflects the influence of the mystical spirituality of men like Valdés and Ochino and that frequently alludes to the doctrine of justification by faith and the Calvinist concept of predestination (which states that the elect are born already destined to be saved and equipped with the capacity for faith, which they must learn to nurture).[48] Colonna's manuscript of sonnets for Michelangelo perhaps best encapsulates the results of this new direction in her Petrarchism, as will be illustrated below.

By the end of the 1530s, a new motivation entered into Colonna's in-

46. One of those who pressed for compromise at Trent was Cardinal Gasparo Contarini, who was later vilified for his apparent embracing of heresy. See Elizabeth G. Gleason, *Gasparo Contarini: Venice, Rome and Reform* (Berkeley: University of California Press, 1993).

47. Concetta Ranieri supports the view that Colonna's interest in *sola fide* was born of the Neapolitan influence of members of the Accademia Pontaniana and not of any contact with Protestant literature in this period. Concetta Ranieri, "Premesse umanistiche alla religiosità di Vittoria Colonna," *Rivista di storia e letteratura religiosa* 32 (1996): 531–48, at 533–34; Ranieri, "Vittoria Colonna e la riforma: Alcune osservazioni critiche," *Studi latini e italiani* 6 (1992): 87–96; and Ferino-Pagden, *Vittoria Colonna*, 225–34.

48. On Calvinist predestination, see Elton, *Reformation Europe*, 151–54.

terest in reform spirituality, engendered by her meeting with Reginald Pole
in Rome cited earlier. Cardinal Pole was also drawn to the doctrine of *sola
fide* and was, like his friend Contarini, instrumental in pushing for a com-
promise with the Protestants at Trent, a move that earned him the attentions
of the Roman Inquisition later in his life.⁴⁹ A number of the same individu-
als who had gathered around Valdés in Naples a few years earlier now con-
gregated around Pole in Rome and at his residence in Viterbo when he was
sent there in 1541 to discuss doctrinal and reform issues, influenced by their
earlier Neapolitan contacts but also by the steady influx into Italy of works
by the Protestant reformers, including those of Luther and Calvin.⁵⁰ This
group, which came to be known as the *ecclesia viterbiensis* because of Pole's res-
idence in Viterbo and also as the Spirituals or *spirituali,* appears to have held
regular meetings in which lay sermons were delivered and discussions were
held dealing with the various articles of faith. Colonna was often present at
such gatherings, moving to Viterbo herself in 1541. By this period, it should
be noted, expressing an interest in Lutheran doctrine was becoming more
dangerous: a number of the individuals involved in the *ecclesia viterbiensis* were
later prosecuted for heresy by the Inquisition or left Italy for Protestant
countries.⁵¹

It has also been convincingly argued that the *spirituali,* at their meetings
in Viterbo, read and discussed the central text of the Italian reform move-
ment, the *Beneficio di Cristo* (apparently written by a Benedictine monk, Bene-
detto da Mantova), before it was first published in 1542 or 1543.⁵² One of

49. On a collection of material relating to Pole and Colonna, which is held in the Vatican's Se-
cret Archive and presumably gathered in preparation for an Inquisitional process against Pole,
see Sergio Pagano and Concetta Ranieri, *Nuovi documenti su Vittoria Colonna e Reginald Pole* (Città
del Vaticano: Archivio Vaticano, 1989).

50. See Silvana Seidel Menchi, "Le traduzioni italiane di Lutero nella prima metà del Cinque-
cento," *Rinascimento* 17 (1977): 31–108. Evidence that Colonna herself read works by Protestant
reformers and was active in promoting their message is provided in Firpo, "Vittoria Colonna,
Giovanni Morone e gli 'spirituali.'"

51. Pietro Carnesecchi was tried for heresy and executed in 1567. For transcriptions of his
three Inquisitional trials, see Giacomo Manzoni, ed., "Estratto del processo di Pietro Carnesec-
chi," *Miscellanea di storia italiana* 10 (1870): 187–573; Massimo Firpo and Dario Marcatto, *Il pro-
cesso inquisitoriale del cardinal Giovanni Morone: Edizione critica.* 5 vols. (Rome: Istituto storico italiano
per l'età moderna e contemporanea, 1981–88). Ochino, Vermigli, and Vergerio all left Italy to
avoid prosecution. The doctrine of *sola fide* was officially declared heretical in 1547. See Silvana
Seidel Menchi, "Italy," in *The Reformation in National Context,* ed. Bob Scribner et al., 181–97
(Cambridge: Cambridge University Press, 1994), 187.

52. The first published edition that we know of is Benedetto da Mantova, *Trattato utilissimo del
beneficio di Giesù Christo crocifisso verso i christiani* (Venice: Bernardino de Bindonis, 1543). On the
publication and circulation of the *Beneficio di Cristo,* see Mantova, *Il Beneficio di Cristo con le versioni
del secolo XVI: Documenti e testimonianze,* ed. Salvatore Caponetto (Florence: Sansoni, 1972), 469–

their number, Marcantonio Flaminio, has been credited with having edited or co-authored the text in the early 1540s, when he brought it with him to Viterbo and most likely consulted the other members of the group for responses and advice. The *Beneficio* went on to attract an enormous readership across Italy both before and after it was condemned by the Council of Trent in 1546 and then placed on the Index of Prohibited Books of 1549.[53] Epitomizing the close connection in this period between the circulation of vernacular literature and reform propaganda, the text presents a jubilant call to arms to the new faith, expressed in a highly evocative and lyrical language that is compelling and arousing, while simultaneously succeeding in clarifying for readers at every level the meaning and significance of the central tenets of the reform movement.[54] Colonna herself was probably exposed to the text in this period, and whether directly or indirectly, both its message and style had a strong influence on her lyric output.

The bond that developed between Colonna and Reginald Pole in this latter period of her life was a profound one, based on their shared concern for spiritual matters and interest in the question of reform, and she clearly relied on him to guide her through this difficult terrain. Her reliance on her friend was not always met with the desired response, however, and a number of her letters testify to Colonna's disappointment at being neglected or abandoned by Pole.[55] In addition, other members of the Viterbo group appear to have doubted the propriety of her intense devotion, accusing her of a love that was "excessive, too maternally carnal."[56] Despite such difficulties Colonna alludes in her poetry to an idealized spiritual bond between them. A sonnet addressed to Pole (in the closing sequence of the manuscript for Michelangelo) describes the importance for her of her friend's role as mentor: "You walk upon the open spacious fields / of heaven, and no shadow or rock / can now delay or obstruct your swift progress. / I, burdened by my

---

98. Also see Tommaso Bozza, *Nuovi studi sulla Riforma in Italia: I, Il Beneficio di Cristo* (Rome: Storia e letteratura, 1976); Caponetto, *The Protestant Reformation in Sixteenth-Century Italy*, 76–94; and Fenlon, *Heresy and Obedience*, 69–88.

53. Mantova, *Il Beneficio di Cristo*, 470.

54. On the connection between the reform movement and published vernacular literature in Italy, see Carlo Dionisotti, "La letteratura italiana nell'età del concilio di Trento," in *Geografia e storia della letteratura italiana*, 183–204 (Turin: Einaudi, 1967).

55. See, for example, Pagano and Ranieri, *Nuovi documenti su Vittoria Colonna e Reginald Pole*, 96, in which Colonna's peevish tone, despite her flattery of her friend, betrays her bitterness at being ignored.

56. "[A]lcuna volta reprendono la mia servitù con Monsig.r., dicendo che è *superchia, troppo maternamente carnale* e simil cose." Cited in Pagano and Ranieri, *Nuovi documenti su Vittoria Colonna e Reginald Pole*, 141–42 (emphasis added).

years, am frozen here; therefore you / who are aflame with divine fire, pray humbly on my behalf / for help from our common father."[57] Both individuals seem to have held fast to the possibility of religious compromise, that is, of retaining a belief in *sola fide* and remaining a Catholic, and Colonna's death in 1547 meant that she was spared the ignominy of the Inquisition's attentions at the end of that decade.

The literary works of these final years of her life, in their frequent references to Lutheran doctrine and their general mystical tenor, clearly speak of Colonna's interest in reform and therefore cannot be fully understood without some knowledge of the context in which they were produced. The manuscript for Michelangelo is perhaps the most condensed and explicit illustration—no doubt in great part due to the private context of its readership—of the manner in which her Petrarchan lyrics came to be wholly spiritual and evangelical and how as a result they turned the genre in a new and previously unexplored direction.[58]

LITERARY WORKS

The publication history of Colonna's poetry in the sixteenth century bears testimony to the unprecedented level of literary fame and success she enjoyed in this era. Also noteworthy, however, is the fact that Colonna herself never claimed any involvement with any of the editions of her work published during her lifetime, suggesting the level of propriety and humility required by the aristocratic woman writer, who cannot admit to a desire for acclaim or publicity and less still for monetary gain. In 1538, a first edition of the poet's *Rime* was published in Parma.[59] A collection of 145 amorous sonnets (the so-called *rime amorose,* although in fact nine of these are mistakenly attributed to Colonna and are by other authors), this work set the standard for the many subsequent editions of her poetry that were issued in the ensuing years and definitively established the public image of Colonna as a

<hr>

57. "Tu per gli aperti spaziosi campi / Del ciel camini, e non più nebbia o pietra / Ritarda o ingombra il tuo spedito corso. / Io, grave d'anni, aghiaccio; or tu ch'avampi / D'alta fiamma celeste, umil m'impetra / Dal comun padre eterno omai soccorso." Sonnet 99, lines 9–14 in this translation.

58. Rinaldina Russell has demonstrated that the final printed edition of Colonna's sonnets of 1546 articulates a more radical commitment to reform than had previously been seen in her published works and thus introduces into a more public context the tendencies already apparent in the private manuscript for Michelangelo. See the discussion in Russell, "L'ultima meditazione di Vittoria Colonna e l' 'Ecclesia Viterbiensis'": *La Parola del Testo; Semestrale di filologia e letteratura italiana e comparata dal medioevo al rinascimento* 4 (2000): 151–66.

59. Colonna, *Rime,* 1982, 258.

mournful widow memorializing her lost consort. As noted above, it appears that the poet's work had become well-known to an erudite courtly audience long before this date (as the eulogy by Ariosto in the 1532 edition of the *Orlando furioso* makes clear), through a carefully controlled process of scribal publication overseen, perhaps, by the poet herself with the help of her literary agents Paolo Giovio (1483–1552) and Carlo Gualteruzzi (1500–77).[60] It was from 1538, however, that a wider public first began to have access to affordable printed editions of the vernacular verses, published in a number of cities on the peninsula.

The amorous sonnets contained in this and other early editions of her work clearly testify to Colonna's debt to Petrarch and also show an intimate knowledge of Dante and of the stylistic and linguistic ideals explored by Bembo in his poetry and prose. Thematically, these sonnets are traditional in their emphasis on the suffering poet who bemoans a lost love, although the gender reversal is of course entirely new and significant and the love that is mourned, unlike its male counterpart, has a legitimate public face. Stylistically, the sonnets are carefully controlled and highly finished, revealing a gravitas of tone and a subtle and gradual development that demand as much of a careful and observant reader as they do of the poet herself.[61] While the subject matter and approach of these early sonnets is perhaps not original (and it would in any case be anachronistic to look for the quality of originality in poetry of this period and in this genre[62]), they clearly reveal Colonna's lyric skill and stylistic control, which marks her as an equal to the finest male poets of her age, an equality that appears to have been recognized and lauded by numerous contemporaries.[63]

60. Giovio and Gualteruzzi both appear to have acted frequently on Colonna's behalf in disseminating her verses and receiving responses to them, presumably in part in order to protect the poet's feminine decorum. More generally, on the role of the literary agent or secretary, see Brian Richardson, "Print or Pen? Modes of Written Publication in Sixteenth-Century Italy," *Italian Studies* 59 (2004): 39–64, at 50–51.

61. Bembo commented on the *gravitas* of Colonna's work, a characteristic he particularly valued. See Dionisotti, "Appunti sul Bembo e su Vittoria Colonna," 261–63. Paolo Giovio also lauded this aspect of her poetry. See Ferino-Pagden, *Vittoria Colonna*, 172–74.

62. On the mistaken view of sixteenth-century Petrarchism as "insincere," based on a misunderstanding of the practice of Renaissance *imitatio*, see Hempfer, "Per una definizione del Petrarchismo," 24–26. More generally on literary imitation in this period, see Martin L. McLaughlin, *Literary Imitation in the Italian Renaissance: The Theory and Practice of Literary Imitation in Italy from Dante to Bembo* (Oxford: Clarendon Press, 1995).

63. On the many instances of praise of and dedication to Colonna in works by contemporaries, see Concetta Ranieri, "Vittoria Colonna: dediche, libri e manoscritti," *Critica letteraria* 1 (1985): 249–70; and Scala, "Encomi e dediche nelle prime relazioni culturali di Vittoria Colonna."

A new publication of 1539 (the fifth edition of the poet's work) appended for the first time a small number of spiritual sonnets to the selection of poems.[64] From this point on, *rime spirituali* were always included in printed editions of the poetry and were highlighted as being particularly new and important on the title pages. In addition, a number of editions now included woodcut illustrations of the poet, clad (quite erroneously) in a nun's habit and kneeling in prayer before a crucifix, as if to underline her impeccable spiritual credentials for any doubtful reader. It seems Colonna's early editors were as aware as she was herself of the immense marketing power of her piety and were keen to foster the link between the poet's public persona and her work. The *rime spirituali* were generally advertised as being a new departure for the poet from this date; nonetheless, the manner in which they grow organically out of her earlier work, D'Avalos prefiguring Christ and the poet's loving bond with him developing naturally into a spiritual union, suggests that Colonna's spiritual project was in place from the very beginning and that her earliest, so-called amorous poetic endeavors were already fostering the later development into overtly religious subject matter. This uniformity of tone and purpose has been remarked upon by previous critics and has been used by some to dismiss Colonna's work, accusing her of repetitiveness and abstraction without perhaps recognizing the important personal and poetic aspirations at the root of her unified approach, which seeks ultimately to find a poetic voice capable of encapsulating her religious faith.[65]

What is undeniable is that, as the number of *rime spirituali* in circulation grows steadily after 1539, the transforming quality of Colonna's lyric enterprise becomes increasingly apparent. In the more mature spiritual verses, reworked and polished by the poet over a number of years, a new and often distinctly un-Petrarchan poetic voice comes to the fore, one that is at times highly sensual and mystical, reflecting the influence of the language of the New Testament as well as of the evangelical religious circles in which Colonna was moving from the 1530s. It seems that we cannot therefore dismiss Colonna as merely the strict and diligent Petrarchan imitator that her earlier amorous poetry might suggest; rather, her mature lyric voice pushes the Petrarchan format in an entirely new direction, in both style and theme, and by anchoring it to a contemporary religious movement and thus conferring

---

64. Colonna, *Rime*, 1982, 259.

65. See for a typical example of such criticism, Vittorio Rossi, *Storia della letteratura italiana. Volume secondo: Dal rinascimento al rinnovamento*, ed. Umberto Bosco (Milan: Dr. Francesco Villardi, 1956), 137. This critic, like many others of his era, also reads Colonna's poetry in a strictly autobiographical vein.

a relevance and immediacy upon a genre better known for its courtliness and isolationism.[66] We must therefore recognize Colonna's status as a poetic innovator in ways that lie quite apart from her gendered approach to her work: her profoundly spiritual Petrarchism was a new take on a well-established genre that would come to be widely imitated by numerous male successors, albeit stripped of its reform resonance, as well as by other women.

Of course it should also be noted that this new spiritual direction to her Petrarchism was Colonna's response to the wider development of both poetry and evangelical literature in this period and did not take place in isolation. In particular, her lyric innovations are a reflection of the notably lyrical language of the Italian reform movement, encapsulated most clearly in a text such as the *Beneficio di Cristo*.[67] Significantly, the alleged co-author of that text, Marcantonio Flaminio, was himself a lyric poet as well as the author of a Latin verse translation of thirty psalms (published in Venice in 1545) that directly responded to Luther's call for new hymns for the new church.[68] Nonetheless, it can be asserted that Colonna occupied a central position as perhaps the most ardent practitioner of the cross-fertilization of Petrarchism and evangelism in the midcentury, and her huge editorial success saw the circulation of her verses to a wide audience across the peninsula. For this reason, the subsequent outpouring of spiritual Petrarchism in the later sixteenth century closely follows the model of Colonna's *canzoniere spirituale*, for example, the poetry of Luca Contile (b. ?–1574) and others.[69]

As testament to her enormous success as a poet, in 1543 a highly unusual edition of Colonna's spiritual sonnets was published, including in it a commentary on the poems by a young scholar from Correggio, Rinaldo Corso (1525–82).[70] This work was unprecedented, constituting not only the first example in this period of a published critical reading of the work of

66. On the lyric abstraction of the Petrarchan genre (that Colonna can be seen to be escaping), see Greene, *The Light in Troy*, 174–76.

67. On the links between Petrarchan lyricism and the evangelical prose works of the mid-sixteenth century, see Abigail Brundin, "Vittoria Colonna and the Poetry of Reform," *Italian Studies* 57 (2002): 61–74, at 63–66.

68. On Flaminio, see Carol Maddison, *Marcantonio Flaminio: Poet, Humanist and Reformer* (London: Routledge and Kegan Paul, 1965), 159–68.

69. On this phenomenon, see Quondam, *Il naso di Laura*, 263–89.

70. The commentary was also reissued in a complete edition, including the *rime amorose*, in 1558. See Monica Bianco, "Le due redazioni del commento di Rinaldo Corso alle *Rime* di Vittoria Colonna," *Studi di filologia italiana* 56 (1998): 271–95; and "Rinaldo Corso e il 'Canzoniere' di Vittoria Colonna," *Italique: Poésie italienne de la Renaissance* 1 (1998): 37–45. For information on Rinaldo Corso, see *DBI*, 29: 687–90; and Riccardo Finzi, *Un Correggese del Rinascimento: Rinaldo Corso, 1525–1582* (Modena: Aedes Muratoriana, 1959).

a female writer, but also of the work of a living writer of either sex.[71] Corso's commentary therefore indicates a serious consideration of Colonna's work by her readers and an effort on the part of contemporary scholarship to locate her poetry within a canonical tradition that linked her to her most prestigious classical and medieval forefathers. In addition to its significance as a sign of the esteem in which her work was held, Corso's commentary also served to highlight the evangelical content of Colonna's spiritual sonnets, through a reading that was alive to the poet's allusions to the doctrines and ideas of the reform movement. Corso himself appears to have had some involvement with groups of reformers in Venice and was employed in Correggio by the other aristocratic woman poet of this era, Veronica Gambara, for whom his commentary was originally prepared and who was herself drawn to the doctrine of *sola fide* and expressed this interest in her poetry.[72] Thus we may hypothesize that Corso was moved to write a commentary on Colonna because of her evident interest in exploring reform spirituality through her poetry, an interest shared by himself and his patron (and also, of course, because of the implicit compliment to Gambara in selecting another female Petrarchist for his scholarly attention), and his sensitive and nuanced reading of the verses drew to the attention of a much wider audience the evangelical content of the sonnets. Whether this publication, and more particularly the later 1558 edition of Corso's commentary on the sonnets, also contributed to Colonna's gradual editorial decline in the latter half of the century can only be left open to hypothesis. Certainly from the 1560s the number of printed editions of her work decreased substantially, perhaps as her link with suspect religious movements became more firmly established in the less tolerant religious environment post-Trent.[73]

Colonna's literary output during her lifetime was not limited to poetry, although it was in this genre that she achieved the greatest level of fame and acclaim. She also wrote a number of prose works that were published during the sixteenth century, the majority composed initially as letters but seemingly always with an eye to eventual dissemination among a wider reader-

---

71. Bembo himself was not honored by a critical commentary until as late as 1729. See Bianco, "Le due redazioni del commento di Rinaldo Corso alle *Rime* di Vittoria Colonna," 273.

72. On Corso's involvement with the reform movement in Venice, see Bianco, "Le due redazioni del commento di Rinaldo Corso alle *Rime* di Vittoria Colonna," 281–82; and Seidel Menchi, "Le traduzioni italiane di Lutero nella prima metà del Cinquecento." On Gambara's interest in reform, see the various articles in Cesare Bozzetti, Pietro Gibellini, and Ennio Sandal, eds. *Veronica Gambara e la poesia del suo tempo nell'Italia settentrionale* (Florence: Olschki, 1989); and William Kennedy, *Authorizing Petrarch* (Ithaca: Cornell University Press, 1994), 134–46.

73. The editorial history of the sonnets will be discussed in more detail below.

ship. The first of these to be published was an edition of three letters on religious topics to her cousin, Costanza D'Avalos Piccolomini, issued in Venice in 1544 and again in 1545.[74] Treating the subject of the potential of the Virgin Mary to act as a positive role model for Catholic women and exploring in addition the figures of Catherine of Alexandria and Mary Magdalene, these letters, with their apparently proto-feminist content and evocative language reminiscent of her spiritual sonnets, embrace the theme of the need for women to find positive religious and behavioral role models from within the examples of their own sex. Clearly this is a theme close to Colonna's own heart in her search for a means of legitimating her position as an outspoken and high-profile literary female. In a letter to Marguerite de Navarre she expresses the difficulty she has had in locating such models in her own country and thus her decision to turn to France and the inspiring model provided by Marguerite herself: "For it seems to me that the examples of our own sex naturally fit us better, and it is more advisable to follow these."[75]

The second of the three published letters in particular is markedly original in its reinterpretation of such female religious figures along new and assertive lines. In the context of a description of a vision the writer has had of Mary embracing her son after the Deposition, Colonna explores her numerous roles and includes among them the unprecedented one of teacher and disseminator of the word of God, as one who is blessed with divine understanding:

> Just think what enlightened words she formed then, what wise and inspiring expressions issued from her saintly mouth, what bountiful and bright rays burned in those divine eyes, with what most astute advice, without contravening any law, she laid down the law for those who heard her, as a true teacher constituted by the first teacher to bring his commandments to the world, which he composed with his own blood.[76]

---

74. On these editions, see Maria Luisa Doglio, "L'occhio interiore e la scrittura nelle 'Litere' di Vittoria Colonna," in *Omaggio a Gianfranco Folena*, 3 vols. (Padua: Editoriale Programma, 1993), 2: 1001–13; and more generally on female epistolography, see Gabriella Zarri, *Per lettera: La scrittura epistolare femminile tra archivio e tipografia, secoli XV–XVII* (Rome: Viella, 1999).

75. "[P]arendomi che gli essempii del suo proprio sesso a ciascuno sian più proportionati, et il seguir l'un l'altro più lecito." Cited in Colonna, *Carteggio*, 186. On the spiritual concerns shared by Colonna and Navarre, see Itala T. C. Rutter, "La scrittura di Vittoria Colonna e Margherita di Navarra: Resistenza e misticismo," *Romance Languages Annual* 3 (1991): 303–8.

76. "Pensa che illuminati accenti allhor formava, che sagge ignite parole uscivan dalla santa bocca, che pietosi et chiari raggi lampeggiavano da quei lumi divini, che rettissimi consigli senza uscir delle leggi davan legge a chi l'udiva, come maestra prima constituita dal maestro

It is unusual and noteworthy that Mary is given language by Colonna in her role as a teacher of other Christians. In direct contravention of her Biblical silence and subservience, Mary takes on here a public vocal role without at any time "contravening any law," as the author is careful to assert.[77] We can well imagine the author of this letter drawing on its positive presentation of Mary's role to legitimize her own authoritative literary stance, both in the context of her letters to her cousin and more broadly in her work as a published writer.[78]

In 1557, another work, entitled *Pianto della Marchesa di Pescara sopra la Passione di Christo . . .*, was published for the first time in Venice, containing two prose meditations by Colonna together with a meditation by Benedetto Varchi (1503–65) and another by an anonymous author (probably Marcantonio Flaminio).[79] Clearly once again reflecting the influence of her evangelical environment upon her religious thought, as well as her sustained interest in the Virgin Mary, Colonna's two contributions to this volume explore the Virgin's relationship with Christ and her role during his ministry and after his death. As in her letters to her cousin, this role is a notably assertive and active one.

The first meditation, the *Pianto* from which the volume takes its name, was originally composed in the early 1540s as a letter to Bernardino Ochino, as various first-person addresses in the manuscript version of the work make clear.[80] In it, the author explores once again a vision of Christ in Mary's arms after the Deposition, a theme also picked up on in her poetry.[81] As in her letter to her cousin, Mary's strength and autonomy are emphasized in the

---

primo a fermare quelli ordini al mondo, che aveva egli fondati col proprio sangue." Cited in Colonna, *Carteggio*, 299.

77. The biblical call for female silence and submission is expressed most clearly in 1 Timothy 2. See for a discussion of this, Constance Jordan, *Renaissance Feminism: Literary Texts and Political Models* (Ithaca: Cornell University Press, 1990), 25–29.

78. For a more detailed discussion of this and the other letters to Costanza, see Abigail Brundin, "Vittoria Colonna and the Virgin Mary," *Modern Language Review* 96 (2001): 61–81, at 76–80.

79. For details of the four sixteenth-century editions of Colonna's *Pianto*, see Eva-Maria Jung-Inglessis, "Il *Pianto della Marchesa di Pescara sopra la Passione di Christo*. Introduzione," *Archivio italiano per la storia della pietà* 10 (1997): 115–47. On the hypothesis concerning Flaminio's authorship of the anonymous piece, see Jung-Inglessis, "Il *Pianto della Marchesa di Pescara*," 122–23; and Simoncelli, *Evangelismo italiano del Cinquecento*, 218–21.

80. See Jung-Inglessis, "Il *Pianto della Marchesa di Pescara*," 141; and Simoncelli, *Evangelismo italiano del Cinquecento*, 211–15. A translation by Susan Haskins of Colonna's *Pianto* is forthcoming in this series.

81. See, for example, sonnet 42 in this translation.

account, including her ability, despite her own acute sorrow, to support and comfort those around her: "She alone had the task of thanking Joseph, soothing John, comforting Mary Magdalene, and of sustaining herself in obedience to him whom she would so happily have followed if it had only been granted to her to do so."[82] While Colonna's representation of the Virgin is a human and earthly one, in line with the position of the reformers who emphasized her humanity over her divinity and her subjection to the authority of Christ, she emphasizes in particular Mary's status as the embodiment of a perfect faith:

> For, since all the treasure that the Christian may obtain is born of a true faith, and since we have received that faith from the Virgin, for without her it would have been extinguished, then we must remember how great is our obligation to her, so huge in fact that this mortal life would never be sufficient to repay even the tiniest fraction of it.[83]

Rather than reducing her significance, as some critics have argued, Colonna's very human vision of Mary in this work can be seen to increase her potency as a model for other women seeking to come to a perfect faith: her role is repositioned in a more intimate relation to the life of every Christian, as she is essentially and eternally "one of us."[84]

This program of reworking Mary's role in order to transform her into an imitable and assertive role model for Catholic women is continued in the second meditation contained in the *Pianto* volume, this time a prayer in the form of a line-by-line response to the "Hail Mary," which explores the very personal relationship between the writer and the Virgin.[85] Mary is cast here as a bountiful intercessor, in line with her traditional role in Catholic popu-

82. "[E]ssa sola havea da ringratiar Ioseph, da sodisfare Giovanni, da confortare Madalena, da sostenere se stessa per ubidire colui, che con tanta allegrezza havrebbe seguito se le fusse stato concesso." See Colonna, *Pianto della Marchesa di Pescara sopra la passione di Christo. Oratione della medesima sopra l'Ave Maria . . . etc.* (Bologna: Manutio, 1557), 9. The multiplicity of Mary's roles is another theme explored in Colonna's poetry. See, for example, sonnets 41 and 95.

83. "Per tanto, nascendo quanto tesoro può havere il Christiano, dalla vera fede; e havendolo ricevuta dalla vergine Maria, che senza lei sarebbe stata estinta; è da pensare, quanto sia l'obligo, che noi le habbiamo, che certamente cosí grande il troveremo, che questa vita mortale non bastarebbe per sodisfare alla millesima parte." Colonna, *Pianto della Marchesa di Pescara,* 11.

84. For a reading of the *Pianto* as a reform-minded work, see Alexander Nagel, *Michelangelo and the Reform of Art* (Cambridge: Cambridge University Press, 2000), 179–87. A more reductive reading of the role of Mary in this work is given in Emidio Campi, *Michelangelo e Vittoria Colonna: Un dialogo artistico-teologico ispirato da Bernardino Ochino, e altri saggi di storia della Riforma* (Turin: Claudiniana, 1994).

85. "Oratione della Marchesa di Pescara sopra l'Ave Maria, alla Madonna," in Colonna, *Pianto della Marchesa di Pescara,* 12–16.

lar worship, and the author maintains a stance characterized by deep humility and self-abnegation. Rather surprisingly, however, Mary's authority in interceding with Christ on behalf of humankind is increased exponentially by the author, so that she appears rather to have the controlling hand in choosing to share her son with others. The Christian must pray to Mary, not only because of her privileged access to Christ and her great pity for humankind, as the tradition dictates, but because she actually governs and channels the intervention of Christ in our lives and is as important as he is in the process of divine redemption: "So many ties of the flesh, chains of the spirit, rays of the intellect and flames of love make of you one single being, that one cannot imagine, nor contemplate, nor serve Christ without Mary."[86] Again, as in the *Pianto*, although the ultimate aim of serving and glorifying Christ is never in doubt, Mary's power and autonomy are clearly highlighted in this work, and its language is notably vibrant and unguarded in lauding her position as an intermediary and her essential role in guaranteeing salvation for humankind. Both these prose meditations and the letters to Costanza illustrate Colonna's developed interest both in exploring literary forms other than the Petrarchan lyric and, more significantly, in articulating a new and far more assertive role for female religious figures, one that is both vocal and authoritative and that finds its exemplification in the wholly human and imitable figure of the Virgin Mary.

THE GIFT MANUSCRIPT FOR MICHELANGELO

Colonna and Michelangelo were introduced to one another in Rome in 1536 or 1538, probably by Michelangelo's close friend Thommaso de' Cavalieri.[87] The precise date of their first meeting is uncertain, in part because of the lack of extant correspondence between them, but by late 1538 or early 1539, when Colonna took up residence in the convent of San Silvestro in Rome, there is no doubt that the pair were in regular contact. Francisco de Hollanda, in his Roman dialogues, describes meetings in the church of San Silvestro which he attended, at which Colonna skillfully questioned her

---

86. "[T]anti legami di carne, tanti vincoli di spirito, tanti lumi d'intelligenza, tanti fuochi di amore, vi fanno una medesima cosa, che non si può imaginare, né riguardare, né servire Christo senza Maria." Colonna, *Pianto della Marchesa di Pescara*, 13.

87. Deoclecio Redig de Campos, "Il Crocifisso di Michelangelo per Vittoria Colonna," in *Atti del Convegno di Studi Michelangioleschi*, 356–65 (Rome: Ateneo, 1966), 356; Ferino-Pagden, *Vittoria Colonna*, 349–73, at 350.

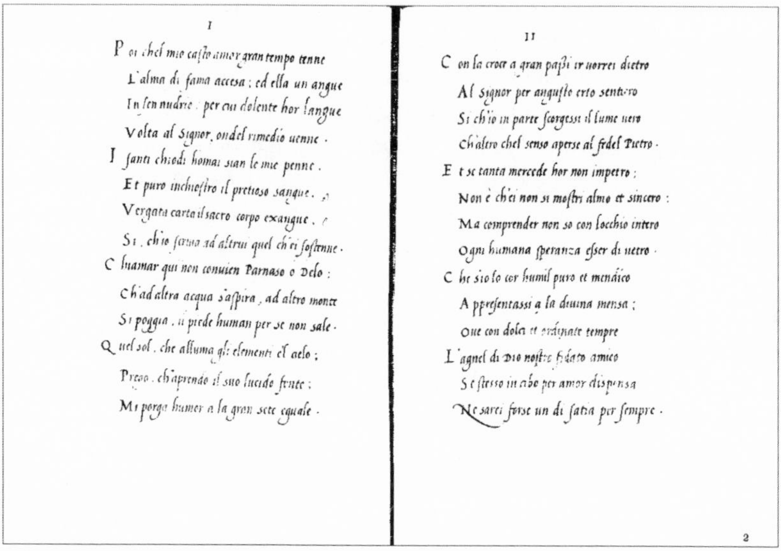

I

P oi chel mio casto amor gran tempo tenne
L'alma di fama accesa; ed ella un angue
In sen nudrie, per cui dolente hor sangue
Volta al Signor, ond'el rimedio uenne.
I santi chiodi homai sian le mie penne.
Et puro inchiostro il pretioso sangue.
Vergata carta il sacro corpo exangue.
Si, ch'io fama ad altrui quel ch'ei sostenne.
C hiamar qui non conuien Parnaso o Delo:
Ch'ad altra acqua s'aspira, ad altro monte
Si poggia, u piede human per se non sale.
Q uel sol, che alluma gli elementi e'l cielo;
Prego, ch'aprenda il suo lucido fonte:
Mi porga humor a la gran sete eguale.

II

C on la croce a gran passi ir uorrei dietro
Al Signor per anguste erto sentiero
Si ch'io in parte scorgessi il lume uero
Ch'altro chel senso aperse al fidel Pietro.
E t se tanta mercede hor non impetro;
Non è ch'ei non si mostri almo et sincero:
Ma comprender non so con l'occhio intero
Ogni humana speranza esser di uetro.
C hi sio lo cor humil puro et menaico
A pprefentassi a la diuina mensa;
Oue con dolci et ordinate tempre
L'agnel di Dio nostre fidato amico
S t stesso in abo per amor dispensa
Ne sarei forse un di satia per sempre.

2

Figure 3 First two pages from Colonna's manuscript (MS Vaticano Latino 11539, folio 1, verso, and folio 2, recto). Courtesy Biblioteca Apostolica Vaticana.

friend Michelangelo on the status of art and the role of the artist, and while his account cannot necessarily be treated as factual it is a clear record of the fame surrounding the friendship between the two, which by the late 1530s was widespread.[88]

While the dynamics of the relationship between Reginald Pole and Vittoria Colonna cast the former very much in the role of guide and mentor, between Michelangelo and Colonna a very different relationship existed. Well read, with a certain knowledge of Latin and possibly of some classical sources as well as a close understanding of the scriptures and of a variety of interpretations thereof (through her contact with the *spirituali* Colonna had access to imported works by prominent reformers from abroad, including works by Luther in translation[89]), Colonna had also benefited from close contact with some of the major religious thinkers of her period in Italy

88. Francesco de Hollanda, "Dialogos en Roma," in *Da Pintura Antigua*, ed. Joaquin de Vasconcellos, 175–277, 2d ed. (Porto: Renascenza Portoguesa, 1930), 175–277. On the trustworthiness of the dialogues as a historical record, see J. B. Bury, *Two Notes on Francisco de Holanda* (London: Warburg Institute, 1981).

89. Pietro Carnesecchi states this in his Inquisition trial. See Colonna, *Carteggio*, 342.

through correspondence and friendships forged in Naples and Rome.[90] She was thus probably in a position of some authority over Michelangelo regarding questions of faith, as well of course as commanding a far higher social status than he did and being already well-known for her skill in poetry, and thus she assumed the role of spiritual guide and source for religious and poetic inspiration in the verses that Michelangelo addressed to her.[91] In one poem in particular, a madrigal entitled "Un uomo in una donna, anzi un dio" (A man within a woman, or rather a god), Colonna's gender is transformed as Michelangelo transmutes her into a man or god, reflecting her strength and leadership:

> A man within a woman, or rather a god
> speaks through her mouth, so that I,
> by having listened to her,
> have been made such that I'll never be my own again.[92]

In this verse, the poet is so grateful for the spiritual inspiration provided by his lady that he prays that he might never be forced to return to his previous earthbound state, for which he now feels only pity. The tone is optimistic, hopeful that salvation will prove to be near at hand. Michelangelo's transformation of Colonna into a man or god as she instructs him in spiritual matters indicates the essentially nongendered nature of their interaction: Colonna's sex does not preclude her from taking a leading role in the relationship. Michelangelo's "masculinized" response to her is a further illustration of the way in which the female poet appears able with great dexterity and skill to modulate the manner of her self-presentation.[93]

90. Firpo, "Vittoria Colonna, Giovanni Morone e gli 'spirituali,'" 248–51. The author points out Colonna's active and central role at Viterbo and the works she read.

91. For an indication of Michelangelo's own theological background and education, see Giorgio Spini, "Per una lettura teologica di Michelangelo," *Protestantesimo* 44 (1989): 2–16; Romeo de Maio, *Michelangelo e la Controriforma* (Rome: Laterza, 1978).

92. "Un uomo in una donna, anzi un dio / per la sua bocca parla, / ond'io per ascoltarla / son fatto tal, che ma' più sarò mio." Cited in Michelangelo Buonarroti, *The Poetry of Michelangelo*, ed. and trans. James M. Saslow (New Haven: Yale University Press, 1991), 398, lines 1–4.

93. An interesting earlier example of this form of gender flexibility is cited in a letter to Colonna from Pope Paul III, in which he agrees to grant her leave to travel on a pilgrimage to the Holy Land. Paul refers to Colonna's bravery in planning such a venture, claiming that she possesses "a manly spirit in a woman's body." The letter is cited in Colonna, *Carteggio*, 131–32; an English translation is given in Marjorie Och, "Vittoria Colonna and the Commission for a *Mary Magdalene* by Titian," in *Beyond Isabella: Secular Women Patrons of Art in Renaissance Italy*, ed. Sheryl E. Reiss and David G. Wilkins, 193–223, Sixteenth-Century Essays and Studies, 54 (Kirksville: Truman State University Press, 2001), 214. There is also, of course, a long-standing misogynistic tradition underpinning the extolling of exemplary females as essentially "manly," clearly

There are a number of other examples of poetic exchanges between Co-
lonna and Michelangelo, which testify to their habit of exploring the spiri-
tual issues that occupied them through the medium of the lyric. In a poem
inscribed by Michelangelo onto a letter to Colonna concerning an artistic
commission, he alludes to the painful state of oscillation in which his soul is
caught, lurching from one choice to another in a misery of spiritual blind-
ness and uncertainty, and looks to his friend to act as his savior in pointing
out the true path to heaven: "Now on the right foot and now on the left,/
shifting back and forth, I search for my salvation."[94] In particular, the clos-
ing statement of this poem is bold, although clothed in an expression of
doubt, as the poet asserts that Christ's sacrifice has brought pardon for all
sinners, an emphasis that reflects the sweet and forgiving Christ of evangeli-
cal texts such as the *Beneficio di Cristo* and the same intimately loving Christ
to whom Colonna appeals in her own verses: "Nor do I know whether hum-
bled sin / holds a lower rank in heaven than sheer good."[95] Colonna's response
to her friend's plea is sonnet 79 in this manuscript, in which she offers him
advice and words of warning on the difficult journey through life. In contrast
to the ardent and devoted tone of Michelangelo's poetic plea to Colonna,
her responsive sonnet appears somewhat chilly, almost as if she suspected
the recipient of being inadequate in faith: "But our great self-love, our weak
faith / in those high and holy invisible things, / slow down our progress to-
wards salvation."[96] The extent to which this sonnet was revised and re-
written, however, testifies to a particularly intense involvement with it on
Colonna's part, and it acts as a clear testimony of the nature of the lyric ex-
changes between the two poets, in which such intimate spiritual anxieties
were aired and to some extent assuaged by Colonna in her position as men-
tor and guide.[97]

There is evidence to suggest that Colonna's interest in reform spiritual-

---

exemplified in works such as Boccaccio's *De mulieribus claris*. For a discussion, see Jordan, *Renais-
sance Feminism*.

94. "Ora in su l'uno, ora in su l'altro piede / variando, cerco della mia salute." Cited in Buonar-
roti, *The Poetry of Michelangelo*, 319. Saslow cites in his edition a later version of the poem, prob-
ably a later reworking. The original letter and poem (cited above) are in a manuscript in the
Biblioteca Apostolica Vaticana, Codice Vaticano Latino 3211, leaf 99.

95. "Né so se minor grado in ciel si tiene / l'umil peccato che 'l superchio bene." Cited (in a
slightly different version) in Buonarroti, *The Poetry of Michelangelo*, 319, lines 13–14.

96. "Ma il molto amore a noi, la poca fede / De l'invisibil cose alte e divine / Ne ritardano il
corso a la mercede." Sonnet 79, lines 12–14.

97. See on Colonna's extensive revisions of this sonnet, Carlo Vecce, "Petrarca, Vittoria,
Michelangelo: Note di commento a testi e varianti di Vittoria Colonna e Michelangelo," *Studi
e problemi di critica testuale* 44 (1992): 101–25, at 114.

ity, inspired by her contact with the *spirituali* in Rome precisely in the period when her friendship with Michelangelo appears to have flourished, may have had some influence on the religious thought of her friend. Certainly, in the poem by Michelangelo cited above, the closing lines emphasize a seemingly evangelical interpretation of the status of the sinner as the poet questions the value of "sheer good" in heaven, implying that God does not take into account our sinfulness but only our faith, as Protestant doctrine maintains. There are in addition other artistic works by Michelangelo that appear to correspond closely to the spiritual impulses that inform Colonna's writing, both in their choice of subject matter and their mode of representation, specifically, three presentation drawings on religious subjects given to Colonna by the artist.[98] The first of these, a *Crucifixion*, was completed some time in 1540 and depicts a *Christus triumphans* undefeated and imbued on the cross with a new and divine life, seemingly intended to inspire, in place of the lamentation of Catholic tradition, joy at the Passion and the jubilant taking up of arms of the militant evangelical, just as is encouraged in a reform movement text such as the *Beneficio di Cristo*.[99] A second drawing of a pietà, thought to have been presented to Colonna in the early 1540s, portrays the same refusal to accept defeat and embrace sorrow, this time in the depiction of Mary's strong and lifelike arms upraised in an ambiguous gesture of intermingled jubilation and mourning and her powerful legs, which support the body of the dead Christ.[100] Finally, a drawing of the *Samaritan Woman at the Well* evokes the passage from John 4 recounting the quick conversion and dedication to the true faith of a woman from Samaria and her subsequent role as preacher spreading the word to others and thus picks up on Colonna's interest in the potential importance of women in spreading news of the new faith, as illustrated in her prose works.[101]

The manuscript of sonnets by Colonna presented in this translation, compiled as a gift for Michelangelo in around 1540 perhaps in response to

---

98. On Michelangelo's use of the genre of presentation drawings in this intimate religious context, see Alexander Nagel, "Gifts for Michelangelo and Vittoria Colonna," *Art Bulletin* 79 (1997): 647–68.

99. See on this drawing, Ferino-Pagden, *Vittoria Colonna*, 413–15. It is now housed in the British Museum in London (Department of Prints and Drawings, catalog no. 1895-9-15-504).

100. Ferino-Pagden, *Vittoria Colonna*, 426–28, now in the Isabella Stewart Gardner Museum in Boston, catalog no. 1.2.o/16. The similarity between this drawing and the emotions of Colonna's *Pianto* has been remarked on by a number of critics. See Campi, *Michelangelo e Vittoria Colonna*; Nagel, "Gifts for Michelangelo and Vittoria Colonna"; Nagel, *Michelangelo and the Reform of Art*, 169–87; and Benedetto Niccolini, "Sulla religiosità di Vittoria Colonna," *Studi e materiali di storia delle religioni* 22 (1949): 89–109.

101. Ferino-Pagden, *Vittoria Colonna*, 445–51. This drawing has not been identified.

(or provoking) his presentation drawings, grows out of this context of mutual poetic and spiritual exploration and, in addition, reflects very clearly the influence on her poetry of the *ecclesia viterbiensis* with which Colonna was closely involved at the time. Allusions to the doctrinal ideas of the reform movement, particularly the doctrine of *sola fide*, abound within the poetic texts in Michelangelo's manuscript, and the exclusive concentration on the poet's relationship with a loving and forgiving Christ is entirely in line with the Christocentrism of reform thought as reflected in a text such as the *Beneficio di Cristo*. The clear reform-minded nature of the work, and the intimate context of its receipt, suggest strongly that the friendship between Michelangelo and Colonna was embedded in a shared interest in just such spiritual issues and perhaps that Michelangelo shared his friend's belief in *sola fide* or that she sought, through her poetry, to convince him of its validity.

In addition, the status of the manuscript as a gift is highly significant and again relates closely to Colonna's involvement with the *spirituali* in this period. Natalie Zemon Davis has asserted that "in a profound sense, the Protestant Reformation was a quarrel about gifts, about whether we can reciprocate to God, about whether we can oblige him, and what this means for what we owe each other."[102] Within the practice of Catholic worship, a complex cycle of giving and reciprocating was in operation through which one could hope to "buy" the salvation of one's own soul or that of a loved one, through, for example, prayer, good works, and regular attendance at confession. Equally, in the sacrifice of mass the Catholic Christian offered the body and blood of Christ to God as a gift to appease his justified anger and to do him honor. It was this notion, that the sacrifice of mass operated as a gift to God to reciprocate him for his original gift of salvation, that was ferociously rejected by the Protestant reformers, who considered it a form of bribery or obligation of God as well as a negative drain on the Christian, who needs to recognize the boundless quality of God's gift and the impossibility of reciprocation.[103] In Protestant ideology, as expressed by Calvin in the *Institutes*, for example, the notion of reciprocity is abandoned or rejected and the gift exchange becomes a one-way process, no longer an eternal cycle of debt and counterdebt, but a flow leading from God down through

102. Davis, "Gifts and Bribes in Sixteenth-Century France," 9. See, more generally, on the context of Renaissance gift exchange, Natalie Zemon Davis, "Beyond the Market: Books as Gifts in Sixteenth-Century France," *Transactions of the Royal Historical Society*, 5th series, 33 (1983): 69–88.

103. On the Protestant debate concerning the institution of Mass, see Jaroslav Pelikan, *The Christian Tradition: A History of the Development of Doctrine*, 5 vols. (Chicago: University of Chicago Press, 1984), 4: 158–61; 189–203.

the Christian brotherhood, who in turn pass it on to the following genera-
tions of the chosen. The true Christian gives unendingly and expects no re-
turn because her return in heaven is already guaranteed.[104]

In this context, a gift such as the evangelically inspired manuscript of
sonnets for Michelangelo from Colonna takes on a religious significance
that moves far beyond the superficial appearance of a mere gesture of friend-
ship and comes to symbolize Colonna's reformed faith in the meritless
bounty of God's love for his elected souls.[105] There is evidence too to sug-
gest that the recipient of this gift, Michelangelo himself, was deeply aware
of the importance of the gesture. In a letter probably composed in 1540,
he thanks Colonna for "things" that she has bestowed upon him and that he
feels unworthy to receive:

> I had wished, my Lady, before accepting the things that you have
> wanted to give me for some time now, to make something for you by
> my own hand in order not to accept them ungratefully: but then, rec-
> ognizing clearly that the grace of God cannot be bought, and to ac-
> cept it uneasily is a mortal sin, I admit that the fault is mine, and will-
> ingly accept these things from you.[106]

Michelangelo's tone in this letter clearly reflects the tendency described
above to view the gift as a reflection of divine grace, something of which the
recipient cannot feel worthy but which he must agree to accept with grate-
ful simplicity. In addition, he clearly refers to his initial desire to reciprocate,
which he has suppressed, recognizing the truth embodied in the doctrine of
sola fide that God's grace cannot be earned and that it is a sin to imagine that
one could deserve it through merit. As he never specifies the nature of "the
things" that so please him, critics have assumed that Colonna's gift consisted
of religious objects of some description. There is no reason, however, why
this letter could not as easily relate to a gift of sonnets, a hand-written and
plainly bound manuscript containing a selection of the poet's most recent,
reform-minded poems. Certainly, the gift manuscript of sonnets that Co-

---

104. Davis, "Gifts and Bribes in Sixteenth-Century France," 9–11.

105. See Nagel, "Gifts for Michelangelo and Vittoria Colonna," 647–48; and Nagel, *Michelan-
gelo and the Reform of Art* , 186–87.

106. "Volevo, Signora, prima che io pigliassi le cose, che Vostra Signoria m'ha più volte volute
dare, per riceverle manco indegnamente che io potevo, far qualche cosa a quella di mia mano:
dipoi, riconosciuto e visto che la grazia di Iddio non si può comperare, e che 'l tenerla a disa-
gio è peccato grandissimo, dico mia colpa, e volentieri dette cose accetto." Cited in Colonna,
Carteggio, 210–11. On this letter from Michelangelo and the reformist gift exchanges between
him and Colonna, see Nagel, "Gifts for Michelangelo and Vittoria Colonna," esp. 650–51.

lonna prepared for her friend was jealously guarded by Michelangelo until his death in 1564, indicating the high value he attached to it.[107]

The manuscript now known to be the gift from Colonna to Michelangelo was first identified in Rome by Enrico Carusi in 1938.[108] Extremely plain in its binding and lacking any illumination, the title page also omits the poet's last name or title as well as the usual epithet of "divine," which was included in all published editions of her work, highlighting the personal and informal nature of the gift. Instead it reads only "Spiritual sonnets by Madam Vittoria." (The addition of the name appears almost as an afterthought, as if it were assumed that the recipient would be well aware of the provenance of this very particular collection.) All the sonnets in the manuscript are *rime spirituali* from the poet's later period of production, only seventeen of which had already been published in printed editions by 1540, when the gift was probably prepared.[109] They are written one per page and numbered chronologically, and the handwriting is that of one of Colonna's own calligraphers, indicating that the poet herself oversaw the preparation of the work.[110]

This collection is not arranged in the manner of earlier *canzonieri* by poets such as Pietro Bembo and Iacopo Sannazaro, which conformed to the

107. In a letter to his nephew Lionardo of March 1551, Michelangelo refuses to loan his manuscript of sonnets to Francesco Fattucci, who has inquired about it, claiming (wrongly) that all the sonnets are already in print. Cited in Domenico Tordi, *Il codice delle Rime di Vittoria Colonna, Marchesa di Pescara, appartenuto a Margherita d'Angoulême, Regina di Navarra* (Pistoia: Flori, 1900), 11. This is not the only copy of Colonna's sonnets that Michelangelo had in his possession; he also owned a copy of the 1558 published edition with commentary, which contains his signature and is now housed in the British Library (catalog no. c.28.a.10).

108. Enrico Carusi, "Un codice sconosciuto delle *Rime spirituali* di Vittoria Colonna, appartenuto forse a Michelangelo Buonarroti," *Atti del IV Congresso Nazionale di Studi Romani* 4 (1938): 231–41. See also the useful article by Carlo Vecce, "Zur Dichtung Michelangelos und Vittoria Colonnas," in Ferino-Pagden, *Vittoria Colonna*, 381–84. Michelangelo's manuscript is now in the Vatican Library, Codice Vaticano Latino 11539.

109. This decision to include only the most mature spiritual sonnets in the manuscript forms a contrast with another gift manuscript of Colonna's sonnets prepared for Marguerite de Navarre at around the same time. For details of the unusual arrangement of Navarre's manuscript, as well as the various arguments for and against its identification, see Brundin, "Vittoria Colonna and the Virgin Mary," esp. 61–64. Russell, "L'ultima meditazione di Vittoria Colonna e l'*Ecclesia Viterbiensis*," 153, mistakenly claims that far more of the sonnets in Michelangelo's manuscript had already been published by 1540 and thus that the collection did not represent a new departure for the poet.

110. See Vecce, "Petrarca, Vittoria, Michelangelo," 104.

model devised by Petrarch, that is, a development from the concerns of an earthly love, through a gradual spiritual awakening, to a final prayer to the Virgin Mary. Here there is no chronological development of the soul, but rather a universal contemplation of the mystery of faith that leads full circle, culminating and beginning in the inevitable fact of the individual and her relationship with Christ.[111] The novelty of this arrangement, which evades the general aspiration toward escape from earthly love to be found in most Petrarchan *canzonieri* and instead celebrates confinement within a dominating and eternal need for spiritual love, marks Colonna's poetic enterprise as distinct from that of her poetic predecessors. The poet no longer bemoans, but rather celebrates her powerlessness faced by the might and wonder of God and abandons herself to his will, as the closing lines of sonnet 21 make clear: "Thus my deeds and my desires will no longer be my own, / but lightly I will move upon celestial wings / wherever the force of his holy love might fling me" (lines 12–14).[112] Such willful self-abandonment is wholly in line with the call of the reformers to devote oneself to faith instead of striving to expunge sin through good works.

In addition, while modern readers have often found fault with Petrarchan lyric collections precisely because of their seeming detachment from reality, in what is seen as a form of courtly escapism into amorous themes and an aristocratic refusal to engage with wider society, in this manuscript the poet's reform spirituality ties her collection closely to the principal religious issues of her day. Many sonnets allude, whether openly or more obscurely, to the doctrine of *sola fide* and its impact upon the individual Christian. In sonnet 2, for example, the poet refers to the fragility of human hope, which must be cast aside in order to trust wholly in God. Sonnet 73 illustrates the utter helplessness of the individual unless God chooses to guide her: "Our minds can only see as much as he chooses / to reveal of himself and can only fly if he lends us wings / and if he clears and banishes the fog for us" (lines 12–14).[113] Sonnet 78 describes the "pure and perfect gift" of faith (line 8) conferred by God and maintains that it is this faith, and not wisdom, learning, or other earthly achievements, that eventually earns salvation. The issue of predestination is examined in, among others, sonnet 8, in which the poet envies the status of the elect and longs to be able to consider herself one of their number. The process of lyric contemplation and the context of

111. See Vecce, "Petrarca, Vittoria, Michelangelo," 105.
112. "Non saranno alor mie l'opre e 'l desire, / Ma lieve andrò con le celesti piume / Ove mi spinge e tira il santo ardore."
113. "Quant'ei si vuol talor mostrar discerne / La mente, e sol quand'ei le presta l'ali / Vola, e mentre le nebbie apre e disgombra."

the manuscript's readership are both deeply private, but the questions Colonna explores and endeavors to illustrate for her reader and herself have a resounding significance for all those caught up by the reverberations of the Reformation in mid—sixteenth-century Europe.

The path-breaking nature of this sonnet sequence in its overall shape and development can be considered to further the argument for the poet's own personal involvement in overseeing the work for Michelangelo. While published editions of Colonna's sonnets from the sixteenth century present a more generic picture of a female poet in mourning for her consort and subsequently finding comfort in religion, this manuscript allows the reader a far more intimate and sustained insight into the questions and issues that most profoundly challenged and moved her at this moment in her life and affords a glimpse into the workings of a very particular friendship. Most crucially, the amorous theme of mourning for the deceased consort has been abandoned altogether and no sonnets referring to an earthly love are included in the collection; rather, the focus is wholly and exclusively on Christ. The poet celebrates a notably corporeal and sensual relationship with her lord. In the opening sonnet she vows to use the parts of his body and the elements of the crucifix as her poetic tools, writing with the nails dipped in his blood for ink and inscribing upon his pale body (sonnet 1, lines 5—7). In sonnet 62 she longs to fly near him, embracing his hem and inhaling his sacred perfume (lines 2—3). Sonnet 21 describes her self-abandon as she strives to be inflamed by a pure faith: "Blindly I call out to the sun, which alone of all things / I worship, and naked I burn for his heavenly gold" (lines 2—3).[114]

There is no sense in this collection of a poet who is merely diligent, working carefully and correctly within the strict limits of Petrarchan imitation (an accusation that has been leveled at Colonna in the past). Rather, although operating undoubtedly from a position of impeccable stylistic decorum and with her poetic model wholly in view at all times, Colonna introduces notes of passion and lyricism that are quite unprecedented within the Petrarchan canon. Certain imagery occurs with a frequency that seems to prefigure later mannerist stylistic developments. The poet strives upward toward the light of Christ, which is warm and secure; on earth she is weighed down by shadows and fog, which are dense and cold; the poet herself is blind and weak, ill and unable to act or feel as she strives to; Christ's communication with the faithful is secret, intimate, and loving as he helps them to untie the bonds around their hearts. Juxtapositions of heat and cold, light and dark, high and low, fire and ice constantly reemphasize the poet's actual state and the divine union that she aspires to and longs for. Yet despite

114. "Cieca il sol cui solo adoro / Invoco, e nuda bramo il celest'oro."

her feeling of being far from achieving a true state of grace, the poems are charged with optimism and hope of imminent renewal, the "true hope" conferred by Christ's love. In addition, as the notes to individual poems will quickly establish, the influence of the biblical language and tone of the New Testament is everywhere detectable in this collection, most crucially in references to the writings of Saint Paul, whose works and thought profoundly influenced the reformers in this period.[115] It is significant that Colonna's commentator, Rinaldo Corso, in his own reading of the spiritual sonnets picks up clearly on this important precedent, citing Pauline literature as a source for a number of ideas and images in the texts.[116]

Significantly, sonnets relating directly to the status of the manuscript as a gift are included in the collection. Sonnet 39 examines the concept of gift-giving in a philosophical vein, in this case the great gift of salvation offered by Christ, and alludes both to the impossibility of reciprocation and to the certainty of receiving the gift, a certainty that is conferred upon the reformed Christian who believes in *sola fide* and predestination: "Man should be humbled and grateful for / the generous gifts, yet so sure of receiving them / that he burns with living faith and love" (lines 9–11).[117] The poet asks herself in the opening lines how this divine conundrum should influence her own behavior: "If it is a greater sign / to seek to offer gifts to others, / or if receiving with pious love / is a secure enough pledge to justify the greater obligation" (lines 1–4).[118] Clearly this question can be seen to relate directly to the act of giving that this manuscript represents as it does to the actions of the manuscript's recipient, who seeks to control his impulse to reciprocate. In a similar vein, sonnets 45 and 98 explore the value of art as a reflection of faith. Sonnet 45 praises the crude primitivism of one of the paintings of the Madonna attributed to Saint Luke in Rome, which reflects the artist's raw faith and his inability adequately to express his divine concept: "His breast

---

115. As noted above, Luther cited Paul as the source for the doctrine of *sola fide*, according to the interpretation of Romans 3:28. See Mullett, *The Catholic Reformation*, 42–43.

116. Particularly relevant is Corso's reading of sonnet 21, in which he notes the poet's emphasis on *sola fide* and refers it to the Pauline notion of faith lived through Christ, as expressed in Galatians 2:20. See Vittoria Colonna, *Tutte le Rime della Illustriss. et Eccellentiss. Signora Vittoria Colonna, Marchesana di Pescara. Con l'Espositione del Signor Rinaldo Corso, nuovamente mandate in luce da Girolamo Ruscelli* (Venice: Giovan Battista et Melchior Sessa Fratelli, 1558), 409–10. On Corso's close knowledge of Pauline literature, and reformist interpretations thereof, see Seidel Menchi, "Le traduzioni italiane di Lutero nella prima metà del Cinquecento."

117. "Onde dai larghi doni umile e grato / L'uom fosse, e dal ricever suo sicuro / Sì che di fede viva e d'amor arda."

118. "[S]e di più legarsi / Il donare ad altrui segno è maggiore, / O se 'l ricever con pietoso amore/Pegno è sicuro assai di più obligarsi."

was so full of the immensity of / his concept, that like a vase overfilled with water / that cannot easily flow out, the great design / came forth bit by bit, partial and imperfect" (lines 5–8).[119] Sonnet 98 praises the poetic style of Pietro Bembo, which unites the best qualities of both nature and art and begs him to turn this great gift to the service of his own faith. The closing two sonnets in the manuscript (102 and 103) both pose questions about the value of Colonna's own poetry as an adequate reflection of her religious faith, claiming that her verses are born of a divine inspiration that acts outside her control and vowing to avoid falling into easy habits but to seek always to renew the living faith that should inflame her poetry.

Petrarchan influences and conceits are of course still everywhere apparent in the sonnets in this collection (as is the important influence of Dante), but the poet's reworking of them is often bold and exciting. In many instances, she is able to redirect the Petrarchan imagery to a markedly evangelical end and thus bend and shape her poetic model to suit her specific needs. In sonnet 22, a familiar Petrarchan topos is borrowed, that of the small bark tossed upon a cruel ocean to represent the soul's difficult journey through life. Petrarch's use of this metaphor is generally negative: in his sonnet no. 189, "Passa la nave mia colma d'oblio" (My ship full of forgetful cargo sails), for example, the sea is rough and stormy, the boat is lost, and the poet despairs of ever reaching port.[120] Colonna employs the same topos in her sonnet but in a far bolder and less rationalistic frame. The enlightened soul launches itself with abandon across the ocean of divine love, in a wholly optimistic vein and safe in the knowledge that this act of faith will be rewarded with a gentle and calm sea: "His waves are always smaller and more gentle / for those who, in a bark of humility upon the great ocean / of his divine grace, freely abandon themselves" (lines 12–14).[121] This kind of example clearly demonstrates the distance that Colonna has moved as a poet from her apparent Petrarchan sources and the influence that the optimistic, Christocentric tenor of her reformed faith has had upon her poetic inspiration.

Aside from striking departures from her Petrarchan roots such as this one, however, a reader will generally need to bear in mind, when approaching a *canzoniere* of such unified thematic purpose and by an ardent and strict

---

119. "[D]e l'immensa idea sì colmo il petto / Avea, che come un vaso d'acqua pregno / Che salir non può fuor, l'alto disegno / A poco a poco uscì manco e imperfetto." This is a theme explored in the context of Michelangelo's own art in Nagel, *Michelangelo and the Reform of Art*.

120. See Francesco Petrarca, *Canzoniere*, ed. Alberto Chiari (Milan: Mondadori, 1985), 314.

121. "Sempre son l'onde sue più dolci e chiare / A chi con umil barca in quel gran fondo / De l'alta sua bontà si lascia andare."

stylist such as Colonna, that great care and attention is required in reading the sonnets in order to draw from them the full effect of their nuanced and subtle messages and particular, grave beauty. This is not always a straight-forward task, not least because we have long lost the practice of reading poetry of this kind, having moved far from an early modern understanding of the importance of literary imitation.[122] While a modern reader may search for poetic "originality" as the key to enjoyment, the true Petrarchist of the Renaissance seeks instead to ally her lyric voice as faithfully as possible with that of her model, all the while gently and gradually bringing forth her own unique poetic concerns. Colonna's oeuvre demands much of an observant reader, who is required not only to tease the overt meaning from the carefully stylized and often convoluted syntax, but also to seek to comprehend the dense and complex thematic allusions that are woven in rich detail into every sonnet.

In conclusion, it is important to make clear that this collection occupies a unique position within the overall panorama of printed and manuscript editions of Colonna's poetry from the sixteenth century. The very act of voluntarily disseminating her work, albeit in this altogether private and exclusive context, was one that was rarely indulged in by the poet. There appear to have been only two other instances in which she knowingly allowed collections of her verses to be passed on to third parties. One was a gift manuscript for Marguerite de Navarre also prepared around 1540 and sent to France via an intermediary, and the second was a manuscript of amorous sonnets, the majority already published in printed collections at the time, which was lent to Francesco della Torre, secretary to Giovanni Matteo Giberti, in 1541.[123] Neither of these other "gifts" bears the imprint of Colonna's own hand to the same extent as Michelangelo's gift. Thus we can consider the manuscript for Michelangelo as representing the poet's personal view of her lyric enterprise to an extent that none of the other collections of her po-

---

122. An interesting study by Amedeo Quondam illustrates, through analysis of anthologies of sixteenth-century Italian poets through the ages, the profound change in poetic taste, which has come about since the early modern period. In particular, poets who enjoyed great editorial success in the Renaissance, such as Colonna and Bembo, have gradually been abandoned in favor of more "original" (but in the context of Petrarchism less successful) writers such as Michelangelo and Gaspara Stampa. See Amedeo Quondam, *Petrarchismo mediato: Per una critica della forma "antologia", Livelli d'uso del sistema linguistico del petrarchismo* (Rome: Bulzoni, 1974).

123. On Navarre's manuscript, see Brundin, "Vittoria Colonna and the Virgin Mary"; Tordi, *Il codice delle Rime di Vittoria Colonna.* On the della Torre loan, see Alan Bullock, "A Hitherto Unexplored Manuscript of 100 Poems by Vittoria Colonna in the Biblioteca Nazionale Centrale, Florence," *Italian Studies* 21 (1966): 42–56; Colonna, *Rime,* 1982, 325–27; and Dionisotti, "Appunti sul Bembo e su Vittoria Colonna," 1: 282–83.

etry from this period do, and a close reading of Michelangelo's manuscript will therefore have much to tell us about Colonna's view of her own function as a poet, in particular of her doubts, despite the unprecedented success and popularity of her work, concerning the viability and legitimacy of a lyric project in which she sought to encapsulate the most profound and intimate aspects of her faith. While the reading public of 1540 was being introduced, via the printed editions of the sonnets, to the image of a pious woman mourning a lost consort, one who sacrificed her personal fame in the interests of celebrating the life of another, Colonna herself in this private manuscript had already moved far beyond that to occupy a new position as the writer of a *canzoniere spirituale* in a deeply evangelical vein, who needed no earthly consort but thought only of the next world and the divine consort with whom she would be united there.

FORTUNES AND INFLUENCE

The many editions of her poetry published during her lifetime and after testify to the popularity of the poetic model devised by Colonna, which was founded on an insistence on the female poet's profound spirituality and her higher moral aim in composing verses which, while they engage with it, also move far beyond the model of the mere love lyric. Alan Bullock's painstaking archival research has produced the first complete modern edition of Colonna's sonnets this century, a work that helps to bring into focus the author's rich and extensive lyric output during her lifetime and also clearly documents her subsequent publication history.[124]

From the first edition in 1538 until her death in 1547, thirteen editions of Colonna's poetry were published, four of these in the year 1539 alone. Of these, the first four contained only a selection of the *rime amorose*, while the subsequent editions contained a selection of both *amorose* and *spirituali* (the latter generally advertised separately on the title page).[125] In addition, Bullock lists in the appendix to his edition eleven sixteenth-century manuscript collections of the verses, in various archives throughout Italy, and more than twenty examples of manuscript anthologies from the period containing a

---

124. See Colonna, *Rime*, 1982; and Alan Bullock, "Vittoria Colonna: Note e aggiunte alla edizione critica del 1982," *Giornale storico della letteratura italiana* 162 (1985): 407–13.

125. All information on Colonna's publication history, for both manuscript and print, can be found in Bullock's invaluable "Nota sul testo" in Colonna, *Rime*, 1982, 223–462. The summary given here does not take into account the inclusion of sonnets by Colonna in printed anthology collections (although Bullock does also provide full details of these).

smaller number of Colonna's poems.[126] His findings suggest a widespread scribal publication of the verses during the period, although the extent of the poet's own involvement in this process remains difficult to ascertain. After her death in 1547, nine further editions of Colonna's poetry were published before the end of the sixteenth century, indicating something of a decline in her popularity (and perhaps more generally in the popularity of the Petrarchan genre), but by no means a radical tailing off. Beyond the end of the sixteenth century, however, the picture looks very different. Over a hundred years passed before another edition of the sonnets was issued, in 1692. This and another late–seventeenth-century edition were followed by only one edition in the eighteenth century, seven in the nineteenth century, and five (including Bullock's) in the twentieth. The impression gleaned from this publication history is of a constant presence being maintained in the literary arena, but one which never recaptured even a vestige of the immense fame and popularity that had qualified the poet's position among her contemporaries.

Such an impression poses the question: why is it that a publishing sensation of the sixteenth century faded into relative obscurity over the following centuries, when so many of her contemporaries continued to enjoy significant fame and popularity? We can link this seeming lack of interest in part, no doubt, to a waning enthusiasm in subsequent eras for the genre in which Colonna wrote, when the courtly conceits of Petrarchism came to seem outmoded and perhaps even self-indulgent. Certainly, in later eras the strict imitation practiced by succeeding generations of Petrarchists was no longer fully understood in the context of the Renaissance literary and linguistic concerns that spawned it, and instead this form of poetry came to be criticized for a perceived repetitiveness, artificiality, and lack of originality.[127] Others of the *Petrarchisti* whose fame in the sixteenth century was great have not fared much better than Colonna in subsequent centuries, most notably Pietro Bembo, whose verses also more or less disappeared from view in the seventeenth century, and who, despite four Italian editions of his poetry in the twentieth century, is still dismissed by some critics as a poet of little literary consequence, more respected by far for his linguistic theories and his neo-Platonic dialogue on love, *Gli asolani*.[128]

---

126. Colonna, *Rime*, 1982, 237–56.

127. The most famous criticism is that of A. Graf: "Il Petrarchismo è una malattia cronica della lettaratura italiana" (Petrarchism is a chronic illness of Italian literature). A. Graf, *Attraverso il Cinquecento* (Turin: Loescher, 1926), 3.

128. See Paolo Trovato, "Per la storia delle *Rime* del Bembo," *Rivista di letteratura italiana* 9 (1991): 465–508.

In addition, one must bear in mind the hypothesis that Colonna's work fell out of favor once the decidedly evangelical reform spirituality evident in her thought could no longer be tolerated by the authorities after the Council of Trent. This would certainly account for the tailing off of editions of the *Rime* after 1560 and their almost total disappearance at the end of the sixteenth century.[129] Significantly, the second edition of Rinaldo Corso's commentary on Colonna's verses, published by Girolamo Ruscelli in 1558, may quite unintentionally have contributed to this falling from favor. Ruscelli's aims in republishing the commentary appear to have been primarily linguistic, and a careful process of editing was carried out on the new edition in order to expunge all of the most overt references to the reform movement from Corso's analysis of the sonnets. Most notably, all references to the name of Bernardino Ochino were deleted, as by 1558 the preacher had been denounced as a heretic and was living in exile.[130] Nonetheless, the tone of the commentary and the arrangement of the poems themselves (which Corso himself seems to have overseen with great care and attention for the 1543 edition of the work) point up the generally evangelical nature of the reading, even in the edited later version. Perhaps, therefore, this reissuing of an undeniably reform-minded reading of Colonna's verses helped to confirm her status as inextricably linked with the *spirituali* and thus tainted posthumously with a degree of heresy, and might inadvertently have alerted the authorities to the heterodox nature of her work.

In addition to historical reasons such as these, however, Colonna's relative fall from favor can be directly attributed to a large extent to the lack of sympathy, on the part of a male critical establishment, for the work of women writers in general and in particular a lack of awareness of the very specific social and literary context of the early modern period, which brought about the development of the sort carefully "marketed" literary persona that we find in a writer like Colonna. It is important, as one assesses the impact of this persona, always to bear in mind the problems and pressures faced by a female writer of her social status, widowed, vulnerable to accusations of impropriety and lack of humility, who sought to establish a voice for herself in such unmarked territory. A highly contextualized reading is demanded by such a writer (while avoiding the all-too-common pitfall of biographism), and on this score Colonna has rarely been afforded to date the attention she fully deserves. And the neglect is not limited of course to

129. See Bianco, "Le due redazioni del commento di Rinaldo Corso alle *Rime* di Vittoria Colonna," 278–80.
130. See on the censoring of the later edition, Bianco, "Le due redazioni del commento di Rinaldo Corso alle *Rime* di Vittoria Colonna."

Colonna; it has been the fate of a number of other woman writers, highly successful in their own lifetimes, to disappear from public view shortly after death.[131]

More recently, in line with the large amount of valuable work being done in order to reclaim and reassess the work of early modern European women writers, Colonna's status and influence is coming to be recognized once again as central to any understanding of the development of a female literary canon in Italy during the Renaissance. The mistaken belief that sufficient critical attention has already been directed at the poet is being dispelled as more profound and intriguing aspects of her literary production are uncovered by scholars and unhelpful stereotypes are finally put aside.[132] It is becoming increasingly apparent, in addition, that the poet's important influence on later women writers cannot be dissociated from her evangelical involvement and interest in reform during her lifetime. By tying her poetry to a reform program, Colonna not only succeeded in escaping from the lyric abstraction and isolation of the Petrarchan courtly ethos, but she also defined a pragmatic and highly effective medium through which secular women writers could legitimately enter the literary arena. As long as writing was at all times dedicated to the service of promoting the true faith (whichever that faith may be in the opinion of the individual writer), a woman could participate in the production of literature on an equal footing with men. Thus Colonna's *canzoniere spirituale*, most clearly elucidated in her gift manuscript for Michelangelo, can be viewed as a new take on a traditional genre and one with particular relevance for women writers.[133]

It is also highly significant that, despite arising from a very particular

---

131. See, for example, the cases of Lucrezia Marinella in Marinella, *The Nobility and Excellence of Women and the Defects and Vices of Men*, ed. and trans. Anne Dunhill, intro. by Letizia Panizza, The Other Voice in Early Modern Europe (Chicago: University of Chicago Press, 1999); and Arcangela Tarabotti in Tarabotti, *Paternal Tyranny*, ed. and trans. Letizia Panizza, The Other Voice in Early Modern Europe (Chicago: University of Chicago Press, 2004).

132. The most important recent work on Colonna is listed in the volume editor's bibliography that follows this introduction.

133. Interesting work has been done, in addition, on the particular appeal of reform to aristocratic women, who were able to adopt more positive and self-affirming roles in a reform context than were usually accorded them: see Natalie Zemon Davis, "City Women and Religious Change," in *Society and Culture in Early Modern France: Eight Essays*, 65–95 (Stanford: Stanford University Press, 1975); Nancy Lyman Roelker, "The Appeal of Calvinism to French Noblewomen in the Sixteenth Century," *Journal of Interdisciplinary History* 2 (1971–72): 391–418; John Lee Thompson, *John Calvin and the Daughters of Sarah: Women in Regular and Exceptional Roles in the Exegesis of Calvin, His Predecessors, and His Contemporaries* (Geneva: Droz, 1992); and Merry E. Weisner, "Beyond Women and the Family: Towards a Gender Analysis of the Reformation," *Sixteenth-Century Journal* 18 (1987): 311–21.

moment in history, when religious thought was undergoing a profound transformation across Europe, the poetic and spiritual model Colonna devised was able to transcend cultural and religious differences and adapt to the very different atmosphere of the Counter-Reformation in Italy. While Colonna herself may have come under suspicion of heresy posthumously, it is a remarkable feature of her legacy that the model she developed and herself embodied, of the pious woman poet and public figure dedicating her literary work to the service of her faith, was, despite its clear evangelical resonance, able to meet the literary needs of later women writers well into the following century and provide them with a suitable model for imitation.[134]

134. On suppositions concerning Inquisitional attention directed at Colonna after her death, see Carlo de Frede, "Vittoria Colonna e il suo processo inquisitoriale postumo," *Atti del Accademia Pontaniana* 37 (1988): 251–83; and Gigliola Fragnito, "Vittoria Colonna e l'Inquisizione," *Benedictina* 37 (1990): 157–72. Note 7 indicates the number of later women writers who referred to Colonna's model in their own literary self-fashioning.

VOLUME EDITOR'S
BIBLIOGRAPHY

PRIMARY SOURCES

Manuscripts

Biblioteca Medicea Laurenziana, Ashburnham 1153, Florence.
Biblioteca Nazionale, Ms.II.IX.30, Florence.
Biblioteca Apostolica Vaticana, Codice Vaticano Latino 3211, Rome.
Biblioteca Apostolica Vaticana, Codice Vaticano Latino 11539, Rome.

Works by Vittoria Colonna: Books

Colonna, Vittoria. *Rime de la Divina Vittoria Colonna Marchesa di Pescara. Nuovamente stampato con privilegio.* Parma: Al Dottissimo Messer Alessandro Vercelli Philippo Pirogallo, 1538.

————. *Rime de la Diva Vettoria* [sic] *Colonna, De Pescara inclita Marchesana, Nuovavamente* [sic] *aggiuntovi .XVI. Sonetti Spirituali, e le sue stanze.* Florence: Nicolo d'Aristotile, detto il Zoppino, da Ferrara, 1539.

————. *Rime de la Divina Vettoria* [sic] *Colonna de pescara inclita Marchesana nuovamente aggiuntovi XXIIII. sonetti Spirituali, e le sue stanze, e uno triompho de la croce di Christo non piu stampato con la sua tavola.* Venice: Per Comin de Trino ad instantia de Nicolo d'Aristotile detto Zoppino, 1540.

————. *Dichiaratione fatta sopra la seconda parte delle Rime della Divina Vittoria Collonna* [sic] *Marchesana di Pescara. Da Rinaldo Corso . . .* Bologna: Gian battista de Phaelli, 1543.

————. *Litere della Divina Vettoria* [sic] *Colonna Marchesana di Pescara alla Duchessa de Amalfi, sopra la vita contemplativa di santa Catherina, Et sopra della attiva santa Maddalena non più viste in luce.* Venice: Alessandro de Viano, Ad instantia di Antonio detto il Cremaschino, 1544.

————. *Litere della divina Vettoria* [sic] *Colonna Marchesana di Pescara alla Duchessa de Amalfi, sopra la vita contemplativa di santa Catherina, Et sopra della attiva santa Maddalena non più viste in luce.* Venice: Giovan Anton. et Pietro fratelli de Nicolini da Sabio, Ad instantia di M. Sebastian Venetiano, 1545.

————. *Pianto della Marchesa di Pescara sopra la passione di Christo. Oratione della medesima sopra l'Ave Maria . . . etc.* Bologna: Manutio, 1557.

————. *Tutte le Rime della Illustriss. et Eccellentiss. Signora Vittoria Colonna, Marchesana di Pescara. Con l'Espositione del Signor Rinaldo Corso, nuovamente mandate in luce da Girolamo Ruscelli.* Venice: Giovan Battista et Melchior Sessa Fratelli, 1558.

————. *Carteggio.* 2d ed. Edited by Ermanno Ferrero and Giuseppe Müller with a supplement by Domenico Tordi. Turin: Ermanno Loescher, 1892.

————. *Rime.* Edited by Alan Bullock. Rome: Laterza, 1982.

————. *Sonetti in morte di Francesco Ferrante d'Avalos, marchese di Pescara: edizione del ms. XIII.G.43 della Biblioteca Nazionale di Napoli.* Edited by Tobia R. Toscano. Milan: Mondadori, 1998.

Works by Other Authors

Alighieri, Dante. *The Divine Comedy.* 3 vols. Edited and translated by John D. Sinclair. New York: Oxford University Press, 1961.

Ariosto, Ludovico. *Orlando furioso.* Classici italiani 27 Edited by Remo Ceserani. Turin: Einaudi, 1962.

————. *Orlando furioso (The Frenzy of Orlando).* 2 vols. Translated by Barbara Reynolds. Harmondsworth: Penguin Books, 1975.

Aristotle. *Metaphysics.* 2 vols. Edited and translated by Christopher Kirwan and David Bostock. Oxford: Clarendon Press, 1993–94.

Augustine, Saint Aurelius. *De genesi contra Manichaeos. On Genesis: Two Books on Genesis against the Manichees; and, On the literal interpretation of Genesis, an unfinished book.* Translated by Roland J. Teske. Washington, DC: Catholic University of America Press, 1991.

————. *De civitate Dei.* Edited and translated by R. W. Dyson. Cambridge: Cambridge University Press, 1998.

Bembo, Pietro. "Delle Prose di M. Pietro Bembo nelle quali si ragiona della volgar lingua." In *Opere in volgare.* Edited by M. Marti, 269–447. Florence: Sansoni, 1961.

Buonarroti, Michelangelo. *The Poetry of Michelangelo.* Edited and translated by James M. Saslow. New Haven: Yale University Press, 1991.

Calvin, Jean. *Institutio Christianae religionis: The Institutes of Christian Religion.* Edited and translated by Tony Lane and Hilary Osborne. London: Hodder and Stoughton, 1986.

Castiglione, Baldassare. *Il libro del cortegiano.* Edited by Ettore Bonora. Milan: Mursia, 1988.

Erasmus, Desiderius. *Ciceronianus.* Edited by A. H. T. Levi. Volume 28 of the *Collected Works of Erasmus.* Literary and Educational Writings, no. 6. Toronto: University of Toronto Press, 1986.

Gambara, Veronica. *Le rime.* Edited by Alan Bullock. Florence: Olschki, 1995.

Giovio, Paolo. *Le vite del gran Capitano e del Marchese di Pescara.* Translated by Ludovico Domenichi. Bari: Laterza, 1931.

————. *Dialogo dell'imprese militari e amorose.* Edited by Maria Luisa Doglio. Rome: Bulzoni, 1978.

Guicciardini, Luigi. *The Sack of Rome.* Edited and translated by James H. McGregor. New York: Italica Press, 1993.

Hollanda, Francesco de. "Dialogos en Roma." In *Da Pintura Antigua.* Edited by Joaquin de Vasconcellos, 175–277. 2d ed. Porto: Renascenza Portoguesa, 1930.

Holy Bible, The. Douay-Rheims Version, Translated from the Latin Vulgate, Diligently Compared with the Hebrew, Greek, and Other Editions in Divers Languages . . . . Fitzwilliam, NH: Loreto Publications, 1941.

Mantova, Benedetto da. *Trattato utilissimo del beneficio di Giesù Christo crocifisso verso i christiani.* Venice: Bernardino de Bindonis, 1543.

————. *Il Beneficio di Cristo con le versioni del secolo XVI, documenti e testimonianze.* Edited by Salvatore Caponetto. Florence: Sansoni, 1972.

Marinella, Lucrezia. *The Nobility and Excellence of Women and the Defects and Vices of Men.* Edited and translated by Anne Dunhill. Introduction by Letizia Panizza. The Other Voice in Early Modern Europe. Chicago: University of Chicago Press, 1999.

Ochino, Bernardino. *Prediche del Reverendo Padre Frate Bernardino Ochino Senese Generale dell'ordine di frati Capuzzini . . . predicate nella Inclita Citta di Vinegia del MDXXXIX.* Venice: A Bindoni and M. Pasini, 1541.

Ovid. *Fasti.* 2d ed. Translated by Sir James George Frazer, revised by G. P. Goold. Cambridge, MA: Harvard University Press; and London: Heinemann, 1989.

Petrarca, Francesco. *Canzoniere.* Edited by Alberto Chiari. Milan: Mondadori, 1985.

————. *Letters of Old Age: Rerum senilium libri I–XVIII.* 2 vols. Translated by A. S. Bernardo, S. Levin, and R. A. Bernardo. Baltimore: Johns Hopkins University Press, 1992.

Plato. *The Republic.* Translated by A. D. Lindsay. London: David Campbell, 1992.

————. *Phaedrus.* Edited and translated by James H. Nichols, Jr. Ithaca, NY; and London: Cornell University Press, 1998.

Pseudo-Bonaventure, Saint. *Meditationes vitae Christi: The miroure of the Blessed Life.* Translated by Nicholas Love. Ilkley, UK: Scholar Press, 1978.

Siena, Caterina da. *Le lettere di S. Caterina da Siena.* Edited by Piero Misciatelli. 6 vols. Florence: Marzocco, 1947.

Stortoni, Laura Anna, ed. *Women Poets of the Italian Renaissance. Courtly Ladies and Courtesans.* Translated by Laura Anna Stortoni and Mary Prentice Lillie. New York: Italica Press.

Tarabotti, Arcangela. *Paternal Tyranny.* Edited and translated by Letizia Panizza. The Other Voice in Early Modern Europe. Chicago: University of Chicago Press, 2004.

Valdés, Juan de. *Alfabeto cristiano.* Edited by Benedetto Croce. Bari: Laterza, 1938.

————. *Lo Evangelio di San Matteo.* Edited by Carlo Ossola. Rome: Bulzoni, 1985.

————. *Two Catechisms.* 2d ed. Translated by William B. and Carol D. Jones. Edited by José C. Nieto. Lawrence, KS: Coronado, 1993.

Virgil. *Eclogues and Georgics.* Translated by David R. Slavitt. Baltimore: Johns Hopkins University Press, 1990.

————. *The Aeneid.* Translated by David West. Harmondsworth: Penguin, 1990.

Voragine, Jacobus de. *The Golden Legend.* Selected and translated by Christopher Stace. Introduction and notes by Richard Hamer. London: Penguin Books, 1998.

SECONDARY SOURCES

Amante, Bruto. *La tomba di Vittoria Colonna e i testamenti finora inediti della poetessa.* Bologna: Ditta Nicola Zanichelli, 1896.

Armour, Peter. "Michelangelo's Two Sisters: Contemplative Life and Active Life in the Final Version of the Monument to Julius II." In *Sguardi sull'Italia: Miscellanea dedi-*

cata a Francesco Villari dalla Society for Italian Studies. Edited by Gino Bedani et al., 55–
83. Exeter: The Society for Italian Studies, 1997.

Bainton, Roland H. *Women of the Reformation in Germany and Italy.* Minneapolis: Augs-
burg, 1971.

Bardazzi, G. "Vittoria Colonna et la voix cachée." *Cahiers de la Faculté des Lettres de l'Uni-
versité de Genève* 4 (1991): 21–3.

Bassanese, Fiora A. *Gaspara Stampa.* Boston: Twayne, 1982.

———. "Vittoria Colonna, Christ and Gender." *Rivista della Civiltà Italiana* 40 (1996):
53–57.

Baxandall, Michael. *Giotto and the Orators: Humanist Observers of Painting in Italy and the
Discovery of Pictorial Composition.* Oxford: Clarendon, 1986.

Benrath, Carl. *Bernardino Ochino of Siena: A Contribution towards the History of the Reforma-
tion.* London: James Nisbet, 1876.

Besami, O., J. Hauser, and G. Sopranzi, eds. Concordances to *Vittoria Colonna e Ga-
leazzo di Tarsia: Le rime.* Archivio tematico della lirica italiana 4. Hildesheim, Zürich,
and New York: Georg Olms Verlag, 1997.

Bianca, Concetta. "Marcello Cervini e Vittoria Colonna." *Lettere italiane* 45 (1993):
427–39.

Bianco, Monica. "Le due redazioni del commento di Rinaldo Corso alle *Rime* di Vit-
toria Colonna." *Studi di filologia italiana* 56 (1998): 271–95.

———. "Rinaldo Corso e il 'Canzoniere' di Vittoria Colonna." *Italique: Poésie italienne
de la Renaissance* 1 (1998): 37–45.

Bornstein, Daniel and Roberto Rusconi, eds. *Women and Religion in Medieval and Renais-
sance Italy.* Translated by Margery J. Schneider. Chicago: University of Chicago
Press, 1996.

Borsetto, Luciana. "Narciso ed Eco. Figura e scrittura nella lirica femminile del
Cinquecento: Esemplificazioni ed appunti." In *Nel cerchio della luna: Figure di donna in
alcuni testi del XVI secolo,* ed. Marina Zancan, 171–233. Venice: Marsilio, 1983.

Bossy, John. *Christianity in the West, 1400–1700.* Oxford: Oxford University Press, 1985.

Bozza, Tommaso. *Nuovi studi sulla Riforma in Italia: I. Il Beneficio di Cristo.* Rome: Storia e
letteratura, 1976.

Bozzetti, Cesare, Pietro Gibellini, and Ennio Sandal, eds. *Veronica Gambara e la poesia
del suo tempo nell'Italia settentrionale.* Florence: Olschki, 1989.

Briganti, Giuliano, ed. *La pittura in Italia. Il Cinquecento.* Vol. 2 of 2. Naples: Electa, 1988.

Brundin, Abigail. "Vittoria Colonna and the Virgin Mary." *Modern Language Review* 96
(2001): 61–81.

———. "Vittoria Colonna and the Poetry of Reform." *Italian Studies* 57 (2002): 61–74.

Bullock, Alan. "A Hitherto Unexplored Manuscript of 100 Poems by Vittoria Co-
lonna in the Biblioteca Nazionale Centrale, Florence." *Italian Studies* 21 (1966):
42–56.

———. "Veronica o Vittoria? Problemi di attribuzione per alcuni sonetti del
Cinquecento." *Studi e problemi di critica testuale* 6 (1973): 115–31.

———. "Vittoria Colonna: Note e aggiunte alla edizione critica del 1982." *Giornale
storico della letteratura italiana* 162 (1985): 407–13.

Bury, J. B. *Two Notes on Francisco de Holanda.* London: Warburg Institute, 1981.

Campi, Emidio. *Michelangelo e Vittoria Colonna: Un dialogo artistico-teologico ispirato da Ber-
nardino Ochino, e altri saggi di storia della Riforma.* Turin: Claudiniana, 1994.

———. "'Non vi si pensa quanto sangue costa': Michelangelo, Vittoria Colonna e

Bernardino Ochino." In *Dall'Accademia neoplatonica fiorentina alla riforma*, 67–135. Florence: Olschki, 1996.

Campos, Deoclecio Redig de. "Il Crocifisso di Michelangelo per Vittoria Colonna." In *Atti del Convegno di Studi Michelangioleschi*, 356–65. Rome: Ateneo, 1966.

Cannata, Nadia. *Il canzoniere a stampa (1470–1530): Tradizione e fortuna di un genere fra storia del libro e letteratura*. Rome: Bagatto Libri, 1996.

Cantimori, Delio. *Umanesimo e religione nel Rinascimento*. Turin: Einaudi, 1975.

————. *Eretici italiani del Cinquecento e altri scritti*. Edited by Adriano Prosperi. Turin: Einaudi, 1992.

Caponetto, Salvatore. *The Protestant Reformation in Sixteenth-Century Italy*. Translated by Anne C. Tedeschi and John Tedeschi. Sixteenth Century Essays and Studies 43. Kirksville, MO: Thomas Jefferson University Press, 1999.

Carroll, Michael P. *Veiled Threats: The Logic of Popular Catholicism in Italy*. Baltimore: Johns Hopkins University Press, 1996.

Carusi, Enrico. "Un codice sconosciuto delle *Rime spirituali* di Vittoria Colonna, appartenuto forse a Michelangelo Buonarroti." *Atti del IV Congresso Nazionale di Studi Romani* 4 (1938): 231–41.

Church, Frederic C. *The Italian Reformers, 1534–1564*. New York: Columbia University Press, 1932.

Cinquini, C. "Rinaldo Corso, editore e commentatore delle *Rime* di Vittoria Colonna." *Aevum* 73 (1999): 669–96.

Cione, E. *Juan de Valdés: La sua vita e il suo pensiero religioso*. 2d ed. Naples: F. Fiorentino, 1963.

Cohn, Samuel K. Jr. *Women in the Streets: Essays on Sex and Power in Renaissance Italy*. Baltimore: Johns Hopkins University Press, 1996.

Collett, Barry. *A Long and Troubled Pilgrimage: The Correspondence of Marguerite d'Angoulême and Vittoria Colonna, 1540–1545*. Studies in Reformed Theology and History, n.s., no.6. Princeton, NJ: Princeton Theological Seminary, 2000.

Corte, Francesco della, ed. *Enciclopedia Virgiliana*. Vol. 1. Rome: Istituto della Enciclopedia Italiana, 1984.

Cox, Virginia. "The Single Self: Feminist Thought and the Marriage Market in Early Modern Venice." *Renaissance Quarterly* 48 (1995): 513–81.

————. "Women Writers and the Canon in Sixteenth-Century Italy: The Case of Vittoria Colonna." In *Strong Voices, Weak History? Medieval and Renaissance Women in their Literary Canons: England, France, Italy*. Edited by Pamela J. Benson and Victoria Kirkham. Ann Arbor: University of Michigan Press, forthcoming.

Cruden, Alexander. *Complete Concordance to the Old and New Testaments*. London: Lutterworth Press, 1930.

Davis, Natalie Zemon. "City Women and Religious Change." In *Society and Culture in Early Modern France: Eight Essays*, 65–95. Stanford: Stanford University Press, 1975.

————. "Beyond the Market: Books as Gifts in Sixteenth-Century France." *Transactions of the Royal Historical Society* 5th series, no. 33 (1983): 69–88.

————. "Gifts and Bribes in Sixteenth-Century France." An Iredell Lecture delivered at Lancaster University on February 14, 1995.

Dionisotti, Carlo. "La letteratura italiana nell'età del concilio di Trento." In *Geografia e storia della letteratura italiana*, 183–204. Turin: Einaudi, 1967.

————. "Appunti sul Bembo e su Vittoria Colonna." In *Miscellanea Augusto Campana*. Edited by Rino Avesani et al., 257–86. Padua: Antenore, 1981.

Dizionario biografico degli italiani (DBI). Rome: Istituto dell'Enciclopedia Italiana, 1960–.

Doglio, Maria Luisa. "L'occhio interiore e la scrittura nelle 'Litere' di Vittoria Colonna." In *Omaggio a Gianfranco Folena*. Vol. 2 of 3, 1001–13. Padua: Editoriale Programma, 1993.

Dunbar, Agnes B. C. *A Dictionary of Saintly Women*. 2 vols. London: George Bell and Sons, 1904.

Dyer, Diane. "Vittoria Colonna's Friendship with the English Cardinal Reginald Pole." *Riscontri* 7 (1985): 45–58.

Elton, G. R. *Reformation Europe, 1517–1559*. 2d ed. Oxford: Blackwell, 1999.

Erdmann, Axel. *My Gracious Silence: Women in the Mirror of Sixteenth-Century Printing in Western Europe*. Luzern: Gilhofer and Rauschberg, 1999.

Fedi, Roberto. "'L'immagine vera': Vittoria Colonna, Michelangelo, e un'idea di canzoniere." *Modern Language Notes* 107 (1992): 46–73.

Fenlon, Dermot. *Heresy and Obedience in Tridentine Italy: Cardinal Pole and the Counter Reformation*. Cambridge: Cambridge University Press, 1972.

Ferino-Pagden, Silvia, ed. *Vittoria Colonna: Dichterin und Muse Michelangelos*. Exhibition catalog. Vienna: Skira, 1997.

Finzi, Riccardo. *Un Correggese del Rinascimento: Rinaldo Corso, 1525–1582*. Modena: Aedes Muratoriana, 1959.

Firpo, Massimo. "Valdesianesimo ed evangelismo: Alle origini dell'*Ecclesia Viterbiensis* (1541)." In *Libri, idee e sentimenti religiosi nel Cinquecento italiano*, 53–71. Istituto di Studi Rinascimentali Ferrara. Ferrara: Panini, 1987.

———. "Vittoria Colonna, Giovanni Morone e gli 'spirituali'." *Rivista di storia e letteratura religiosa* 24 (1988): 211–61.

———. *Tra Alumbrados e "spirituali": Studi su Juan de Valdés e il valdesianesimo nella crisi religiosa del '500 italiano*. Florence: Olschki, 1990.

Firpo, Massimo, and Dario Marcatto. *Il processo inquisitoriale del cardinal Giovanni Morone. Edizione critica*. 5 vols. Rome: Istituto storico italiano per l'età moderna e contemporanea, 1981–88.

Fontana, Bartolommeo. "Nuovi documenti vaticano intorno a Vittoria Colonna." *Archivio della R. Società Romana di Storia Patria* 10 (1887): 595–628.

Fragnito, Gigliola. "Appunti e documenti: Gli 'Spirituali' e la fuga di Bernardino Ochino." *Rivista storica italiana* 84 (1972): 777–813.

———. "Vittoria Colonna e l'Inquisizione." *Benedictina* 37 (1990): 157–72.

Frede, Carlo de. "Vittoria Colonna e il suo processo inquisitoriale postumo." *Atti del Accademia Pontaniana* 37 (1988): 251–83.

Freedberg, David. *The Power of Images: Studies in the History and Theory of Response*. Chicago: University of Chicago Press, 1989.

Galdi, Francesco. *Vittoria Colonna dal lato della neuro-psicopatologia*. Portici: Spedalieri, 1898.

Gibaldi, Joseph. "Vittoria Colonna: Child, Woman, Poet." In *Women Writers of the Renaissance and Reformation*. Edited by Katherine M. Wilson, 22–46. Athens, GA, and London: University of Georgia Press, 1987.

Gilson, Etienne. *Thomism: The Philosophy of Thomas Aquinas*. Toronto: Pontifical Institute of Medieval Studies, 2002.

Giusti, Paola, and Pierluigi Leone de Castris. *Pittura del Cinquecento a Napoli*. Vol. 1 of 2. Naples: Electa, 1988.

Gleason, Elisabeth G. *Gasparo Contarini: Venice, Rome and Reform.* Berkeley: University of California Press, 1993.

Goldscheider, Ludwig, ed. *Michelangelo's Drawings.* London: Phaidon, 1951.

Graf, A. *Attraverso il Cinquecento.* Turin: Loescher, 1926.

Graef, Hilda. *Mary: A History of Doctrine and Devotion.* 2d ed. London: Sheed and Ward, 1987.

Greenblatt, Stephen. *Renaissance Self-Fashioning: From More to Shakespeare.* Chicago: University of Chicago Press, 1980.

Greene, Roland. *Post-Petrarchism: Origins and Innovations of the Western Lyric Sequence.* Princeton: Princeton University Press, 1991.

Greene, Thomas M. *The Light in Troy: Imitation and Discovery in Renaissance Poetry.* New Haven: Yale University Press, 1982.

Grubbs, Judith Evans. *Women and the Law in the Roman Empire: A Sourcebook on Marriage, Divorce and Widowhood.* London: Routledge, 2002.

Gui, Francesco. *L'attesa del Concilio: Vittoria Colonna e Reginald Pole nel movimento degli "spirituali."* Storia e società. Rome: Editoria Università Elettronica, 1998.

Hall, James. *Dictionary of Subjects and Symbols in Art.* Rev. ed. London: John Murray, 1984.

Hare, Christopher. *Men and Women of the Italian Reformation.* London: Stanley Paul, 1914.

Haskins, Susan. *Mary Magdalene: Myth and Metaphor.* London: Harper Collins, 1993.

Hempfer, Klaus W. "Per una definizione del Petrarchismo." In *Dynamique d'une expansion culturelle: Pétrarque en Europe XIVe–XXe siècle; Actes du XXVIe congrès international du CEFI, Turin et Chambéry, 11–15 décembre 1995.* Edited by Pierre Blanc, 23–52. Bibliothèque Franco Simone 30. Paris: Honoré Champion, 2001.

Jenkins-Blaisdell, Charmarie. "Renée de France between Reform and Counter-Reform." *Archive for Reformation History* 63 (1972): 196–226.

Jerrold, Maude. *Vittoria Colonna, Her Friends and Her Times.* New York: Freeport, 1906.

Joannides, Paul. *Michelangelo and His Influence: Drawings from Windsor Castle.* Exhibition catalog. London: Lund Humphries, 1996.

Jordan, Constance. *Renaissance Feminism: Literary Texts and Political Models.* Ithaca, NY: Cornell University Press, 1990.

Jung, Eva-Maria. "Vittoria Colonna: Between Reformation and Counter-Reformation." *Review of Religion* 15 (1951): 144–59.

Jung-Inglessis, Eva-Maria. "Il Pianto della Marchesa di Pescara sopra la Passione di Christo. Introduzione." *Archivio italiano per la storia della pietà* 10 (1997): 115–47.

Kennedy, William J. *Authorizing Petrarch.* Ithaca and London: Cornell University Press, 1994.

Ladner, Gerhart B. *The Idea of Reform: Its Impact on Christian Thought and Action in the Age of the Fathers.* Cambridge, MA: Harvard University Press, 1959.

Maddison, Carol. *Marcantonio Flaminio: Poet, Humanist and Reformer.* London: Routledge and Kegan Paul, 1965.

Maio, Romeo de. *Michelangelo e la Controriforma.* Rome: Laterza, 1978.

Manzoni, Giacomo, ed. "Estratto del processo di Pietro Carnesecchi." *Miscellanea di storia italiana* 10 (1870): 187–573.

Mayer, Thomas F. *Reginald Pole: Prince and Prophet.* Cambridge: Cambridge University Press, 2000.

Mazzetti, Mila. "La poesia come vocazione morale: Vittoria Colonna." *Rassegna della letteratura italiana* 77 (1973): 58–99.

McAuliffe, Dennis. "Vittoria Colonna and Renaissance Poetics, Convention, and

Society." In *Il Rinascimento: Aspetti e problemi attuali.* Edited by Vittore Branca et al., 531–41. Florence: Olschki, 1982.

———. "Neoplatonism in Vittoria Colonna's Poetry: From the Secular to the Divine." In *Ficino and Renaissance Neoplatonism.* Edited by K. Eisenbickler and O. Z. Pugliese, 101–12. Toronto: University of Toronto Press, 1986.

———. "The Language of Spiritual Renewal in the Poetry of Pre-Tridentine Rome: The Case of Vittoria Colonna as Advocate for Reform." *Rivista della Civiltà Italiana* 40 (1996): 196–99.

McLaughlin, Martin L. *Literary Imitation in the Italian Renaissance. The Theory and Practice of Literary Imitation in Italy from Dante to Bembo.* Oxford: Clarendon Press, 1995.

Menzies, Lucy. *The Saints in Italy.* London: Medici Society, 1924.

Merrill, R. V. "Platonism in Petrarch's *Canzoniere.*" *Modern Philology* 27 (1929–30): 161–74.

Moro, Giovanni. "Le Commentaire de Rinaldo Corso sur les *Rimes* de Vittoria Colonna: Une Encyclopédie pour les 'très nobles Dames.'" In *Les Commentaires et la Naissance de la Critique Littéraire.* Edited by Gisèle Mathieu-Castellani and Michel Plaisance, 195–202. Paris: Aux amateurs de livres, 1990.

Moroni, Ornella. *Carlo Gualteruzzi (1500–1577) e i corrispondenti.* Studi e Testi 307. Città del Vaticano: Biblioteca Apostolica Vaticana, 1984.

Mullett, Michael A. *The Catholic Reformation.* London: Routledge, 1999.

Murray, Peter, and Linda Murray. *The Oxford Companion to Christian Art and Architecture.* Oxford: Oxford University Press, 1996.

Mussio, Thomas E. "The Augustinian Conflict in the Lyrics of Michelangelo: Michelangelo Reading Petrarch." *Italica* 74 (1997): 339–59.

Nagel, Alexander. "Gifts for Michelangelo and Vittoria Colonna." *Art Bulletin* 79 (1997): 647–68.

———. *Michelangelo and the Reform of Art.* Cambridge: Cambridge University Press, 2000.

Niccolini, Benedetto. "Sulla religiosità di Vittoria Colonna." *Studi e materiali di storia delle religioni* 22 (1949): 89–109.

Nieto, José C. *Juan de Valdés and the Origins of the Spanish and Italian Reformation.* Geneva: Droz, 1970.

Nobbio Mollaretti, Raffaela. *Vittoria Colonna e Michelangelo: Nel quinto centenario della sua nascita, 1490–1990.* Florence: Firenze libri, 1990.

O'Carroll, Michael. *Theotokos: A Theological Encyclopedia of the Blessed Virgin Mary.* Wilmington, DE: Michael Glazier, 1983.

Och, Marjorie. "Vittoria Colonna and the Commission for a *Mary Magdalene* by Titian." In *Beyond Isabella: Secular Women Patrons of Art in Renaissance Italy.* Edited by Sheryl E. Reiss and David G. Wilkins, 193–223. Sixteenth-Century Essays and Studies 54. Kirksville, MO: Truman State University Press, 2001.

———. "Portrait Medals of Vittoria Colonna: Representing the Learned Woman." In *Women as Sites of Culture: Women's Roles in Cultural Formation from the Renaissance to the Twentieth Century.* Edited by Susan Shifrin, 153–66. Aldershot: Ashgate, 2002.

O'Malley, John W. *Praise and Blame in Renaissance Rome: Rhetoric, Doctrine, and Reform in the Sacred Orators of the Papal Court, c. 1450–1521.* Durham, NC: Duke University Press, 1979.

Ordine, Nucio. "Vittoria Colonna nell'*Orlando Furioso.*" *Studi e problemi di critica testuale* 42 (1991): 55–92.

Pagano, Sergio, and Concetta Ranieri. *Nuovi documenti su Vittoria Colonna e Reginald Pole.* Città del Vaticano: Archivio Vaticano, 1989.

Pelikan, Jaroslav. *The Christian Tradition. A History of the Development of Doctrine.* 5 vols. Chicago: University of Chicago Press, 1984.

―――. *Mary through the Centuries: Her Place in the History of Culture.* New Haven: Yale University Press, 1998.

Prosperi, Adriano, and Carlo Ginzburg. *Giochi di pazienza: Un seminario sul "Beneficio di Cristo."* Turin: Einaudi, 1975.

Quondam, Amedeo. *Petrarchismo mediato: Per una critica della forma "antologia"; Livelli d'uso del sistema linguistico del petrarchismo.* Rome: Bulzoni, 1974.

―――, ed. *Le "carte messaggiere": Retorica e modelli di comunicazione epistolare: per un indice dei libri di lettere del Cinquecento.* Rome: Bulzoni, 1981.

―――. *Il naso di Laura: Lingua e poesia lirica nella tradizione del Classicismo.* Ferrara: Panini, 1991.

Rabitti, Giovanna. "Linee per il ritratto di Chiara Matraini." *Studi e problemi di critica testuale* 22 (1981): 141–65.

―――. "La metafora e l'esistenza nella poesia di Chiara Matraini." *Studi e problemi di critica testuale* 27 (1983): 109–45.

―――. "Vittoria Colonna, Bembo e Firenze: Un caso di ricezione e qualche postilla." *Studi e problemi di critica testuale* 44 (1992): 127–55.

―――. "Lyric poetry, 1500–1650." Translated by Abigail Brundin. In *A History of Women's Writing in Italy.* Edited by Letizia Panizza and Sharon Wood, 37–51. Cambridge: Cambridge University Press, 2000

―――. "Vittoria Colonna as Role Model for Cinquecento Women Poets." In *Women in Italian Renaissance Culture and Society.* Edited by Letizia Panizza, 478–97. Oxford: European Humanities Research Centre, 2000.

Ranieri, Concetta. "Ancora sul carteggio tra Pietro Bembo e Vittoria Colonna." *Giornale Italiano di Filologia* 14 (1983): 133–52.

―――. "Vittoria Colonna: Dediche, libri e manoscritti." *Critica letteraria* 1 (1985): 249–70.

―――. "Vittoria Colonna e la riforma: Alcune osservazioni critiche." *Studi latini e italiani* 6 (1992): 87–96.

―――. "Premesse umanistiche alla religiosità di Vittoria Colonna." *Rivista di storia e letteratura religiosa* 32 (1996): 531–48.

―――. "Imprestiti platonici nella formazione religiosa di Vittoria Colonna." In *Presenze eterodosse nel Viterbese tra Quattro e Cinquecento.* Edited by V. De Caprio and C. Ranieri, 193–212. Rome: Archivio Giodo Izzi, 2000.

Reumont, Alfredo. *Vittoria Colonna: Vita, fede e poesia nel secolo decimosesto.* Translated by Giuseppe Müller and Ermanno Ferrero. Turin: Ermanno Loescher, 1883.

Richardson, Brian. "Print or Pen? Modes of Written Publication in Sixteenth-Century Italy." *Italian Studies* 59 (2004): 39–64.

Roberts, Gareth. *The Mirror of Alchemy: Alchemical Ideas and Images in Manuscripts and Books from Antiquity to the Seventeenth Century.* Toronto: University of Toronto Press, 1995.

Roelker, Nancy Lyman. "The Appeal of Calvinism to French Noblewomen in the Sixteenth Century." *Journal of Interdisciplinary History* 2 (1971–72): 391–418.

Roscoe, H. *Vittoria Colonna: Her Life and Poems.* London: MacMillan, 1868.

Rosenthal, Margaret F. *The Honest Courtesan: Veronica Franco, Citizen and Writer in Sixteenth-Century Venice.* Chicago: University of Chicago Press, 1992.

Rossi, Vittorio. *Storia della letteratura italiana: Volume secondo, Dal rinascimento al rinnovamento.* Edited by Umberto Bosco. Milan: Dr. Francesco Villardi, 1956.

Russell, Rinaldina. "The Mind's Pursuit of the Divine: A Survey of Secular and Religious Themes in Vittoria Colonna's Sonnets." *Forum Italicum* 26 (1992): 14–27.

———, ed. *Italian Women Writers: A Bio-Bibliographical Sourcebook.* London: Greenwood, 1994.

———. "L'ultima meditazione di Vittoria Colonna e l' 'Ecclesia Viterbiensis'": *La Parola del Testo; Semestrale di filologia e letteratura italiana e comparata dal medioevo al rinascimento* 4 (2000): 151–66.

———. "Vittoria Colonna's Sonnets on the Virgin Mary." In *Maria Virgine nella letteratura italiana.* Edited by Florinda M. Iannace, 125–37. Stony Brook, NY: Forum Italicum, 2000.

Rutter, Itala T. C. "La scrittura di Vittoria Colonna e Margherita di Navarra: Resistenza e misticismo." *Romance Languages Annual* 3 (1991): 303–8.

Sabbatino, Pasquale. *Il modello bembiano a Napoli nel Cinquecento.* Naples: Ferraro, 1986.

Saulnier, V. L. "Marguerite de Navarre, Vittoria Colonna et quelques autres amis italiens de 1540." In *Mélanges à la Mémoire de Franco Simone: France et Italie dans la culture européene: I, Moyen Age et Renaissance,* 281–95. Geneva: Slatkine, 1980.

Scala, Mirella. "Encomi e dediche nelle prime relazioni culturali di Vittoria Colonna." *Periodico della società storica comense* 54 (1990): 95–112.

Scaraffia, Lucetta, and Gabriella Zarri, eds. *Donne e fede: Santità e vita religiosa in Italia.* Rome: Laterza, 1994.

Shifrin, Susan, ed. *Women as Sites of Culture.* Aldershot: Ashgate, 2002.

Schoedel, William R. *Ignatius of Antioch: A Commentary on the Letters of Ignatius of Antioch.* Edited by Helmut Koester. Philadelphia: Fortress Press, 1985.

Schurr, Claudia Elizabeth. *Vittoria Colonna und Michelangelo Buonarroti: Künstler und Liebespaar der Renaissance.* Tübingen: Gunter Narr Verlag, 2001.

Schutte, Ann Jacobson. "The *Lettere Volgari* and the Crisis of Evangelism in Italy." *Renaissance Quarterly* 28 (1975): 639–88.

———. *Pier Paolo Vergerio: The Making of an Italian Reformer.* Geneva: Droz, 1977.

———. "Printing, Piety, and the People in Italy: The First Thirty Years." *Archiv für Reformationsgeschichte* 71 (1980): 5–19.

Segre, C., and C. Ossola, eds. *Antologia della poesia italiana.* Vol. 2. *Quattrocento-Settecento.* Turin: Einaudi-Gallimard, 1998.

Seidel Menchi, Silvana. "Le traduzioni italiane di Lutero nella prima metà del Cinquecento." *Rinascimento* 17 (1977): 31–108.

———. "Italy." In *The Reformation in National Context.* Edited by Bob Scribner et al., 181–97. Cambridge: Cambridge University Press, 1994.

Simoncelli, Paolo. *Il caso Reginald Pole: Eresia e santità nelle polemiche religiose del Cinquecento.* Rome: Edizioni di Storia e Letteratura, 1977.

———. "Pietro Bembo e l'evangelismo italiano." *Critica storica* 15 (1978): 1–63.

———. *Evangelismo italiano del Cinquecento: Questione religiosa e nicodemismo politico.* Rome: Istituto storico italiano per l'età moderna e contemporanea, 1979.

Spini, Giorgio. "Per una lettura teologica di Michelangelo." *Protestantesimo* 44 (1989): 2–16.

Squarotti, Giorgio Barberi. "Michelangelo e Vittoria Colonna." In *Michelangelo e Dante.* Milan: Electa, 1995.

Summers, David. *Michelangelo and the Language of Art.* Princeton: Princeton University Press, 1981.

Tacchi-Venturi, Pietro. *Nuove lettere inedite di Vittoria Colonna.* Rome: Tipografia Poliglotta, 1901.

―――. *Vittoria Colonna Fautrice della riforma cattolica secondo alcune sue lettere inedite.* Rome: Tipografia Poliglotta, 1901.

Therault, Suzanne. *Un cénacle humaniste de la Renaissance autour de Vittoria Colonna châtelaine d'Ischia.* Paris: Didier; and Florence: Sansoni Antiquariato, 1968.

Thompson, John Lee. *John Calvin and the Daughters of Sarah: Women in Regular and Exceptional Roles in the Exegesis of Calvin, His Predecessors, and His Contemporaries.* Geneva: Droz, 1992.

Tordi, Domenico. "Vittoria Colonna in Orvieto durante la guerra del sale." *Bolletino della Società Umbra di Storia Patria* 1 (1895): 473–533.

―――. *Il codice delle Rime di Vittoria Colonna, Marchesa di Pescara, appartenuto a Margherita d'Angoulême, Regina di Navarra.* Pistoia: Flori, 1900.

Toscano, Tobia. "Due 'allievi' di Vittoria Colonna: Luigi Tansillo e Alfonso d'Avalos." *Critica letteraria* 16 (1988): 739–73.

Trovato, Paolo. "Per la storia delle *Rime* del Bembo." *Rivista di letteratura italiana* 9 (1991): 465–508.

Valerio, Adriana. "Bibbia, ardimento, coscienza femminile: Vittoria Colonna." In *Cristianesimo al femminile: Donne protagoniste nella storia della Chiesa,* 151–70. Naples: M. D'Auria, 1990.

Vecce, Carlo. "Paolo Giovio e Vittoria Colonna." *Periodico della Società Storica Comense* 54 (1990): 67–93.

―――. "Petrarca, Vittoria, Michelangelo: Note di commento a testi e varianti di Vittoria Colonna e Michelangelo." *Studi e problemi di critica testuale* 44 (1992): 101–25.

―――. "Vittoria Colonna: Il codice epistolare della poesia femminile." *Critica letteraria* 21 (1993): 3–34.

―――. "Zur Dichtung Michelangelos und Vittoria Colonnas." In *Vittoria Colona: Dichterin und Muse Michelangelos.* Edited by Silvia Ferino-Pagden, 381–4. Catalog to the exhibition at the Kunsthistorisches Museum, Vienna, February 25–May 25, 1997. Vienna: Skira, 1997.

Walker, D. P. *Spiritual and Demonic Magic: From Ficino to Campanella.* London: Sutton Publishing, 2000.

Warner, Marina. *Alone of All Her Sex: The Myth and Cult of the Virgin Mary.* New York: Vintage Books, 1983.

Weinberg, Bernard. *A History of Literary Criticism in the Italian Renaissance.* 2 vols. Chicago: University of Chicago Press, 1961.

Weisner, Merry E. "Beyond Women and the Family: Towards a Gender Analysis of the Reformation." *Sixteenth-Century Journal* 18 (1987): 311–21.

―――. *Women and Gender in Early Modern Europe.* Cambridge: Cambridge University Press, 1993.

Wilde, Johannes. *Italian Drawings in the Department of Prints and Drawings in the British Museum: Michelangelo and His Studio.* London: Trustees of the British Museum, 1953.

Zancan, Marina, ed. *Nel cerchio della luna: Figure di donna in alcuni testi del XVI secolo.* Venice: Marsilio, 1983.

Zarri, Gabriella, ed. *Donna, disciplina, creanza cristiana dal XV al XVII secolo: Studi e testi a stampa.* Rome: Edizioni di storia e letteratura, 1996.

―――, ed. *Per lettera: La scrittura epistolare femminile tra archivio e tipografia, secoli XV–XVII.* Rome: Viella, 1999.

SONNETS FOR MICHELANGELO

1. S1:1 (1538), fol. 1v[1]

 Poi che 'l mio casto amor gran tempo tenne
L'alma di fama accesa, ed ella un angue
In sen nudriò per cui dolente or langue
Volta al Signor, onde 'l rimedio venne,

 I santi chiodi omai sian le mie penne,
E puro inchiostro il prezioso sangue,
Vergata carta il sacro corpo exangue,
Sì ch'io scriva ad altrui quel ch'ei sostenne.

 Chiamar qui non convien Parnaso o Delo,
Ch'ad altra aqua s'aspira, ad altro monte
Si poggia, u' piede uman per sé non sale.

 Quel sol, che alluma gli elementi e 'l cielo,
Prego ch'aprendo il suo lucido fonte
Mi porga umor a la gran sete eguale.

2. S1:5 (1538), fol. 2r

 Con la croce a gran passi ir vorrei dietro
Al Signor per angusto erto sentiero,
Sì ch'io in parte scorgessi il lume vero
Ch'altro che 'l senso aperse al fedel Pietro;

 E se tanta mercede or non impetro
Non è ch'ei non si mostri almo e sincero,
Ma comprender non so con l'occhio intero
Ogni umana speranza esser di vetro.

 Che s'io lo cor umil puro e mendico
Appresentassi a la divina mensa,
Ove con dolci e ordinate tempre

SONNETS FOR MICHELANGELO

1. S1:1 (1538), fol. 1v[1]
  Since my chaste love for many years
kept my soul aflame with the desire for fame,[2] and it nourished
a serpent in my breast so that now my heart languishes
in pain turned towards God, who alone can help me,
  let the holy nails from now on be my quills,
and the precious blood my pure ink,
my lined paper the sacred lifeless body,[3]
so that I may write down for others all that he suffered.[4]
  It is not right here to invoke Parnassus or Delos,[5]
for I aspire to cross other waters, to ascend
other mountains that human feet cannot climb unaided.
  I pray to the sun, which lights up the earth and the
heavens, that letting forth his shining spring
he pours down upon me a draught equal to my great thirst.

2. S1:5 (1538), fol. 2r
  I long to stride behind my Lord
bearing his cross along the steep and narrow path,[6]
and thus make out in part the one true light,
which opened more than just the eyes of faithful Peter;[7]
  and if I am not now granted so great a reward
it is not because God is ungenerous or insincere,
but because I fail to understand completely
that all human hope is as fragile as glass.[8]
  If I were to present my humble heart
in purest supplication before the divine table,[9]
where with sweet and orderly constitution

L'Angel di Dio, nostro fidato amico,
Se stesso in cibo per amor dispensa,
Ne sarei forse un dì sazia per sempre.

3. S1:54 (1539), fol. 2v
  Quel pietoso miracol grande, ond'io
Sento, la sua mercé, due parti estreme,
Il divino et l'uman, sì giunte inseme
Ch'è Dio vero uomo e l'uomo è vero Dio,
  Erge tant'alto il mio basso desio
E scalda in modo la mia fredda speme
Che 'l cor libero e franco più non geme
Sotto 'l carco terreno indegno e rio.
  Con la piagata man dolce e soave
Giogo m'ha posto al collo, e lieve peso
Mi mostra or dentro al suo bel lume chiaro;
  A l'alme umili con secreta chiave
Apre 'l tesoro suo, del qual è avaro
Ad ogni cor d'altere voglie acceso.

4. S1:93 (1538), fol. 3r
  Di vero lume abisso immenso e puro,
Con l'alta tua pietà, le luci amiche
Rivolgi a questi quasi vil formiche,
Saggi del mondo, c'hanno il cor sì duro.
  Rompi de l'ignoranza il grosso muro
Ch'ancor li copre di quelle ombre antiche
Del vecchio Adamo, fredde empie nemiche
Al caldo raggio tuo chiaro e sicuro,
  Tal che rendendo al Pastor santo onore,
Vestiti sol di te con fede viva,
Abbian la legge tua scritta nel core,
  Sì che dei propri affetti ogni alma priva
Voli con l'ale del divino amore
A la celeste tua beata riva.

5. S1:50 (1542), fol. 3v
  Quando, vostra mercé, quasi presente
Scorge la fede viva ad una ad una
L'alme gratie divine, e poi le aduna
Tutte in un punto il cor lieto e ardente,

the angel of God, our trusted friend,
offers himself through his love to be our food,[10]
one day my appetite may perhaps be forever satiated.

3. S1:54 (1539), fol. 2v
The wondrous and holy miracle by which,
through his mercy, I perceive two opposed beings,
one divine and one human, so fused into one
that God becomes a true man and man a true God,[11]
causes my lowly desire to soar so high
and in the same way so inflames my chilly hope
that my free and candid heart no longer trembles
beneath the evil, worthless burdens of the world.
With his sweet, gentle, wounded hand
he has placed a yoke around my neck, and in the beautiful
clear light I see it is an easy weight to bear;[12]
to all humble souls with his secret key
he opens up his treasure,[13] jealously guarded
from any heart inspired by proud ambition.

4. S1:93 (1538), fol. 3r
From within a vast pure well of the true light,[14]
through your mercy, you turn your loving eyes
upon these lowly, crawling ants, who are so
full of worldly wisdom and hard of heart.
Break down the thick wall of ignorance
which still casts over them Adam's
ancient shadows,[15] chilly and persistent enemies
of the clarity and healing of your warm gaze,
so that, paying holy tribute to the Eternal Shepherd,[16]
and clothed in you alone with living faith,
they may bear your law inscribed upon their hearts,[17]
and every soul liberated from selfish desires
may fly upon wings of holy love
up to your blessed celestial shore.[18]

5. S1:50 (1542), fol. 3v
When, through your mercy, our living faith
makes out as if close at hand, one by one,
the divine life-giving graces, and then the ardent and
joyful heart assembles them together in one place,

Tirar da tanto amor l'alma si sente,
Che quanto giace qui sotto la luna,
La morte, il mondo, e buona e rea fortuna,
Riman poi sotto l'amorosa mente.

E mentre servon l'ali al gran pensero
Or sul mare, or sul fiume, or sovra 'l monte,
Veggio il sol di là su splender fra noi,

E quando Dio quando uom far qua giù conte
L'immortal glorie, e coi bei raggi suoi
Disparir l'ombre e dimostrarsi il vero.

6. S1:83 (1539), fol. 4r

Se quanto è inferma e da sé vil con sano
Occhio mirasse l'uom nostra natura,
Ch'al crescer e scemar de la misura
Prescritta al corpo altri s'adopra invano,

De le bisogne sue l'ingegno umano
Al Padre eterno con la mente pura,
Che veste i gigli et degli augelli ha cura,
Porrebbe lieto ogni pensiero in mano.

Ché se tutto il ben vero ha in se raccolto
Lui brami e ami, e prenda solo a sdegno
Volger le luci altrove un gentil core;

Col lato aperto su dal santo legno
Ne chiama sempre, pieno il petto e 'l volto
D'infinita pieta, d'immenso amore.

7. S1:7 (1538), fol. 4v

Da Dio mandata, angelica mia scorta,
Volgi per dritto calle al ciel la mente,
E quando l'alma al suo cader consente
Riprendi 'l freno e 'l pie' lasso conforta,

Sì che a le nozze eterne non sia morta
Ogni mia luce, ma con lampa ardente,
Chiamata dal Signor, saggia, prudente,
Aperta al giunger mio trovi la porta.

E perché 'l cor l'aspetti ad'or ad'ora
Per girli incontro lietamente armato
Di puro acceso amor, di viva fede,

the soul feels itself borne up by so much love
that all things that dwell here beneath the moon,
death, the world, and fortune both good and evil,
are lost from view to the enlightened mind.

And as we take flight on the wings of great ideals
over the oceans, the rivers, and the mountains,
I see the celestial sun shine here around us,

while as God or man [19] he heaps his eternal glory
upon us, and his divine rays of light
banish the shadows and reveal the truth.[20]

6. S1:83 (1539), fol. 4r

If man were to look with a clear vision upon
the sickly and vile state of human nature,
instead of striving, as some do in vain, against
the waxing and waning of our prescribed time on earth,

the human spirit would, with a pure intention,
gratefully surrender every thought
of its own gain to our eternal Father,
who alone clothes the lilies and feeds the birds.[21]

If he has gathered within himself all truth and virtue,
then a gentle heart[22] must love him and burn for him alone,[23]
and disdain to direct its gaze elsewhere;

wounded in one side, he calls eternally
down from the holy cross, his breast and his face
charged with infinite pity and unending love.[24]

7. S1:7 (1538), fol. 4v

My angelic escort, sent to me by God,[25]
guide my mind along the straight path to heaven,[26]
and whenever my spirit allows itself to stumble
then restrain me and restore my weary feet,

so that at the eternal marriage
my light is not extinguished, but with a brightly burning lamp,
summoned by my Lord, wise and prudent,
I find the door open, awaiting my arrival.[27]

And so that my heart may expect him at every hour
and move to meet him joyfully, armed
with pure burning love and with living faith,

Poich'hai di me la cura, ed ei ti crede,
Mostrami i segni, quasi interna aurora,
Nel venir del mio sol chiaro et beato.

8. S2:32 (1840), fol. 5r
Anime elette, in cui da l'ampie e chiare
Cristalline del cielo onde secrete
Ristagna ogni or per farvi sempre liete
De la bontà di Dio più largo mare,
Breve stilla di quelle in queste amare
Nostre del mondo estinguer può la sete
Ai cori ingordi, e le lor voglie quete
Render che de' lor danni son sì avare.
Or che del lato aperto le sante acque
Non sempre tanto lavan quanto ponno
Le macchie nostre, insin nel vivo impresse,
Pregate lui che con le voci stesse
Con le quai chiamar l'uom al ciel li piacque,
Lo svegli omai dal grave interno sonno.

9. S2:22 (1539), fol. 5v
Rinasca in te il mio cor quest'almo giorno
Che nacque a noi colei di cui nascesti,
L'animo excelso tuo l'ale ne presti
Per gir volando al vero alto soggiorno.
Di mille rai da pria consperso intorno
Era 'l suo mortal velo, e mille desti
Sempre al ben far pensieri alti ed onesti,
Poi dentro il fer di maggior lume adorno.
So ch'ella prega te per noi, ma, o pio
Signor, prega tu lei che preghi in modo
Ch'io senta oprar in me sua vital forza,
Ond'io sciogliendo anzi spezzando 'l nodo
Che qui mi lega, questa umana scorza
Serva a lo spirto, e sol lo spirto a Dio.

10. S1:55 (1539), fol. 6r
Con che saggio consiglio e sottil cura
Dee l'uom d'intorno, dentro e lungi e presso
Guardar, ornar e pulir l'alma spesso
Con severo occhio e con giusta misura,

since you are sent to guide me, and he trusts you,
show me the signs, like an internal dawn,
of the coming of my bright and blessed sun.[28]

8. S2:32 (1840), fol. 5r
    Elected souls,[29] in whom the broad, clear,
secret, crystal waves of heaven
fill ever deeper a wide ocean of God's bounty
to guarantee you eternal joy,[30]
    one meager drop from those waters mixed into these
bitter worldly ones of ours can vanquish the thirst
in all eager hearts[31] and assuage our desires,
which so avidly seek their own damnation.
    The holy water flowing from his open wound
does not always entirely wash away
our sins, which are imprinted on our living flesh,[32]
    so pray to him that with those very voices
with which it pleased him to call men to heaven,[33]
he awakens us now from this deep spiritual sleep.

9. S2:22 (1539), fol. 5v
    Let my heart be reborn in you on this glorious day
on which she who bore you was herself born,[34]
and may your divine being lend my heart wings
to fly up to its true lofty resting place.
    Her mortal body was from the beginning surrounded
by a thousand rays of light, and you gave her
a thousand noble and honest inspirations to do good,
which made that body shine with yet a greater light within.
    I know that she prays to you on our behalf,[35] but,
Holy Father, pray to her that through her prayers
her vital energy may fill my being,[36]
    so that I may untie or even break apart the knots
that bind me to this place, and this mortal shell
will serve my spirit alone, and my spirit only God.

10. S1:55 (1539), fol. 6r
    With wise probity and minute care
man must, within and without, from far and near,
observe, enrich, and purge his soul often
with a stern eye and with just moderation,

Sapendo che di Dio per la man pura
Del santo amor v'è sempre il volto impresso
Sì, che convien che 'n noi veggia se stesso,
Nè macchie il fallo uman la sua figura.
    Lontan da sé l'imagin falsa sgombri
E s'onori altamente de la vera
Colui che del gran padre è figlio umile,
    E del divino amor tanto s'ingombri
Che si purghi e rinovi, onde l'altera
Luce non scopra in lui più cosa vile.

11. S1:18 (1539), fol. 6v

Cibo, del cui meraviglioso effetto
L'alma con l'occhio interno dentro vede
L'alta cagion divina e acquista fede
Che sei Dio vero e suo verace obietto:
    Nudrita del tuo ardor, con umil petto
Quasi del ciel sicura indegna erede,
Vorrei là su far gloriose prede
Per forza d'un sol puro acceso affetto.
    Ch'a te furar si possa il tuo bel regno
Con violenta man ne mostri, e poi
Ne dai te stesso in grazioso pegno;
    Tutto sol per far noi divenir tuoi
Facesti, e pur da noi s'usa ogni ingegno
Ed ogni poder nostro incontro a noi.

12. S1:8 (1539), fol. 7r

Tempo è pur ch'io, con la precinta vesta,
Con l'orecchie e con gli occhi avidi intenti
E con le faci in man vive e ardenti,
Aspetti il caro sposo ardita e presta
    Per onorarlo riverente, onesta,
Avendo al cor gli altri desiri spenti,
E brami l'amor suo, l'ira paventi,
Sì ch'ei mi trovi a la vigilia desta.
    Non per li ricchi suoi doni infiniti
Ne men per le soavi alte parole,
Onde vita immortal lieto m'offerse,

knowing that by the pure hand of divine love
the face of God is eternally marked so clearly upon him,
that God can see himself reflected in us,
and his image must not be defiled by our human sin.[37]
     He who is a humble son to the great father,
let him push false icons far from himself
and venerate only true ones,
     so that he is so overcome by divine love
that he is purged and renewed, and the holy
light can reveal no more vile stains upon him.

11. S1:18 (1539), fol. 6v
     Holy sustenance,[38] of whose marvellous effects
the soul with its inner eye perceives
the lofty divine cause and renews its faith
that you are the true God and our soul's one object:
     nurtured by your fire, clothed with humility,
I am almost assured, although unworthy of heaven's grace,[39]
and long to make great conquests in the sky
armed only with a pure and ardent love.
     You show us that violent hands can assault
your holy kingdom, yet then
in gracious pledge you offer yourself;[40]
     all this you did so that we may become yours,
and still we employ all our cunning
and all our strength against ourselves.

12. S1:8 (1539), fol. 7r
     The time has come when I too, with my robe belted tightly,[41]
with my eyes and ears open and alert,
my torch grasped in my hands burning with a bright flame,
must await my beloved husband, joyful and ready
     to honor him reverently, chastely,
having quashed all other desires within my heart,
and I must burn for his love, fear his anger,
and hope that he may find me prepared for the holy vigil.[42]
     Not for the sake of his infinite abundant gifts,
nor for his wise and divine words,
with which joyfully he offered me eternal life,

Ma perché la man santa non m'additi,
"Ecco la cieca, a cui non si scoverse
Con tanti chiari raggi il suo bel sole."

13. S1:92 (1539), fol. 7v
     Del mondo e del nimico folle e vano
Far il contrasto, e de l'iniquia morte,
Signor, aprendo le tartaree porte
Sol con la nuda tua piegata mano;
     Del crudele aversario il fero insano
Furor legar, e le tue luci scorte
Esser ai santi padri a l'alta corte,
U' lor condusse il valor piu che umano;
     Grand'opra fu di re saggio e prudente.
Ma legar i contrari miei pensieri,
Aprir per forza l'indurato petto,
     Far ch'in me sian l'ardenti voglie spente
Onde vadano al ciel i desir veri,
Sol de la tua bontà fie vero effetto.

14. S1:57 (1542), fol. 8r
     S'io, mossa con Zacheo da intenso affetto
Per mirar quel gran sol che 'n ciel fa giorno,
M'alzassi tanto che le turbe intorno
Non fesser ombra al mio basso intelletto,
     Sperar potrei che questo indegno petto
Gli fosse albergo, e 'n quel dolce soggiorno
M'aprisse raggio il suo bel lume adorno
Ch'io provassi altro che mondan diletto;
     Tal che lieta ed umil nel gran convito
Gli apparecchiassi una candida fede
Per mensa e poi per cibo l'alma e 'l core,
     Si ch'ei dicesse, "Omai da te sbandito
Sia il vizio, che con larga ampia mercede
Oggi t'ha fatto salva il mio valore."

15. S1:95 (1538), fol. 8v
     Padre nostro e del ciel, con quant'amore,
Grazia, lume, dolcezza, in vari modi
Dal mondo e da se stesso l'uomo snodi,
Onde libero a te rivolga il core.

but so that his holy hand may not hold me up as an example,
saying, "Here is the blind woman, who failed to discern
her own beautiful sun despite his many bright rays."[43]

13. S1:92 (1539), fol. 7v
O Lord, you vanquished our world, our
proud and brutal enemy, and iniquitous death,
by opening the infernal gates [44]
with your naked wounded hand alone;
and you overcame the shameless frenzied fury
of our cruel adversary, and your shining eyes escorted
the holy fathers to the court on high,
whither they were led by your superhuman power;[45]
all this was indeed the great work of a wise and prudent king.
But when you draw together my confused thoughts,
and break open by force my hardened heart,
and cause my burning desires to be calmed
so that all true longing is channeled up to heaven,
all this is the work of your goodness alone.[46]

14. S1:57 (1542), fol. 8r
If I, together with Zacchaeus,[47] moved by intense desire
to gaze upon that great sun that lights up the sky,
raised myself high enough that the surrounding crowds
could not overshadow even my feeble understanding,
I could then hope that my unworthy breast
might give him shelter, and in his sweet sojourn there
his wondrous great brightness would light a spark within me
so that I felt an otherworldly rapture;
and then joyfully, humbly, at the eternal banquet
I would lay down for him my sincere faith
as the table and my soul and heart as his food,
and he would say to me, "From now on
let vice be banished from your heart, for with great and boundless mercy
my virtue today has been your salvation."

15. S1:95 (1538), fol. 8v
O heavenly Father, with what love,
grace, light, sweetness and in how many ways do you
untie man from the world and his desires,
so that he may turn his heart freely towards you.

Rivolto poi, di puro interno ardore
L'accendi e leghi con più forti nodi;
Poscia lo fermi con sì saldi chiodi
Ch'ogni aspra morte gli par vivo onore.
    Dal pensier fermo poi ne cresce fede,
Da la fe' lume, e da la luce speme,
E dal vero sperar fuochi più vivi,
    Onde non più rubello il voler cede
A lo spirto, anzi al ciel volano inseme
D'ogni cura mortal sdegnosi e schivi.

16. S1 : 132 (1542), fol. 9r
    D'altro che di diamante o duro smalto
Avesti scudo, alor che l'empie e fere
Del superbo nimico invide schiere
Mossero in ciel quell'orgoglioso assalto,
    Angel, per la cui forza elle il mal salto
Fer da la luce eterna a l'ombre nere,
E 'l tuo bel pregio fur le grazie vere
Di non peccar, o dono eccelso e alto.
    Cagion di gloria a l'onorate squadre
Fosti tu, Giesu mio, mia viva luce,
Ch'accendesti a Michel l'ardir invitto;
    Che vide al chiaro specchio del gran padre
Come sareste sempre e'n quel conflitto
De l'angelo e de l'uom possente duce.

17. S1 : 98 (1542), fol. 9v
    Di breve povertà larga ricchezza
Esempio a' servi tuoi, Signor, mostrasti
Con l'opre, e poi con le parole usasti
Semplice gravitate, umile altezza,
    E d'ambe due con pura alma dolcezza
Sì vivo del tuo sol raggio mandasti;
Ch'ebber poi con desii purgati e casti
D'aspramente morir somma vaghezza,
    Acciò che 'l grido tuo grande e possente,
Che chiama l'uom dal ciel a vera vita,
Fosse per lor dal sordo mondo inteso;

Once he has turned, with a pure internal flame
you set him alight, and you tether him with far stronger bonds;
then you fix him with such secure nails
that even a cruel death seems to him a high honor.
From loyal thoughts faith then grows,
from that faith light, and from the light hope,
then from true hope yet brighter fires,
for our desires no longer rebel but cede
to the spirit, and together they fly up to the heavens
rejecting and disdaining all mortal cares.[48]

16. S1:132 (1542), fol. 9r

When the proud, ungodly, and envious army
of your arrogant enemy set in motion its insolent assault
on the heavens,[49] at that time your shield was made
from more than diamonds or hard enamel,
O angel, whose strength forced their unhappy fall
from the eternal light into dark shadows,[50]
and your priceless reward was the one true virtue
of sinlessness, a divine and wondrous gift.
But the true author of victory for those honored troops
was you, Christ Jesus, my living light,[51]
for you inspired Michael's unswerving love;
and he saw in God's clear mirror
that you would eternally be the powerful victor
in the battle between men and angels.[52]

17. S1:98 (1542), fol. 9v

Lord, you demonstrated to your servants the way
to gain from brief poverty great riches
through the example of your deeds, and then you spoke
words of simple gravity and humble pride,[53]
and through both, with pure abundant sweetness,
you sent out such a bright ray of your sun
that, all desires chastened and purged,
their greatest longing was for bitter death,
and thus your great and powerful cry,
which from the heavens calls men to the true life,
could be heard by them from the unheeding world;

Onde spirando il santo foco acceso
Ne mostrar la virtù viva e ardente
Del vero e de l'amor, ch'era smarrita.

18. S1:51 (1538), fol. 10r

Se ne die' lampa il ciel chiara e lucente
Per metter fuoco in terra, acciò ch'egli arda
Per nostro ben, qual ghiaccio or ne ritarda
Che non s'infiammi ogni gelata mente?
    È forte la virtù, l'esca possente,
Largo il Signor che con dritto occhio guarda
Qual alma è più veloce e qual più tarda
A correr per purgarsi al lume ardente.
    Guerra, disunion la viva face
Minaccia e sfida a morte ed a martiri,
Per riunirne poscia a la sua pace;
    Accende 'l pianto in noi, move i sospiri,
Consuma in terra quanto al senso piace,
Sol per far lieti in ciel nostri desiri.

19. S1:10 (1539), fol. 10v

Spiego vèr voi mia luce indarno l'ale
Prima che 'l caldo vostro interno vento
M'apra l'aria d'intorno, ora ch'io sento
Vincer da novo ardir l'antico male.
    Che giunga a l'infinito opra mortale
Vostro dono è, Signor, che 'n un momento
La può far degna, ch'io da me pavento
Di cader col pensier quand'ei più sale.
    Bramo quell'invisibil chiaro lume
Che scaccia dense nebbie e quell'accesa
Secreta fiamma ch'ogni giel consuma,
    Perché poi sgombra del terren costume,
Tutta al divino onor l'anima intesa,
Si mova al volo altero in altra piuma.

20. S1:12 (1542), fol. 11r

Padre eterno del ciel, se, tua mercede,
Vivo ramo son io ne l'ampia e vera
Vite ch'abbraccia il mondo e chiusa intera
Vuol la nostra virtù seco per fede,

and as this blessed burning flame radiated light,
it illuminated the living, holy virtues
of truth and love, which had been lost to us.[54]

18. S1:51 (1538), fol. 10r
　　If the heavens gave up a bright, shining light
to set fire to the earth, so that it burns
for our salvation, what ice now delays
the igniting of our frozen minds?[55]
　　Virtue is strong, the tinder powerful,
God is bountiful and watches with an unflinching eye
to see which soul moves swiftly and which delays
to purge itself in that loving heat.
　　War and strife menace the beautiful flame
and incite death and martyrdom on earth,
but then reunite us in heavenly peace;
　　our cries well up in us, our sighs break out,
all sensual pleasure is consumed on earth,
so that our longing may be satisfied in heaven.

19. S1:10 (1539), fol. 10v
　　I bend my wings towards your light in vain
until the warm breath of your spirit
opens a way through the air around me
and I feel my ancient sin overcome by fresh hope.[56]
　　Your gift, Lord, is that a mortal being can attain
the infinite, for you can in one instant
make it worthy, yet I fear that my aspiring thoughts
are more in danger of falling the higher they rise.[57]
　　I yearn for the clear invisible light
that banishes thick fog and for the hot
secret flame that melts all ice,
　　so that, liberated from earthly ties,
with my soul turned wholly to honoring my God,
I may take flight towards heaven upon new wings.

20. S1:12 (1542), fol. 11r
　　Eternal heavenly Father, as, by your mercy,
I am a living branch on the broad vine of truth,
which embraces the world[58] and enfolds in its girth
our virtue offered up through faith,[59]

L'occhio divino tuo languir mi vede
Per l'ombra di mie frondi intorno nera,
S'a la soave eterna primavera
Il quasi secco umor verde non riede.

Purgami, sì ch'io rimanendo teco
Mi cibi ogni or de la rugiada santa
E rinfreschi col pianto la radice.

Verità sei; dicesti d'esser meco;
Vien dunque lieto, ond'io frutto felice
Faccia in te degno di sì cara pianta.

21. S1:52 (1542), fol. 11v

Debile e 'nferma a la salute vera
Ricorro, e cieca il sol cui solo adoro
Invoco, e nuda bramo il celest'oro
E vo al suo foco fredda in pura cera;

E quanto in sé disfida, tanto spera
L'alma in quel d'ogni ben vivo tesoro,
Che la può far con largo ampio ristoro
Sana, ricca, al suo caldo arder sincera.

Onde con questi doni e questo ardire
Lo veggia non col mio ma col suo lume,
L'ami e ringratii col suo stesso amore.

Non saranno alor mie l'opre e 'l desire,
Ma lieve andrò con le celesti piume
Ove mi spinge e tira il santo ardore.

22. S1:84 (1542), fol. 12r

Tra gelo e nebbia corro a Dio sovente
Per foco e lume, ond'i ghiacci disciolti
Siano e gli ombrosi veli aperti e tolti
Con la divina luce e fiamma ardente;

E se fredda ed oscura è ancor la mente,
Pur son tutti i pensieri al ciel rivolti,
E par che dentro in gran silenzio ascolti
Un suon che sol ne l'anima si sente,

E dice, "Non temer, che venne al mondo
Giesù, d'eterno ben largo ampio mare,
Per far leggiero ogni gravoso pondo;

your divine eye will see me languishing
in the dark shadows that surround my leafy tendrils,
if in your sweet eternal spring
my parched sap cannot restore its fresh green color.

    Cleanse my soul, so that close by your side
I am nourished eternally by your holy dew
and my roots are refreshed with tears.

    You are the truth; you promised to be with me;[60]
come to me joyfully, so that I may grow
sweet fruits in you worthy of this blessed vine.[61]

21. S1:52 (1542), fol. 11v
    Weak and infirm I run towards true salvation,
and blindly I call out to the sun, which alone of all things
I worship, and naked I burn for his heavenly gold[62]
and approach his flames fashioned in pure, cold wax;[63]

    and however much I distrust myself, so much more
then does my soul trust in his wondrous gift,
which has the great healing power to make me
healthy, enriched, and whole in his loving fires.

    Thus, once armed with these gifts and this burning ardor,
I may behold him not through my own powers of vision but through his,
and may love and worship him through the power of his love for me.[64]

    Thus my deeds and my desires will no longer be my own,
but lightly I will move upon celestial wings
wherever the force of his holy love might fling me.[65]

22. S1:84 (1542), fol. 12r
    I often run through cold and mist toward God's
heat and light, which melt away the ice
and tear apart and banish the shadowy veils
through the power of holy light and ardent flames;[66]

    and if my mind remains chilly and dark,
yet all my thoughts are turned to heaven,
and deep within myself in a profound silence I seem to hear
a sound that can only be heard within my soul,

    and it tells me, "Do not be afraid, for Jesus came
into the world, wide and ample sea of eternal good,
to relieve us of our heavy burdens;[67]

Sempre son l'onde sue più dolci e chiare
A chi con umil barca in quel gran fondo
De l'alta sua bontà si lascia andare."

23. S1:53 (1542), fol. 12v
Vorrei che 'l vero sol, cui sempre invoco,
Mandasse un lampo eterno entro la mente,
E non sì breve raggio, che sovente
La va illustrando intorno a poco a poco;
E non scaldasse 'l cor quel santo foco
Da lungi con scintille tarde e lente,
Ma dentro lo struggesse viva ardente
Fiamma senza aspettar tempo ne loco.
Lo spirto è ben dal caldo ardor compunto,
E sereno dal bel lume il desio,
Ma non ho da me forze a l'alta impresa.
Deh! fa, signor, con un miracol ch'io
Mi veggia intorno lucida in un punto
E tutta dentro in ogni parte accesa.

24. S1:134 (1546), fol. 13r
Alta umiltade, e sopra l'altre cara
Virtuti a Dio, le cui parole e opre
Dimostran quanti bei secreti scopre
La sua mercede a chi da lui t'impara;
Se tu sei dolce è ben più tanto amara
La tua aversaria, ch'ogni ben ricopre
E più armata talor par che s'adopre
Contra di te che sei virtù sì rara.
Tu combatti per pace, ella per ira;
Ella cerca il suo onore, e tu la gloria
Di colui che concede il campo e l'armi.
Non può fallir la tua sicura mira,
Perch'l piede erri o la man si disarmi,
Ché vive entro 'l tuo cor la tua vittoria.

25. S1:11 (1546), fol. 13v
Il ciel, la terra, ogni elemento rende
Testimon d'alta causa, e che superna
Virtù li regga, acciò che l'uom discerna
Che 'l valor di là su fra noi s'estende.

his waves are always smaller and more gentle
for those who, in a bark of humility upon the great ocean
of his divine grace, freely abandon themselves."[68]

23. S1:53 (1542), fol. 12v
    I wish that the true sun, upon which I eternally call,
would send an endless stream of light into my mind,
instead of this weak ray, which sometimes
barely manages to cast a glow;
    I wish that the holy fire did not warm my heart
only from afar with spent and feeble sparks,
but instead that a searing flame would devour my breast
without respect for time or place.
    My spirit is truly mortified by the gentle flames,
and my longing is requited by the beautiful light,
yet still I lack the strength for this great undertaking.
    Lord, perform a miracle so that I
may find my being encircled by your light[69]
and all within me burning with your fire.

24. S1:134 (1546), fol. 13r
    Great humility, God's preferred of all
the virtues,[70] whose words and deeds
demonstrate how many wondrous secrets are revealed
in his mercy to those who learn your worth from him;
    if you are sweet then all the more bitter
is your adversary,[71] who conceals all good
and seems to take up arms with greater strength
against you because you are so rare a virtue.
    You fight through peace, she fights through discord;
she seeks her own reward, you honor him
alone who bestows the field and the arms.
    Your certain aim cannot miss its target,
even if the foot errs or the hand drops its weapon,
for your victory dwells within your heart.

25. S1:11 (1546), fol. 13v
    The heavens, the earth, each element bears
witness to the divine cause, and each one shows that a supreme
power rules over it, and thus man can discern
that celestial forces reign here on earth.

Questo admirar fa il saggio, e non l'accende
Al vero ardor ne la sua parte interna,
Ma ben l'infiamma quella umile eterna
Bontà ch'in croce sol se stessa offende.
    Questa può far prigion l'alto intelletto,
Legar la saggia voglia, che non preme
Sì dolce nodo al cor gentil intorno;
    Anzi ogni uman pensier sgombra del petto
Sicuro già de la gioiosa speme
Che gl'impromette un sempiterno giorno.

26. S1:121 (1538), fol. 14r
    Donna accesa animosa, e da l'errante
Vulgo lontana in solitario albergo,
Parmi lieta veder lasciando a tergo
Quanto non piace al primo eterno amante,
    E fermato il desio fermar le piante
Sovra un gran monte; ond'io mi specchio e tergo
Nel bello esempio e 'l pensier drizzo e ergo
Dietro l'orme beate e l'opre sante.
    L'alta spelonca sua quest'aspro scoglio
Mi rappresenta, ma da lunge il sole
Che vicin l'infiammava il cor mi scalda.
    Da ghiaccio e nodo vil pur l'alzo e scioglio,
Ond'ella, a pie di lui ch'adora e cole,
Lo leghi con catena ardente e salda.

27. S2:2 (unpub.), fol. 14v
    Non senza alta cagion la prima antica
Legge il suo paradiso a noi figura
Di latte e mel, perché candida pura
Fede e soave amor l'alma nudrica,
    E 'n guisa d'ape, natural nimica
D'ogni amaro sapor, con bella cura
Da ciascun fior d'intorno il dolce fura,
Per dare in frutto altrui la sua fatica.
    E quasi agnello il latte umil riceve,
Perch'altri l'abbia in maggior copia quando
L'avezza a forte cibo il buon pastore;

A wise man will admire these clear signs,
yet they will not inspire his inner spirit to holy love,
but instead the wise are inflamed by that eternal humble
goodness that wounds itself alone upon the cross.

Thus is the haughty intellect imprisoned
and wise desire tamed, but such a sweet bond
does not damage the gentle heart it binds;

instead all mortal thoughts are purged from a mind
that is already focused on the joyful hope
offered by the promise of eternal life.[72]

26. S1:121 (1538), fol. 14r

I seem to see a woman of passion and spirit,
far from the errant crowd in her lonely dwelling[73]
and joyous in turning away from
all the things rejected by her one true lover,[74]

and I see her halting her desires and setting her feet
upon a high mountain; therefore I mirror and purify myself
in her wondrous example and urge on and raise up my thoughts,
following in her blessed footsteps and imitating her holy deeds.

This cruel rock represents for me her
lofty cave,[75] but the sun that inflamed her
from so close heats my own heart from far off.

I struggle here to free my heart from cold ice and tight knots,
so that she, kneeling at the feet of the one she adores and worships,
may bind it with the strong chains of love.[76]

27. S2:2 (unpub.), fol. 14v

Not without some higher wisdom the ancient
law describes God's paradise to us as fashioned
from milk and honey, because true pure
faith and gentle love nourish the soul,[77]

and in the guise of a bee, the natural enemy
of bitter flavors, with wondrous care
our Lord extracts sweet nectar from flowers growing all around,
so that through his labors the fruits of others may grow plump.[78]

As meek as a lamb Christ humbly receives the milk,
so that others may drink a greater abundance when
the good shepherd weans them onto stronger food;[79]

Onde poi sazia e grande in tempo breve,
Le sue dolcezze e se stessa sdegnando,
Fermi in Dio l'occhio al suo divino onore.

28. S1:56 (1546), fol. 15r
Il buon pastor, con opre e voci pronte
Al nostro ben, molt'anni ha richiamato
Il gregge suo dal periglioso prato
U' smarrito era, al bel sicuro monte.
Poi su le spalle, per far chiare et conte
L'accese voglie, in croce l'ha portato,
E di chiodi e di spine insieme ornato
Sparge di sangue e d'acqua un vivo fonte
Onde si pasca, si ristori, e onore
Renda al gran Padre, e per un pianto breve
Mandar vuol in oblio ben lungo errore.
Gran nebbia copre un cor, gran sasso e greve
Il preme, s'a tal lume e tanto ardore
Non è di molle cera o bianca neve.

29. S1:19 (1546), fol. 15v
Anima, il Signor viene, omai disgombra
Le nebbie intorno e sol t'orna d'amore
E di fede, onde i pensier, la mente e 'l core
A l'alta luce sua non faccian ombra.
Il nostro oprar sovente impaccia e 'ngombra
Lo albergo; onde ricorri al suo valore,
La cui virtù da noi fuga l'errore
Che la sua bella imagin macchia e ombra.
Essendo ei re del ciel, disse ch'allora
Sente le vere sue delizie quando
Con noi parte i divini alti tesori;
Così metter convien noi stessi in bando,
Tal ch'al mondo al piacer falso si mora
E 'n lui si viva e lui s'ami ed onori.

30. S1:23 (1546), fol. 16r
Apra 'l sen, Giove, e di sue grazie tante
Faccia che 'l mondo in ogni parte abonde,
sì che l'anime poi ricche e feconde
Sian tutte di virtute amiche e sante.

then having quickly become satiated and robust,
spurning this nectar and all earthly desires,
the soul must fix its eyes on the divinity of God.

28. S1:56 (1546), fol. 15r
    The good shepherd, eager to protect us
with deeds and words, has for many years been calling
his flock from the dangerous field
where it had wandered, to a beautiful and secure mountain pasture.[80]
    Then, to demonstrate with utmost clarity his great desire,
he bore his charges upon his shoulders to the cross,
and, decorated with both nails and thorns,
he poured down a living fountain of blood and water[81]
    where we can feed and restore ourselves and do honor
to our eternal Father, and thus with a brief lament
our ancient sin is banished into oblivion.
    Great shadows must cover our hearts, huge and heavy stones
weigh down upon them, if in such bright light and intense heat
we do not melt as soft wax or white snow.[82]

29. S1:19 (1546), fol. 15v
    O my soul, the Lord is coming, now chase away
the mists that surround you and clothe yourself only in love
and in faith, so that your thoughts, spirit, and heart
do not cast shadows upon his holy light.
    Our deeds too often darken and weigh down
this earthly resting place; turn then to his example,
his virtue that shuns our sins,
which would stain and cloud his pristine image.[83]
    As he is king of heaven, he tells us
that he feels true joy only when
he shares with us his wondrous and divine treasures;[84]
    thus we must exile ourselves from these
worldly concerns, so that vain pleasure dies in us
and we learn to live in him and love and honor him.

30. S1:23 (1546), fol. 16r
    May Jove open his heart and bring the abundance
of his many graces to all the world,[85]
so that our souls may become enriched and fertile
with pure and holy virtues.[86]

Soave primavera orni ed ammante
La terra e corran puro nettar l'onde;
Copra di gemme il mar l'altere sponde,
Ed ogni scoglio sia vago diamante,
    Per onorar il giorno aventuroso
Che ne die' il parto eternamente eletto
Per apportar vera salute a noi;
    A cantar come in veste umana ascoso
Venne l'immortal Dio, discenda poi
Da l'angeliche squadre il più perfetto.

31. S1:27 (1546), fol. 16v

Se 'l breve suon, che sol quest'aer frale
Circonda e move, e l'aura, che raccoglie
Lo spirto dentro e poi l'apre e discioglie
Soavemente in voce egra e mortale,
    Con tal dolcezza il cor sovente assale
Che d'ogni cura vil s'erge e ritoglie,
Sprona, accende il pensier, drizza le voglie
Per gir volando al ciel con leggier ale,
    Che fia quando udirà con vivo zelo
La celeste harmonia l'anima pura,
Sol con l'orecchia interna attenta al vero
    Dinanzi al suo fattor nel primo cielo,
U' non si perde mai l'ampia misura
Né si discorda il bel concento altero?

32. S1:124 (1539), fol. 17r

Dietro al divino tuo gran capitano,
Seguendo l'orma bella, ardito intrasti
Fra perigliose insidie, aspri contrasti,
Con l'arme sol de l'umiltade in mano;
    Mentre 'l mondo sprezzando, e nudo e piano,
Solo de la tua croce ricco, andasti
Per deserti selvaggi, a noi mostrasti
Quanto arda il divin raggio un cor umano;
    Divo Francesco, a cui l'alto Signore
Nel cor l'istoria di sua man dipinse
Del celeste vèr noi sì grand'amore;

Sweet spring adorn and carpet
the earth, and waves of pure nectar swell the oceans;
let the sea strew her proud shores with gems,
and let every rock be carved from perfect diamonds,
to venerate that blessed day
that saw the divinely elected birth
that brought true salvation to us all;[87]
to sing of how, disguised in human form,
immortal God descended,[88] let he who is
most perfect among the angelic throngs descend.[89]

31. S1:27 (1546), fol. 16v
If the faint sound, which alone stirs and
moves the frail air, and the breeze, which gathers
up the spirit and then opens and melts it
softly in a weak mortal whisper,
often assail the heart with such a gentle touch
that it rises up, shedding all vile cares,
and spur on and inflame the mind and stiffen the resolve
to fly toward heaven on bright wings,
what then will the pure heart do when, fired with hope,
with the inner ear tuned to the truth,
it hears the music of the celestial choirs[90]
before our maker in the heavens above,
where the steady rhythm is never broken
and the heavenly harmony never grows discordant?[91]

32. S1:124 (1539), fol. 17r
Behind your blessed great captain,[92]
bravely following his inspiring path, you encountered
dangerous traps, bitter struggles,
bearing in your hand only the weapon of humility;
disdaining the world, naked and gentle,
your cross your only treasure, you went on through
savage deserts, and thus you showed us how greatly
the divine fire can inflame a human heart;
holy Francis,[93] in whose heart
the Lord God with his own hand wrote the story
of his heavenly and abundant love for us;

Poi seco t'abbracciò tanto e distrinse
Che scolpiò dentro sì, ch'apparver fore
Le piaghe, ond'ei la morte e 'l mondo vinse.

33. S1:123 (1546), fol. 17
Francesco, in cui sì come in umil cera
Con sigillo d'amor sì vive impresse
Le sue piaghe Iesù, che sol t'elesse
A mostrarne di sé l'imagin vera,
    Quanto ti strinse ed a te quanto intera
Die' la sua forma e le virtuti istesse,
Onde fra noi per la sua sposa eresse
Il tempio e 'l seggio e l'alma insegna altera.
    Povertade, umil vita e l'altre tante
Grazie l'alzaro al più sublime stato,
Quanto or per suoi contrari è bassa e vile;
    L'amasti in terra, or prega in ciel, beato
Spirto, ch'ella ritorni omai pura gentile
Ai pensieri, ai desiri, a l'opre sante.

34. S1:29 (1546), fol. 18r
Vorrei che sempre un grido alto e possente
Risonasse, Giesù, dentro al mio core,
E l'opre e le parole anco di fore
Mostrasser fede viva e speme ardente.
    L'anima eletta, che i bei segni sente
In se medesma del celeste ardore,
Giesù vede, ode e 'ntende, il cui valore
Alluma, infiamma, purga, apre la mente,
    E dal chiamarlo assai fermo ed ornato
Abito acquista tal, che la natura
Per vero cibo suo mai sempre il brama;
    Onde a l'ultima guerra, a noi sì dura,
De l'oste antico, sol di fede armato
Già per lungo uso il cor da sé lo chiama.

35. S1:130 (1546), fol. 18v
Beati voi, cui tempo né fatica
Può far lo spirto vostro afflitto o stanco,
Né per la notte il dì viene a voi manco,
Né copre nebbia il sol che vi nudrica.

then he embraced and held you so tightly that
within you were carved the wounds, which appeared upon your flesh,
with which he conquered death and the world.[94]

33. S1 : 123 (1546), fol. 17
        Francis, in whom as if in humble wax
with the stamp of love Jesus imprinted his wounds
so clearly and elected you alone
to show yourself in his true image,[95]
        how tightly he held you, and how wholly
he gave you his form and his own virtues,
and then among us for his wife he erected
the temple, the throne, and the sustaining noble emblem.[96]
        Your poverty, your humble life, and your other many
graces raised her to the most sublime state,
while now opposing vices have made her low and vile;
        you loved her on earth, now pray in heaven, blessed
spirit, that she may return again pure and gentle
to good thoughts, desires, and sacred works.[97]

34. S1 : 29 (1546), fol. 18r
        I long for a high and strident call,
Lord Jesus, which would ring out eternally within my heart,
and that my deeds and words might shine forth,
revealing my living faith and burning hope.
        The elected soul, who feels the wondrous heat
of the celestial fire within,
sees, hears, and understands Jesus, whose virtue
lights up, inflames, purges, and opens the mind,[98]
        and by calling out to him it acquires
such a rich and pure habit, that the spirit
burns ever more for holy sustenance;
        thus in that final battle with the ancient enemy,[99]
so difficult for us, armed with pure faith alone,
the heart through long practice calls out unaided to Christ.[100]

35. S1 : 130 (1546), fol. 18v
        You blessed ones,[101] whose spirits are never
afflicted or exhausted by time or by toil,
night can never obscure the light of your day,
nor is the sun that nourishes you ever masked by clouds.

Per laberinti o reti non s'intrica
Il vostro piede, ma sicuro e franco
Sta in porto, né vi rende il pelo bianco
La vita grave o ver la morte amica.
 Un sol foco il desio nudrisce e 'ncende,
E 'l dolce desiar non ange il core,
Né la sazietà fastidio rende.
 Gradito è a maggior gloria chi più amore
Ebbe a Dio in terra, né l'invidia offende
L'un perché l'altro abbia più grande onore.

36. S1:113 (1546), fol. 19r
 Potess'io in questa acerba atra tempesta
Del travagliato mondo entrar ne l'arca
Col caro a Dio Noè, poich'altra barca
Non giova a l'acqua perigliosa infesta;
 O con la schiera ebrea, ch'ardita e presta
L'aperto rosso mar sicura varca,
E poi sul lito, del gran peso scarca,
Ringrazia Dio cantando in gioia e 'n festa;
 O con Pietro il mio core, alor ch'io sento
Cader la fede al sollevar de l'onde,
Da la divina man sentisse alzarsi;
 E s'al lor l'esser mio già non risponde,
Non è il favor del ciel scemato o spento
Né quei soccorsi fur mai tardi o scarsi.

37. S1:112 (1546), fol. 19v
 Il porvi Dio ne l'arca e farvi poi
Padre del miglior gente, già non sono
Cagione ond'io, Noè, di voi ragiono,
Né 'l fido aprirvi i gran secreti suoi;
 Ma che fra tanto numero sol voi
Riguardasse dal ciel per giusto e buono
E 'n voce e 'n opra lo mostrasse, è un dono
Che d'invidia e d'amor infiamma or noi.
 Quand'ei l'odio e lo sdegno discoverse
Al mondo, che ne l'ira sua si giacque,
Con dolce amor e pace a voi s'offerse,

Your foot is not entangled in labyrinths
or nets, but you remain always in port
safely and humbly,[102] and your hair does not grow white
at the harshness of life or thoughts of friendly death.

A single fire feeds and inflames your desire,
and sweet desiring does not torment your heart,
nor does satiety cause you disgust.

Destined for greater glory in heaven is he who loved God
more on earth, and one is not afflicted by jealousy
because another is honored more highly.[103]

36. S1 : 113 (1546), fol. 19r

I wish that in the harsh, lowering storm
of this tormented world I could climb aboard the ark
with Noah, blessed by God, for no other boat
will survive in these dangerous, infested waters;[104]

or else move together with the Jewish ranks,
who with bold haste safely traverse the yawning Red Sea,
and on the opposite shore, freed from their terrible burden,
give thanks to God, celebrating with joyful songs;[105]

or else with Peter, when I feel my faith
shrinking from the threatening waves,
I wish that I could find my heart too lifted up by the divine hand;[106]

but if my state is not similar to these,
it is not that heaven's favor has ceased to be bountiful
or that such miracles were ever rare or scarce.[107]

37. S1 : 112 (1546), fol. 19v

God's placing you in the ark and making you
father of a blessed race, these are not the
reasons why I speak of you, Noah,
nor his trusting you with his great secrets;

but that among such a great multitude you alone
were seen by the heavens to be just and true
and that he showed this in word and deed, this is a gift
that inflames us still with envy and with love.[108]

When God uncovered the hatred and spite
in the world and it lay subject to his wrath,
he offered himself to you with gentle love and peace,

E mentre ch'allargò del furor l'acque
Con l'onde de la grazia vi coverse,
Cotanto il vostro ben oprar gli piacque.

38. S2:31 (unpub.), fol. 20r
　　Penso ch'in ciel, con puri e lieti canti,
Si celebri oggi l'onorato giorno
Nel quale a la lor patria fer ritorno
Per Iesù Cristo i gloriosi santi,
　　E che di lui le lode, i pregi e i vanti
Sian di vedere il paradiso adorno
Di tanti lumi, e come d'ogn'intorno
Un raggio del suo sol gli orni e ammanti,
　　E che le veste del finissimo oro
Sian, quasi di rubin fregiate asperse
De l'innocente suo sangue beato,
　　E 'l fonte del divin largo tesoro
Irrigandoli tutti esca dal lato,
Che sol la sua bontade al mondo aperse.

39. S2:12 (unpub.), fol. 20v
　　Suol nascer dubbio se di più legarsi
Il donare ad altrui segno è maggiore,
O se 'l ricever con pietoso amore
Pegno è sicuro assai di più obligarsi;
　　Ma il vero amante, Dio, che non mai scarsi
Fece partiti, a noi diede il suo amore
Divino e per sé prese il nostro errore
Umano e volse in terra mortal farsi,
　　Onde dai larghi doni umile e grato
L'uom fosse, e dal ricever suo sicuro
Sì che di fede viva e d'amor arda;
　　Ma la tanta sua luce il nostro oscuro
Occhio, da color falsi qui turbato,
Quanto risplende più, meno riguarda.

40. S1:119 (1546), fol. 21r
　　Non sol per la sua mente e pura e retta
Il martir primo in Dio le luci fisse
Tenne, pregando sì ch'al ciel prescrisse
Il far del suo morir degna vendetta;

and while in a fury he spread abroad the waters,
he covered you only with the waves of his grace,
because your good deeds pleased him so.

38. S2:31 (unpub.), fol. 20r
    I believe that in heaven, with pure and joyful song,
today they celebrate the noble day
when the glorious saints return to their homelands
in the name of Jesus Christ,[109]
    and the worship of Christ, the prayers and music,
ring out to see paradise ablaze
with so many lights, and as if from every corner
a ray of his sun adorns and covers the throng,
    and every robe is made of finest gold,
decorated with sprinklings of rubies
fashioned from his innocent holy blood,
    and the fountain of great holy treasure
pours from his side, bathing all around,[110]
for he alone opened his bounty to the world.

39. S2:12 (unpub.), fol. 20v
    A doubt arises if it is a greater sign
to seek to offer gifts to others,
or if receiving with pious love
is a secure enough pledge to justify the greater obligation;[111]
    for God, the true lover,[112] who never offered
poor rewards, gave to us his divine
love and took our human error as his own
and chose to come to earth in mortal form,
    so that man should be humbled and grateful for
the generous gifts, yet so sure of receiving them
that he burns with living faith and love;[113]
    but in our dark eyes, blinded here
by false colors, the brighter his great light
burns, the less easily we can see it.[114]

40. S1:119 (1546), fol. 21r
    The first martyr kept his eyes fixed on God,[115]
not only because his mind was pure and good,
praying that the heavens would convert his death
into a justified vengeance;

Anzi ogni pietra a lui dolce saetta
Parea che 'l ciel più largamente aprisse,
Or li parean corone intorno fisse
Da lui per gloria sua ciascuna eletta.
     Per suoi nemici orò, né mercé impetra
Madre con tal desio per figlio caro
Quanto ei pregò per lor con dolce amore;
     Né mai lucida gemma ad uomo avaro
Fu in pregio sì come a lui quella pietra,
Che più dritto li giunse in mezzo 'l core.

41. S1 : 17 (1546), fol. 21v
     Quando quell'empio tradimento aperse
Iesù contra sé ordito al caro amato
Discepolo, in silenzio il suo turbato
Aspetto quasi a gli altri il discoperse,
     Ma il buon maestro il suo petto gli offerse;
E pria che fosse il duolo oltra passato
Dal core e 'l viso avesse ancor bagnato,
Il sonno chiuse l'occhio e il duol coverse,
     Ond'ei cadde in sul dolce letto, e volo
Non fece augel già mai tant'alto quanto
Volò in questo cader l'aquila altera.
     Dio li mostrò se stesso e li fu solo
E luce e specchio, mentre ebbe quel santo
Riposo in braccio a l'alta pace vera.

42. S1 : 108 (1546), fol. 22r
     Vergine e madre, il tuo figlio sul petto
Stringesti morto, ma il fido pensero
Scorgea la gloria e 'l bel trionfo altero
Ch'ei riportava d'ogni spirto eletto.
     L'aspre sue piaghe e il dolce umile aspetto
T'accendeva il tormento acerbo e fero,
Poi la vittoria grande e l'onor vero
Portava a l'alma nuovo alto diletto.
     E so che in quella umanità sentisti
Che Dio non la lasciava, anzi avea cura
Di ritornarla gloriosa e viva;

but also because every stone that struck him seemed a sweet
arrow that rent the heavens ever wider,[116]
or else he saw them as crowns bestowed by him,
in his glory, on each of the chosen ones.
    He prayed for his enemies, and a mother would not
pray more ardently for mercy for her own son
than he prayed for them with sweet love;
    nor was a precious gem ever more prized
by an avaricious man than that stone was to him,
which penetrated straight to the center of his heart.

41. S1 : 17 (1546), fol. 21v
    When Jesus revealed to his dearly beloved
disciple the enormous betrayal that would be committed
against him, in silence his ravaged
features almost revealed his suffering to the other men,
    but the good master offered him his breast;[117]
and before the pain had left his
heart and the tears dried upon his face,
sleep closed his eyes and numbed his torment,[118]
    and thus he fell upon a soft bed,
and no eagle ever flew
as high as the divine eagle in that moment of his falling.[119]
    God revealed himself and was for him
both a light and a mirror, while he rested
in holy repose in the arms of a sacred and true peace.

42. S1 : 108 (1546), fol. 22r
    Virgin and mother, you clasped your dead son
upon your breast, but in your faithful mind
you saw the glory and the holy victory
that he brought to every elected soul.
    His bitter wounds and sweet humble countenance
increased your harsh and potent torment,
but the great triumph of true honor
brought to your soul a new and pure delight.
    I know you saw that God
had not left his soul in that mortal body, but rather
would be certain to resurrect it into glorious life;

Ma perché vera madre il partoristi,
Credo che insino a la tua sepoltura
Di madre avesti il cor d'ogni ben priva.

43. S1:107 (1546), fol. 22v
    Quando vedeste, Madre, a poco a poco
A Iesù dolce in croce il bel splendore
Fuggir da gli occhi e in sua vece l'amore
Sfavillar d'ogn'intorno ardente fuoco,
    Credo che i vostri spirti andar nel loco
D' suoi per riportarne al vostro core
Quei che v'eran più cari, ma brev'ore
Vi fur concesse al doloroso gioco,
    Ché la morte li chiuse, onde s'aperse
La strada a noi del ciel, prima serrata
Mille e più lustri da la colpa antica.
    Lo scudo de la fede in voi sofferse
Il mortal colpo, onde ogni alma ben nata
Nel favor vostro sua speme nudrica.

44. S1:105 (1546), fol. 23r
    Con che pietosa carità sovente
Apria 'l gran figlio i bei concetti a voi,
Madre divina, e con che fe' nei suoi
Precetti andaste voi più sempre ardente.
    Il vostro santo amor prima fu in mente
Di Dio fermato e in carne qui fra noi
Ristretto e in ciel con maggior nodo poi
Rinovato, più saldo e più possente.
    S'ei nacque, s'ei morì, s'egli andò in cielo,
Per compagna, rifugio, ancella e madre
Seco vi scorgò con umile affetto;
    Ed ora il dolce sposo e l'alto padre
Col caro figlio a voi rendon perfetto
Guidardon del vostro almo e puro zelo.

45. S2:23 (unpub.), fol. 23v
    Mentre che quanto dentro avea concetto
Dei misteri di Dio ne facea degno
La vergin Luca, oprava egli ogni ingegno
Per formar vero il bel divino aspetto,

yet because you bore him as a human mother,
I believe that from that moment until death
your maternal heart was robbed of any joy.[120]

43. S1 : 107 (1546), fol. 22v
    Holy Mother, when you saw the living
light gradually draining from the eyes of your
sweet crucified son and in its place a great fire
of love leap up on every side,
    I believe that your spirit went to the place
of his spirit and tried to recover what was dearest in him
within your own heart, but only a few brief
hours were granted you for this painful task,
    as death closed his eyes and opened wide
for us the path to heaven,[121] which had been barred
by original sin for many thousands of years.
    The shield of faith in you withstood
the mortal blow,[122] and every elected soul
nurtures its hope in your favor.[123]

44. S1 : 105 (1546), fol. 23r
    Blessed mother, with holy charity your divine
son would often explain to you his wondrous concepts,
and you followed him, burning with ever more
passionate faith in his teachings.[124]
    Your saintly love was first born in the mind
of God and confined in flesh among us here
and then in the heavens renewed with greater bonds,
making it more secure and powerful.[125]
    At his birth, at his death, when he rose into heaven,
he found you at his side, his companion, refuge, servant,
and mother, filled with humility and love;
    and now your sweet husband, the eternal father
and beloved son,[126] bestows upon you
a perfect reward for your pure and dedicated faith.[127]

45. S2 : 23 (unpub.), fol. 23v
    While his inner understanding of the
mysteries of God conferred nobility upon Luke's virgin,
he mustered all possible skill
to render true to life that sweet holy countenance,[128]

Ma de l'immensa idea sì colmo il petto
Avea, che come un vaso d'acqua pregno
Che salir non può fuor, l'alto disegno
A poco a poco uscì manco e imperfetto.

In parte finse l'aer dolce e grave;
Quel vivo no 'l mostrò, forse sdegnando
De l'arte i gravi lumi e la fiera ombra.

Basta che 'l modo umil, l'atto soave
A Dio rivolge, accende, move, e quando
Si mira il cor d'ogni atra nebbia sgombra.

46. S2 : 30 (unpub.), fol. 24r

Se piace a l'occhio di veder volando
Venir falconi per l'aere, lasciati
Da lor signori a la rapina usati,
Solo il suo cibo e se medesmi amando,

Quanto gode il pensiero oggi mirando
Undici mila bei guerrieri alati,
Dal ciel di palme e di corone armati,
Venir la preda lor lieti cercando;

Poscia gioir con gli altri angeli inseme
Tutti d'aver unite in tanto amore
Undici mila vergini prudenti.

Onde la lode e 'l frutto de la speme
Fu de le donne e di quei lumi ardenti
Il gaudio ancor, ma sol di Dio l'onore.

47. S2 : 3 (unpub.), fol. 24v

Scorgean li spirti eletti sempre in cielo
Del gran sole i bei rai, ma non reflessi
Da lo specchio mortal, né meno impressi
Su l'imagin del nostro umano velo,

Onde in quell'antro, anzi pur sacro Delo
U' nacque il vero Apollo, e chiari e spessi
Folgoravan splendori, or per se stessi
Ardenti ed or per noi d'un puro zelo,

Guardavano il bel figlio e la gran madre,
Ch'avean fatto di lor degna la terra,
Dio ringraziando e l'alta ardente face

but his breast was so full of the immensity of
his concept that, like a vase overfilled with water
that cannot easily flow out, the great design
came forth bit by bit, partial and imperfect.
    Some shade of her sweet and grave air was captured;
yet she is not lifelike, perhaps because he scorned
the polished lights and haughty shades of artifice.[129]
    It is enough that her gentle air, her humility,
when we gaze upon it, turns our hearts to God,
inflames and moves them, cleanses them of gloomy shadows.

46. S2:30 (unpub.), fol. 24r
    If the eye delights in seeing falcons
come sweeping through the air, released
by their masters and intent upon their prey,
caring only for themselves and their own nourishment,
    how much then must the mind delight today in seeing
eleven thousand beautiful winged warriors,
descending from the sky, armed with palms and crowns,
hunting joyfully for their prey;[130]
    and to see them celebrate with all the other angels
the great love that has united as one
these eleven thousand wise virgins.
    Therefore great praise and bright rewards belonged
to these women and continued celebration to
those shining lights, but all honor belongs to God alone.[131]

47. S2:3 (unpub.), fol. 24v
    The elected spirits could always make out in the heavens
the wondrous rays of the great sun, not reflected
merely in our mortal mirror,[132] nor less still imprinted
upon the image of our human veil,
    in which, in that lowly cavern, or rather the sacred and splendid Delos
where the true Apollo was born,[133] many splendors
shone clear and abundant, the pure beauty of their light
shining sometimes for us, sometimes for themselves alone,
    they watched the beautiful son and his divine mother,
who had made the earth worthy of them,
giving thanks to God and to the luminous essence

Del santo spirto, e in mille e mille squadre
Cantavan ch'era vinta l'aspra guerra
E data ai buoni al mondo eterna pace.

48. S1 : 117 (1546), fol. 25r
    Quante dolcezze, Andrea, Dio ti scoverse
Alor che salutandol di lontano
Adorasti il supplizio empio inumano
Ove al padre il Signor per noi s'offerse.
    Col santo fuoco ei proprio il cor t'aperse,
E vi raccolse con la forte mano
Dentro l'alte virtù, che il nostro insano
Voler manda di fuor vaghe e disperse.
    Onde ne l'aspra croce il dolce e 'l chiaro
Del ciel vedesti e quella immortal vita,
Che parve a gli altri ciechi dura morte.
    La tua fortezza celere e spedita
Vittoria elesse per vie dritte e corte,
Che fanno il viver bello e 'l morir caro.

49. S1 : 133 (1546), fol. 25v
    Quanta gioia, tu segno e stella ardente,
Alor che i vivi bei raggi fermaste
Sul tugurio felice, al cor mandaste
De i saggi re del bel ricco oriente.
    E voi, quanto più basso il re possente
Fasciato, picciolin, pover trovaste,
Più grande, alto il vedeste e più l'amaste,
Ch'al ciel tanta umiltà v'alzò la mente.
    Il loco, gli animali, il freddo e 'l fieno
Davano, e i panni vili, e il duro letto,
De l'alta sua bontà sicuro segno;
    E per la stella e per lo chiaro aspetto
De la potenzia, avendo in mano il pegno,
L'adoraste col cor di gaudio pieno.

50. S1 : 25 (1546), fol. 26r
    Puri innocenti, il vostro invitto e forte
Duca parte, e vi lascia soli inermi,
E vuol che i vostri petti siano schermi
A le sue spalle, o benedetta sorte!

of the Holy Spirit, and in legions of thousands
they sang that the end of the bitter war had come
and that the good people on earth had inherited eternal peace.[134]

48. S1:117 (1546), fol. 25r

What gentleness God discovered in you, Andrew,[135]
when, saluting him from afar,
you worshiped that great and inhuman torment
with which our Lord offered himself to his father for us.

He opened your heart with his holy fire,
and with his strong hand he gathered within you
the divine virtues, which our own unsound
desires scatter abroad, far from us.

Thus on the bitter cross you saw the sweetness
and the clarity of heaven and the immortal life,
which to other, blind men appeared to be only cruel death.[136]

In your strength you chose a swift and easy
victory by way of straight and short roads,
which make living beautiful and death welcome.

49. S1:133 (1546), fol. 25v

How much joy you brought to the hearts
of the wise kings from the magnificent East,
O sign and burning star, when you fixed your beautiful
living rays upon that happy lowly hut.[137]

And you kings, how much more did you love your own great king,
how much higher and more powerful did you consider him,
the more lowly you found him then, swaddled, tiny and poor,
and his great humility lifted your souls to heaven.

The stable, the animals, the cold, and the hay,
and his poor rags, and his hard bed,
all were a sure sign of his celestial grace;[138]

then, your hearts filled with joy, you worshiped
that star and the sweet countenance
of our Lord, holding your gifts before you.

50. S1:25 (1546), fol. 26r

Pure innocent ones, your fearless and brave
leader is departing,[139] leaving you alone and unprotected,
and he wishes you to use your breasts as shields
behind him. O blessed fortune![140]

Erode con le voglie inque e torte
Incide e spezza i bei teneri germi,
Ed ei ne rende a voi gli eterni e fermi
Frutti e vita immortal per breve morte.
    Voi senza fede, deste il pianto solo
Per parola ai martiri, e egli ornati
V'ha di celesti palme e santi allori;
    A pena eran su gli omer vostri nati
I vanni, o cari e pargoletti amori,
Ch'alzaste infino al cielo il primo volo.

51. S1 : 103 (1546), fol. 26v
    Donna, dal ciel gradita a tanto onore,
Che il tuo seno il figliuol di Dio nudriva,
Or com'ei non t'ardeva e non t'apriva
Con la divina bocca il petto e 'l core?
    Or non si sciolse l'alma, e dentro e fore
Ciascun tuo spirto ed ogni parte viva
Col latte insieme a un punto non s'univa
Per gir tosto a nudrir l'alto Signore?
    Ma non conviene andar coi stretti umani
Termini a misurar gli ordini vostri,
Troppo al nostro veder larghi e lontani;
    Dio morì in terra; or nei superni chiostri
L'uom mortal vive, ma ben corti e vani
Sono a saperne il modo i pensier nostri.

52. S1 : 104 (1546), fol. 27r
    Un foco sol la donna nostra accese
Divino in terra, e quello in ciel l'accende;
Quella stessa bontà chiara or comprende
L'intelletto, che in parte già comprese.
    Le parole, che pria l'orecchia intese,
Per celeste armonia l'anima intende;
Con Dio immortal quel grado ora in ciel prende
Di madre che con l'uom qui mortal prese.
    Cangiar obbietto o variar pensero
Uopo non le fu mai, perché i bei sensi
Fosser da la ragion ripresi e vinti;

Herod's iniquitous and twisted desires
cut down and smash these tender young shoots,
and he confers upon you the eternal and sure
fruits of eternal life through a swift death.
        Faithless,[141] you raise your cries
as your only reply to this torment, and Christ has adorned you
with celestial palms and sacred laurel crowns;
        the wings had hardly sprouted upon your
shoulders, O sweet tiny cherubs,[142]
than your very first flight raised you to the heavens.

51. S1 : 103 (1546), fol. 26v
        Lady, blessed by the heavens with such high honor,
whose breast nourished the son of God himself,
how is it that his divine mouth did not scorch
or rend your breast and your heart?
        Did your soul not melt away,
and within and without your spirits and all
living parts not flow out in your milk
and speed to nurture your holy Lord?[143]
        Yet we must not measure in our imperfect human
terms your task, which lies far beyond
and above our base understanding;[144]
        God died upon this earth; now in the heavenly cloisters
the mortal man lives on,[145] yet our thoughts
are too weak and frail to understand these things.

52. S1 : 104 (1546), fol. 27r
        One holy fire alone inflamed Our Lady
here on earth, and the same one warms her in heaven;
and her mind now understands that clear and wondrous bounty,
which in part it already perceived.[146]
        The words, which her ears heard on earth,
her soul now understands in their celestial harmonies;
and now she assumes her role in heaven as mother
to immortal God, as she was mother to the mortal man.
        She never felt the need to alter her path or
change her mind for her clear senses
to be sustained and overcome by reason;

Ch'infin dal primo giorno solo al vero
Aperse gli occhi, e li spirti ebbe accensi
Sempre d'un foco ripurgati e cinti.

53. S1:101 (1546), fol. 27v

Stella del nostro mar chiara e sicura,
Che il sol del paradiso in terra ornasti
Del mortal sacro manto, anzi adombrasti
Col virginal velo la sua luce pura,

Chi guarda al gran miracol più non cura
Del mondo vile e i vari empi contrasti
Sdegna de l'oste antico, poi ch'armasti
D'invitta alta virtù nostra natura.

Veggio il figliuol di Dio nudrirsi al seno
D'una vergine e madre, ed ora insieme
Risplender con la veste umana in cielo,

Onde là su nel sempre bel sereno
Al beato s'accende il vivo zelo,
Al fedel servo qui la cara speme.

54. S1:129 (1546), fol. 28r

Udir vorrei con puri alti pensieri
La vostra guerra in ciel, spirti beati,
Non di ferro o d'orgoglio o d'ira armati,
Ma di concetti in Dio stabili e veri

Contra i nemici, che in se stessi alteri
Insuperbir dal proprio amor legati
Contra il principio lor ciechi ed ingrati
Sol per imagin false arditi e feri.

Ma se ben per la patria e per l'onore
Di Dio v'armaste, e per la pace eterna,
D'altra maggior virtù fu la vittoria;

Voi v'inchinaste a l'infinito amore
Di Iesù dolce, onde il Padre superna
Grazia concesse a voi per la sua gloria.

55. S2:34 (unpub.), fol. 28v

Quando io sento da pura amica voce,
Che mi risuona spesso in mezzo al core,
Dirmi, "Risguarda, ingrata, ecco il Signore
Cui le tue colpe han posto in su la croce!"

for from the first day she opened her eyes
only to the truth, and she kept her spirit inflamed
by a single fire, purged and protected.[147]

53. S1:101 (1546), fol. 27v
    Clear and sure star of our sea,[148]
you who adorned the heavenly sun here on earth
with a sacred mortal mantle and even tempered
its strong pure light with your virginal veil,[149]
    he who beholds this great miracle no longer
heeds the vile world and scorns the many ungodly
assaults of our ancient enemy,[150] since you arm
our nature with courage and noble virtue.
    I see the son of God nourish himself at the breast
of a virgin mother, and now I see
their mortal forms shine above us together in heaven,[151]
    so that in paradise, in heavenly peace,
the blessed one is filled with great zeal,
and here on earth, his faithful servant with joyous hope.

54. S1:129 (1546), fol. 28r
    I would like to witness with a pure and noble mind
your war in the heavens, blessed spirits,[152]
armed not with iron, nor with pride or anger,
but with sound and true knowledge of God,
    waged against your enemies, who, puffed up with pride
and united by self-love, turned in anger
against their prince, blind and ungrateful
and burning only in the worship of false images.
    But if indeed you armed yourselves for your kingdom,
and for the honor of God, and for eternal peace,
the victory was for a greater virtue still;
    you bowed down before the infinite love
of sweet Jesus, and thus our Father bestowed
heavenly grace upon you in his glory.

55. S2:34 (unpub.), fol. 28v
    When I hear the clear loving voice,
which often sounds out in the depths of my heart,
telling me, "Look, ungrateful one, here is the Lord
who was placed upon the cross for your sins!"

Alzo gli occhi al bel segno, e grave atroce
Pena m'assale sì che dal timore
Vinta cade la speme, ma in brevi ore
Giova tanto la fe' ch'ei più non noce.

La qual col pensier vero al cor risponde
Che convien gloriarsi in quella ardente
Opra d'alta pietà, ch'al ciel ne spinge,

E che il peccato umilia, non confonde,
Se 'l peccator il cor, l'alma e la mente
Ne la bontà di Dio chiude e ristringe.

56. S2:19 (unpub.), fol. 29r

Questa d'odiar la morte antica usanza
Nasce sovente in noi, ciechi mortali,
Dal non aver su gli omer le grandi ali
Ferme de la divina alta speranza,

Né 'n quella pietra, ch'ogni stima avanza
Di sodezza, ma solo in questi frali
Fondamenti di rena a tutti i mali
esposti, edificar la nostra stanza;

Onde con fede anchor per grazia spera
L'alma in Dio forte aver per segno caro
Quella, ch'a i più superbi è più nemica,

E non che sia col braccio empio ed avaro
De le mie spoglie lieta, anzi io sia altera
D'usare in gloria mia la sua fatica.

57. S1:22 (1546), fol. 29v

Felice giorno, a noi festo e giocondo,
Quando offerse il Signor del sacro e puro
Corpo nudrirne e render l'uom sicuro
Di star sempre con lui nel cieco mondo,

E che per tal virtù leggiero il pondo
Fòra de' nostri mali; e 'l popul duro
Quel divino parlar velato oscuro
Intese mal col core empio ed immondo.

Onde sol meraviglia e grande orrore
Diede al superbo quella alta mercede
Di dar per cibo nostro a noi se stesso,

to this wondrous sign I raise my eyes, and a deep awful
pity overwhelms me so that, undone by fear,
my hope collapses vanquished, yet in a few short hours
my faith is so renewed that it can no longer be damaged.[153]

    Thus, with a pure mind my faith replies to my heart
that one must rejoice in this loving deed
of great mercy, which carries us to heaven,[154]

    and that sin humbles us, but does not lead us astray,
as long as the sinner encloses and confines
within the bounty of God his heart, soul, and mind.[155]

56. S2:19 (unpub.), fol. 29r

    The ancient tradition of fearing death
often arises within us, blind mortals,
because we do not carry upon our backs the great solid
wings of divine celestial hope[156]

    and because we fail to construct our houses
upon that rock, more firm than any other,
but only upon these weak foundations of sand,
exposed to every cruel element;[157]

    so the soul trusts faithfully in God,
through his grace, that the one sign that the
proudest await most fearfully will be his strength and hope[158]

    and that my profane and avaricious arm
will not hoard this mortal bounty, but instead that I may
be proud to turn his suffering to my own glory.[159]

57. S1:22 (1546), fol. 29v

    Happy day, joyful and wondrous for us,
on which God offered up his sacred and pure
body as nourishment and made man sure
of his eternal presence in this blind world,[160]

    so that through such virtue he renders weightless
the burden of our sins; yet the hardened race of men
barely understood the subtle nuances of
his divine speech in their godless and impure hearts.

    Thus only awe and then immense horror
was given to the proud man by Christ's infinite mercy
in offering himself to us to be our food,[161]

E solo a quei che l'odio con l'amore
Avean vinto, e la legge con la fede,
Il dono che dà vita al cor fu impresso.

58. S1:20 (1546), fol. 30r

La reverenza affrena, il grande amore
Mi sprona spesso al glorioso effetto
Di dare albergo a Dio dentro al mio petto,
Gradito, sua mercede, a tanto onore.
    Il gel de le mie colpe e 'l vivo ardore
Suo verso noi fan dubbio a l'intelletto;
Questo arma, quello spegne in me l'affetto,
L'uno a la speme va, l'altro al timore.
    Ma la fede fra i dubbi ardita e franca
Chiede il cibo de l'alma, onde si sforza
D'accostarsi a quel sol candida e bianca,
    Perché mentre ella vive in questa scorza
Terrena ha la virtù debile e stanca
Se 'l nudrimento suo non la rinforza.

59. S1:3 (1546), fol. 30v

Parrà forse ad alcun che non ben sano
sia il mio parlar de l'invisibil cose,
Tanto a l'occhio mortal lontane ascose,
Che son sopra l'ingegno e corso umano.
    Non han, credo, costor guardato al piano
De l'umiltade, e quanto alte e pompose
Spoglie riporti e ch'io de le ventose
Glorie del mondo avrei diletto in vano.
    La fede erge il desire e 'nseme i grandi
Oblighi eterni al mio dolce Signore,
Sì ch'io vorrei lodarlo in tutti i modi.
    Lui che move il pensier prego che mandi
Virtù che sciolga e spezzi i duri nodi
A la mia lingua, onde gli renda onore.

60. S1:9 (1546), fol. 31r

Quando dal lume, il cui vivo splendore
Rende il petto fedel chiaro e sicuro,
Si dissolve per grazia il ghiaccio duro
Che sovente si gela intorno al core,

and only those who had overcome hatred
with love, and vanquished the law through faith,
felt the imprint on their hearts of this life-affirming gift.[162]

58. S1:20 (1546), fol. 30r
    Reverence holds me back, but great love
often urges me on to the glorious end
of welcoming God into the refuge of my breast,
to which, by his mercy, he grants such high honor.[163]
    The ice of my own sins and the burning fire
of his love for us confuse my mind;[164]
the one fortifies, the other dampens my ardor,
one charges my hope, the other my fear.
    But among such doubts a bold and sincere faith
asks for sustenance from my soul and then pushes on
towards the bright clarity of that sun,
    for while faith lives in this earthly
shell her virtue is weak and frail
if his nourishment does not replenish her strength.[165]

59. S1:3 (1546), fol. 30v
    Perhaps it will appear to some that my talking
of those invisible things is not entirely healthy,
things that are so distant and hidden from mortal eyes,
far above the minds and lives of men.
    Those people, I believe, have not looked at the actions
of humility, how she rejects all proud and overblown
prizes so that I would revel in vain
in the empty glories of this world.[166]
    Faith lifts up my desire and my great
eternal debt to my sweet Lord,
so that I yearn to praise him in every possible way.
    He who guides our thoughts I pray may send
me virtue to untie and break the hard knots
that bind my tongue so that I may honor him.[167]

60. S1:9 (1546), fol. 31r
    When that light, whose bright splendor
fills the faithful breast with hope and peace,
through its grace melts the hard ice
that often freezes around my heart,

Sento ai bei lampi del possente ardore
Cader de le mie colpe il manto oscuro,
E vestirmi in quel punto il chiaro e puro
De l'innocentia prima e primo amore.
E se ben con segreta e fida chiave
Serro quel raggio, è sì schivo e sottile
Ch'un sol basso pensier par che lo sdegni,
Onde leggier se 'n vola; io mesta e grave
Rimango e pregol che d'ogni ombra vile
Mi spogli onde tornar tosto si degni.

61. S1:30 (1546), fol. 31v
Vedea l'alto Signor, ch'ardendo langue
Del nostro amor, tutti i rimedi scarsi
Per noi s'ei non scendea qui in terra a farsi
Uomo e donarci in croce il proprio sangue.
Ivi si vede aver, nudo e exangue,
Disarmati i nimici e rotti e sparsi
Lor fieri artigli, e non può più vantarsi
Del primo inganno il rio pestifero angue.
Novo trionfo e in modo novo nota
Vittoria, che morendo ei vinse e sciolse
Legato e preso i suoi contrari nodi.
Ben fu d'ogni superbo orgoglio vota
Questa alta gloria, onde in se stesso volse
Insegnarne umiltate in tutti i modi.

62. S1:60 (1546), fol. 32r
Fido pensier, se intrar non pòi sovente
Entro 'l cor di Iesù, basciali fore
Il sacro lembo, o pur senti l'odore;
Volagli intorno ogni or più vivo ardente.
S'altro non miri, avrai sempre presente
Il suo bel lume che il tuo proprio errore
Sol t'allontana, e perde ogni valore
L'alma se non lo scorge, ascolta e sente.
Non ti smarrir, rinforza il vago volo,
Che quando ei dà il desio non molto tarda
A dar virtù per giunger tosto a l'opra.

I feel in the lovely rays of that powerful fire
the dark mantle of my sins fall away,[168]
and at that moment I am clothed in the garment
of innocence and pure, clear, first love.[169]
But if with a secret and faithful key
I lock up that ray, it is so reluctant and so frail
that one single base thought seems to wound it,
    and as a breath it flies away;[170] and I am left,
sad and bereft, to pray that I may be cleansed of every
foul shadow so that it may soon return to me.

61. S1:30 (1546), fol. 31v
    The Lord on high saw, as he languished
in longing for our love, scant hope of cure
for us unless he descended here to earth and became
man and offered up his own blood upon the cross.
    Thus, naked and bleeding, he was able
to disarm his enemies and destroy and scatter
their haughty weapons, and the evil venomous serpent
can now no longer boast of his original deceit.[171]
    This is a new triumph and a new kind of worthy
victory, that he conquered through death
and, bound and tied, that he unbound these other knots.
    This great glory was accomplished without any trace
of insolent pride, so that by his own example he could
teach us of humility in every way.[172]

62. S1:60 (1546), fol. 32r
    Faithful spirit, if you cannot often enter
within the heart of Jesus then embrace from without
his sacred hem, or else inhale his perfume;[173]
fly near him every hour more charged with love.[174]
    If you see nothing else you will always be close to
his sacred light, which alone can distance you from your
own sin, and your soul loses all its worth
if it does not behold him, listen to him, and feel him.
    Do not lose your way, but renew your eager flight,
so that when he grants you the desire he will not delay long
in giving you the virtue to accomplish your aims.

Vuol la nostra salute, e bada e guarda
L'ardito suo guerrier come s'adopra
S'ei si vede al periglio inerme e solo.

63. S1:67 (1546), fol. 32v
    Già si rinverde la gioiosa speme,
Che quasi secca era da me sbandita,
Di veder l'alma e ben dal ciel gradita
Terra che il gran sepolcro adorna e preme.
    Odo ch'or gente intrepida non teme
Tormenti o morte, anzi vien tanto ardita
A la fede, da noi quasi smarrita,
Che 'l sangue loro a gli altri è vivo seme
    Sì fecondo che sol dodici eletti
Fatto han che mille e mille ad alta voce
Chiamano il buon signor già loro ignoto,
    Ed a scorno di noi, con vivi effetti
Il segno umil de l'onorata croce
Faran con maggior gloria al mondo noto.

64. S1:131 (1546), fol. 33r
    Angel beato, a cui 'l gran Padre expresse
L'antico patto, e poi con noi quel nodo
Che die' la pace, la salute e 'l modo
D'osservar l'alme sue larghe promesse:
    Colui ch'al grande ufficio pria t'elesse
Con l'alma inchino e con la mente lodo,
E de l'alta ambasciata ancora io godo
Che 'n quel virgineo cor sì ben s'impresse.
    Ma vorrei mi mostrassi il volto e i gesti,
L'umil risposta e quel casto timore,
L'ardente carità, la fede viva
    De la donna del cielo, e con che onesti
Desiri ascolti, accetti, onori e scriva
I divini precetti entro nel core.

65. S1:125 (1546), fol. 33v
    Se 'l nome, in voce expresso o ver dipinto,
Di Iesù dolce arma di tal valore
Un fedel servo suo ch'ogni vigore
Ha sempre in guerra d'alta speme cinto,

He longs for our salvation, so watch and heed
how his brave warrior defends himself
when he must face danger unarmed and alone.[175]

63. S1:67 (1546), fol. 32v

 My joyous hope renews itself already,
a hope I had relinquished and allowed to fade,
of visiting the fertile and much blessed
land that that noble grave honors and protects.[176]
 I hear that some intrepid people no longer fear
suffering or death, but rather come with such passion
to the faith that we have almost lost
that their blood acts as a potent and fertile seed
 to other men;[177] twelve alone of the elect
have caused thousands and thousands to call out
in a great voice to the Lord, who was unknown to them before,[178]
 and now, despite us, with great acclaim
they will make known the humble sign of the noble cross
more gloriously to all the world.

64. S1:131 (1546), fol. 33r

 Blessed angel,[179] to whom our Holy Father explained
the ancient pact and then revealed his bond with us
that brought peace, salvation, and the means
to fulfil his life-affirming generous promises:
 To him who first elected you to that great office
my soul bows down, and my spirit worships him,[180]
and I still celebrate the wondrous visitation
that left so strong a seal upon the Virgin's heart.
 Yet I wish you could show me the face and gestures,
the humble reply and chaste fear,
the great charity and burning faith
 of the queen of heaven, so that with an honest will
I may listen, accept, honor, and inscribe
those divine precepts within my own heart.[181]

65. S1:125 (1546), fol. 33v

 If the very name of sweet Jesus, spoken aloud
or else inscribed, arms his faithful servant
with such valor that in battle his courage
is always girded about with divine hope,

Quanto più arditamente Ignazio spinto
Fu al tormento, a le bestie ed al dolore,
Avendol sculto in lettre d'oro al core
Sicuro alor di più non esser vinto.
    Ché né fuoco, né dente, né saetta
Potean entrar fra cotal scudo e lui,
Sì forte e interna fu la sua difesa.
    Il mortal velo era in poter altrui,
Ma l'alma invitta già sicura eletta
Stava col suo Iesù d'amore accesa.

66. S1:61 (1546), fol. 34r

Poi che la vera ed invisibil luce
N'apparve chiara in Cristo, ond'or per fede
L'eterna eredità, l'ampia mercede
Fra l'aperte sue piaghe a noi traluce,
    Qual scorta infida e cieco error ne 'nduce
A por su l'alta gloriosa sede
De l'alma il senso, che sol ombra vede,
Avendo in terra Dio per guida e duce?
    La cui virtù, con l'orma e con l'esempio,
Con la moderna istoria e con l'antica,
Ne chiama e sprona al destro ed erto calle,
    Ma questo laberinto obliquo ed empio,
Che porta sempre in più profonda valle,
Il cieco veder nostro ogni ora intrica.

67. S1:85 (1546), fol. 34v

Se del mio sol divino lo splendente
Lume nel mezzo giorno puro altero
Rappresentasse ogni ora il bel pensiero,
Fuor d'ogni nube, a l'amorosa mente,
    Uopo non fòra mai la cieca gente
Cercare in questo o in quell'altro emispero
Ne l'amate sue stelle un raggio vero,
Che ne mostrasse il suo bel lume ardente.
    Ma la nebbia dei sensi a noi sì spesso
L'asconde, che l'interna vista inferma
Quel fulgor cerca in altra minor luce;

how much more ardently was Ignatius carried
to his torment, to the wild beasts and to suffering,
since he had carved it in letters of gold upon his heart
and thus was certain that he could never be vanquished.[182]

    For neither fire, nor fang, nor arrow
could come between that shield and him,[183]
so powerful and solid within himself was his defense.

    His mortal veil was in the hands of others,
but his unconquered soul was already safe
and blessed beside his Lord Jesus, radiant with love.

66. S1:61 (1546), fol. 34r
    Since the true and invisible light
appeared clearly in Christ[184] and now, through faith,
our eternal inheritance, his bounteous mercy
shines out at us from his open wounds,

    then what ungodly motivation or blind error leads us
to place upon the glorious high throne
of the soul the senses, which can detect only shadows,[185]
since we have God for our guide and master on earth?[186]

    His virtue, through his deeds and example,
through the lessons of ancient and modern history,
calls out and urges us onto the true straight path,[187]

    but this unholy and perplexing labyrinth,
which leads us into an ever-deeper valley,[188]
confuses our blinded sight at every moment.

67. S1:85 (1546), fol. 34v
    If the resplendent light of my divine sun,
pure and sublime in the midday,[189]
were always to represent perfect understanding,
free from any clouds, to the loving mind,

    then the blind race of men would never need
to search throughout this hemisphere or that,
among their beloved stars, for one true ray
to reveal its beautiful living fire.

    But the fog that cloaks our senses too often
hides it from us[190] so that our unsound inner eye
seeks that radiance in some other, lesser light;

Ché se ben come debil non è ferma,
Fermo è il desio ch'ad un fin la conduce
Or ne le stelle, ed or nel sole istesso.

68. S1:94 (1546), fol. 35r

Le braccia aprendo in croce e l'alme e pure
Piaghe largo, Signore, apristi il cielo,
Il limbo, i sassi, i monumenti, il velo
Posto a nostri occhi, e l'ombre e le figure.
Le menti umane infino allora oscure
Illuminasti, e dileguando il gelo
Le riempiesti d'un ardente zelo,
Ch'aperse poi le sacre tue scritture.
Mostrossi il dolce imperio e la bontade,
Che parve ascosa in quei tanti precetti
De l'aspra e giusta legge del timore.
O desiata pace, o benedetti
Giorni felici, o liberal pietade,
Che ne scoperse grazia, lume, amore!

69. S1:58 (1546), fol. 35v

Se con l'armi celesti avess'io vinto
Me stessa, i sensi, e la ragione umana,
Andrei con altro spirto alta e lontana
Dal mondo e dal suo onor falso e dipinto.
Su l'ali de la fede il pensier, cinto
Di speme omai non più caduca e vana,
Sarebbe fuor di questa valle insana
Da verace virtude alzato e spinto.
Ben ho già fermo l'occhio al miglior fine
Del nostro corso, ma non volo ancora
Per lo destro sentier salda e leggiera;
Veggio i segni del sol, scorgo l'aurora,
Ma per li sacri giri a le divine
Stanze non entro in quella luce vera.

70. S1:59 (1546), fol. 36r

La innocenzia da noi pel nostro errore
Veggio punire, e il ricco Signor degno
Con infamia morir nudo sul legno
Per ritornarne in sul perduto onore.

but if the eye is weak and uncertain,
the desire is firm that leads it to one end,
first to the stars, then up to the sun itself.[191]

68. S1:94 (1546), fol. 35r

    Opening wide your arms upon the cross and your blessed
and pure wounds, O Lord, you opened the heavens
and limbo, rent the rocks, monuments, and the veil
that cloaked our eyes, the shadows and figures.[192]

    All human minds, until then immersed in darkness,
you enlightened, and melting the ice
you filled them with a burning fervor,
revealing the meaning of your sacred texts.

    You showed them your sweet kingdom and your
kindness, which seemed to be hidden by the many rules
dictated by the harsh but just law of fear.[193]

    O welcome peace, O blessed
and happy days, O bountiful pity,
which conferred upon us grace, light, and love!

69. S1:58 (1546), fol. 35v

    If with celestial arms I had overcome
myself, my senses, and my mortal reason,[194]
then I would fly with a new spirit high and far
from this world and its false, spurious honor.

    Upon the wings of faith my mind, encircled
with a hope that was no longer frail or vain,
would be raised and urged on by true virtue
beyond this raging vale.

    I already have my eye firmly fixed upon the true end
of our life's journey, but I do not yet fly
steady and light along the right path;

    I glimpse the sun's rays, I can make out the dawn,
but through the celestial spheres around the heavenly temple
I have not emerged into the true light.[195]

70. S1:59 (1546), fol. 36r

    I see the innocent punished by us
through our own error, and our great noble Lord
die in infamy, naked upon the cross,
to return to his lost honor.

  Veggio offender con odio il vero amore
E ferir l'umiltà con fiero sdegno,
Usar di crudeltade ogni aspro segno
Contra colui che per pietà sol more.
  Alor l'alta bontà di Dio si stese
In parte al mondo, ond'ogni fedel petto
Si fe' più forte a le più acerbe offese;
  Paulo, Dionisio, ed ogni alto intelletto
Si die' prigione al vero alor ch'intese
La mirabil cagion di tanto effetto.

71. S1:62 (1546), fol. 36v
  Se le dolcezze, che dal vivo fonte
Divino stillan dentro a un gentil core,
Apparissero al mondo ancor di fore
Con bella pace in puro ardor congionte,
  Forse sarebbon più palesi e conte
Le cagion da sdegnar ricchezza e onore,
Onde i più saggi scalzi, ebri d'amore,
Andrebbon con la croce a l'erto monte
  Per sentir con la morte dolce vita
Non solo eternamente, ma in quel punto
Ch'a gli altri di lasciar questa ombra spiace.
  Quando lo spirto vive a Dio congiunto,
Con umil voglia al suo voler unita,
L'aperta guerra gli è segreta pace.

72. S1:64 (1546), fol. 37r
  In forma di musaico un alto muro
D'animate scintille alate e preste,
Con catene d'amor sì ben conteste,
Che l'una porge a l'altra il lume puro
  Senz'ombra che vi formi il chiaro e scuro,
Ma sol vivo splendor del sol celeste
Che le adorna, incolora, ordina e veste,
D'intorno a Dio col mio pensier figuro.
  E quella poi, che in velo uman per gloria
Seconda onora il ciel, più presso al vero
Lume del figlio ed a la luce prima,

I see that true love is sullied by hatred
and humility is wounded by proud disdain;
harsh acts of cruelty are turned
against the one who died for pity alone.

At that time the wondrous bounty of God was offered
in part to the world, so that all faithful hearts
were fortified against the most bitter of assaults;

Paul,[196] Dionysius,[197] and all great minds
captured the truth once they had understood
the miraculous cause of such an effect.

71. S1:62 (1546), fol. 36v

If the sweet bounty, which flows out from the holy
living fountain into the noble heart,[198]
could still be seen in this world by mortal eyes,
united with sweet peace in pure love,

perhaps the reasons for rejecting riches and honors
would become more manifest and clear
and the wisest men would walk barefoot and drunk
with love, bearing their crosses up the steep mountain

to experience the sweetness of life through death
not only in all eternity, but at that moment
when others are loath to quit this shadowy veil.[199]

When the spirit lives united with God,
its humble desire at one with God's desire,
even open war is its secret peace.

72. S1:64 (1546), fol. 37r

A high wall, in the form of a mosaic
of lively sparks, flying rapidly
and so tightly bound by chains of love,[200]
that one casts upon the other a pure light

without any shadows to give *chiaroscuro*,[201]
but only resplendent light from the heavenly sun,
which decorates, colors, arranges, and adorns them,
all this I envision in my mind surrounding God.

And then I imagine her, whom heaven honors
in human form as second in glory, closest to the true
light of the son and the first light,[202]

La cui beltà non mai vivo pensiero
Ombrar potea, non che ritrar memoria
In carte, e men lodarla ingegno in rima.

73. S1:65 (1546), fol. 37v

Quasi rotonda palla accesa intorno
Di mille stelle veggio, e un sol che splende
Fra lor con tal virtù che ogni or le accende,
Non come il nostro che le spegne il giorno.
Or quando fia che l'alma in quel soggiorno
Segua il pensier, che tanto in su s'estende?
Che spesso quel che in ciel piglia non rende
A la memoria poi nel suo ritorno.
Ond'io dipingo in carte una fosca ombra
Per quel sol vivo, e de le cose eterne
Parlo fra noi con voci rotte e frali.
Quant'ei si vuol talor mostrar discerne
La mente, e sol quand'ei le presta l'ali
Vola, e mentre le nebbie apre e disgombra.

74. S1:118 (1546), fol. 38r

A la durezza di Tomaso offerse
Il buon Signor la piaga, e tai gli diede
Ardenti rai ch'a vera ed umil fede
L'indurato suo cor tosto converse.
L'antica e nova legge gli scoverse
In un momento, ond'ei si vidde erede
Del ciel, dicendo, "È mio ciò ch'ei possede,
Sì e quei mio che tanto ben m'aperse!"
Ond'ei li disse poi, "Maggior è il merto
Di creder l'invisibile, per quella
Virtù che non ha in sé ragione umana."
Il ciel fu a lui col bel costato aperto,
A noi la strada assai più corta e piana
Per fede di trovar l'orma sua bella.

75. S1:63 (1546), fol. 38v

Per le vittorie qui rimangon spente
Talor le virtù prime, per ch'altera
Contra de l'altra la vittrice schiera
Mostra il superbo sdegno e l'ira ardente.

whose beauty no living thought
could ever draw, nor could memory ever commit it
to paper, much less the intellect describe it in verse.[203]

73. S1:65 (1546), fol. 37v

    I see what seems to be a sphere, lit up around
by a thousand stars, and a sun, which shines
among them with such brightness that it lights them at all times,
not like our own, which hides their light in daytime.[204]
    But when will it be that my soul will follow my mind,
which strives to rise so high, to that place?
For often the things my mind sees in heaven are not
retained in my memory when it returns to earth.
    Thus I inscribe upon these pages a dark shadow
instead of that dazzling sun, and I speak to others here
of heavenly things with broken and inadequate words.[205]
    Our minds can only see as much as he chooses
to reveal of himself and can fly only if he lends us wings
and if he clears and banishes the fog for us.[206]

74. S1:118 (1546), fol. 38r

    In response to Thomas's stubborn will,
the good Lord offered him his wound and shined such burning and
rays upon him that his hardened heart was swiftly
converted to a true and humble faith.[207]
    In one instant the ancient and modern laws
were revealed to him, so that he saw that he was to inherit
the heavens, and he exclaimed, "All that he has is mine,
and those rays that opened my eyes belong to me!"[208]
    And then Christ said to him, "It is of greater merit
to believe in the invisible through the virtue
that is not possessed of human reason."[209]
    The blessed rib opened up the heavens to him,
and to us the shorter and straighter road by far,
which leads us, through faith, to follow in his footsteps.

75. S1:63 (1546), fol. 38v

    For the sake of earthly victories, primary virtues
are sometimes forsworn, in order that
the victorious army can proudly show its enemies
its haughty scorn and blazing anger.

Scintilla alor di carità non sente,
Né de l'alta umiltà la gloria vera;
Sempre le par che 'l ciel le rida, e spera
Con l'altrui sangue assicurar la mente.
Ma al vero Dio, quand'ei fatto uom qui vinse
L'inferno e 'l mondo, di luce infinita
Lampeggiar sempre le virtù divine;
L'umiltà lo spogliò, l'amor lo avinse
Di laccio, e in croce con chiodi e con spine
Diede a lui morte, a tutti gli altri vita.

76. S1:76 (1546), fol. 39r
Se per serbar la notte il vivo ardore
Dei carboni, da noi la sera accensi
Nel legno incenerito arso, conviensi
Coprirli sì che non si mostrin fuore;
Quanto più si conviene a tutte l'ore
Chiuder in modo d'ogn'intorno i sensi,
Che sian ministri a serbar vivi e intensi
I bei spirti divini entro nel core.
Se s'apre in questa fredda notte oscura
Per noi la porta a l'inimico vento,
Le scintille del cor dureran poco;
Ordinar ne convien con sottil cura
Il senso, onde non sia da l'alma spento
Per le insidie di fuor l'interno foco.

77. S1:77 (1546), fol. 39v
Veggio in croce il mio Dio nudo e disteso
Coi piedi e man chiodate e il destro lato
Aperto e il capo sol di spine ornato,
E da vil gente d'ogni parte offeso,
Avendo su le spalle il grave peso
De le colpe del mondo; e in tale stato
La morte e l'aversario stuolo irato
Vincer solo col cor d'amore acceso.
Pazienza, umiltà, vero ubidire
Con l'altre alme virtuti eran le stelle
D'intorno al sol de la sua caritade,

Then no flicker of pity is felt,
nor the true glory of noble humility;
instead it believes that the heavens mock
and hopes to calm its anguish through another's blood.
    But the true God, when he was made man
and conquered hell and the world, his divine virtues
shone always with eternal light;
    humility stripped him naked, love bound him
with cords, and upon the cross with nails and thorns
brought him death, and to all of humankind life.[210]

76. S1:76 (1546), fol. 39r
    If, to conserve the lively heat of coals
through the night, we light them in the evening
beneath the burnt ashes of dry wood, it is important
to cover them so that no trace can be seen;[211]
    how much more important is it then at all times
to shut off our senses from their surroundings,
so that they may serve as wakeful and alert ministers
to those beautiful, divine spirits that inhabit our hearts.
    If, in this cold dark night, the door opens
to allow the cruel wind in to us,
the sparks of fire in our hearts will not burn for long;
    with delicate care we must prepare
our senses, so that the internal fire within the soul
is not extinguished by assaults from without.

77. S1:77 (1546), fol. 39v
    I see my Lord naked and hung upon the cross
with nails driven through his feet and hands and his right side
cut open and his head adorned only with thorns,
tormented on all sides by a vile throng,
    while he bears upon his shoulders the heavy burden
of the world's sins; and yet in this state
I see him conquer death and his angry band of enemies
with his heart alone, aflame with love.[212]
    Patience, humility, true obedience,
together with the other life-giving virtues, were the stars
encircling the sun of his pity,

Onde ne l'aspra pugna e questa e quelle
Fecer più chiara, dopo il bel morire,
La gloria de l'eterna sua bontade.

78. S1:78 (1546), fol. 40r
Questo vèr noi maraviglioso effetto
Di morir Dio su l'aspra croce excede
Ogni umana virtute, onde no 'l vede
Col suo valor l'uman nostro intelletto.
Entra del bel misterio in mortal petto
Quel grande o picciol raggio, che concede
La sopra natural divina fede,
Dono solo di Dio puro e perfetto.
Onde quel ch'avrà in lui le luci fisse,
Non quel ch'intese meglio o che più lesse
Volumi in terra, in ciel sarà beato.
In carte questa legge non si scrisse,
Ma con la stampa sua nel cor purgato
Col fuoco del suo amor Iesù l'impresse.

79. S1:97 (1546), fol. 40v
Non potrò dire, o mio dolce conforto,
Che non sia destro il luogo, e i tempi e l'ore,
Per far chiaro con l'opre un tale ardore,
Quale è il desio che dentro acceso porto.
Ma se ben questo o quel picciol diporto
Sottrae dal sempre procurarvi onore
I sensi, ho pur per grazia fermo il core
Non mai drizzar la vela ad altro porto.
M'accorgo or che nel mondo e sterpi e spine
Torcer non ponno al saggio il destro piede
Dal sentier dritto s'antivede il fine;
Ma il molto amore a noi, la poca fede
De l'invisibil cose alte e divine,
Ne ritardano il corso a la mercede.

80. S1:80 (1546), fol. 41r
L'occhio grande e divino, il cui valore
Non vide, né vedrà, ma sempre vede,
Toglie dal petto ardente sua mercede
I dubbi del servil freddo timore,

so that in the bitter battle the sun and stars
lit up more brightly, after his blessed death,
the glory of his eternal grace.

78. S1:78 (1546), fol. 40r
    God's incredible gesture towards us
of dying upon the cruel cross exceeds the scope
of any human virtue, so that our earth-bound
intellect cannot comprehend its worth.[213]
    Some great or tiny ray of this beautiful mystery
enters into our mortal breast and confers
a divine and superhuman faith,
a pure and perfect gift from God alone.[214]
    Thus he who can fix his eyes upon God,
not he who better understood or who read more
books on earth, will be blessed in heaven.[215]
    This law was not written upon paper,
but rather it was imprinted by Jesus with his seal
and with the fire of his love upon the purified heart.[216]

79. S1:97 (1546), fol. 40v
    I cannot say, O my sweet comfort,[217]
that the place is not opportune, the moment or the hour,
to clarify with action such a passion,
the desire that I bear brightly lit within my being.
    But if this or that little pastime
distracts my senses from always honoring you,
still through your grace I have a firm heart
and never turn my bark towards another port.[218]
    I now understand that in this world pricks and thorns
cannot turn the sure foot of the wise man
from his straight path if he foresees its end;
    but our great self-love, our weak faith
in those high and holy invisible things,
slow down our progress towards salvation.

80. S1:80 (1546), fol. 41r
    His great divine eye,[219] whose virtue
has not seen, nor will see, but sees eternally,
through its mercy takes from the loving heart
the doubts created by cold, servile fear,

Sapendo che i momenti tutti e l'ore,
Le parole, i pensier, l'opre e la fede
Discerne, né velar altrui concede
Per inganni o per forza un puro core.

Sicuri del suo dolce e giusto impero,
Non come il primo padre e la sua donna
Debbiam del nostro error biasmare altrui,

Ma con la speme accesa e dolor vero
Aprir dentro passando oltra la gonna
I falli nostri a solo a sol con lui.

81. S1:28 (1546), fol. 41v

Vorrei l'orecchia aver qui chiusa e sorda,
Per udir coi pensier più fermi e intenti
L'alte angeliche voci e i dolci accenti
Che certa pace in vero amor concorda.

Spira un aer vital fra corda e corda
Divino e puro in quei vivi instrumenti,
E sì move ad un fine i lor concenti,
Che l'eterna armonia mai non discorda.

Amore alza le voci amor le abbassa,
Ordina e batte egual l'ampia misura
Che non mai fuor del segno in van percote.

Sempre è più dolce il suon se ben ei passa
Per le mutanze in più diverse note,
Ché chi compone il canto ivi n'ha cura.

82. S1:106 (1546), fol. 42r

L'alto consiglio, alor ch'elegger volse
Madre a Dio in terra, con divina cura,
Vedendo già cader nostra natura,
Lei sola tenne e 'n grembo a sé l'accolse.

Dal giusto sdegno suo colui la tolse,
Che sol forma le leggi e 'l ciel misura,
E fuor d'ombra d'error, candida et pura,
Dal nodo universal non mai la sciolse.

Perché non la legò, né meno in forse
La lasciò di cader, ma caro in mano
Sempre serbò quel bel cristallo intero,

knowing that it can discern all moments and hours,
all words, thoughts, deeds, and faith
nor does it allow anyone to conceal
a pure heart through subterfuge or force.

 Certain of his sweet and just reign,
not like the first father and his lady
should we blame others for our error,[220]

 but with ardent hope and true suffering
we must open ourselves up, passing beyond the flesh
to reveal our sins to him alone.

81. S1:28 (1546), fol. 41v
 I wish my mortal ear to be closed and deaf,
so that with a stronger and more concentrated mind
I can hear the high angelic voices and sweet tones
that harmonize certain peace with true love.[221]

 A living breeze moves from chord to chord,
holy and pure among those living instruments,
and draws to a common end the harmonies,
so that the eternal music is never out of key.

 Love raises those voices and love lowers them,
it orders and regulates the universal rhythm
so that it never sounds in vain or out of time.

 The music is always sweeter when it passes
through sequences of changing notes
and the composer of the song controls each element.[222]

82. S1:106 (1546), fol. 42r
 The holy wisdom, when he wished to elect
a mother for God on earth, with divine care,
seeing that our nature was already fallen,
selected her alone and gathered her into his lap.[223]

 He saved her from his righteous condemnation,
he who alone creates laws and lays out the heavens,
and free from any shadow of sin, honest and pure,
he never unbound her from the universal knot.[224]

 Because he never bound her or
let her fall, but lovingly he kept that beautiful crystal[225]
always whole and sheltered in his palm,

E per far l'ordin suo più dritto il torse
Per altro solo a lui noto sentero,
E lo condusse al camin nostro umano.

83. S1 : 122 (1546), fol. 42v

Su l'alte eterne rote il pie' fermasti,
Donna immortal, quando col santo ardire
Quella de la fortuna e del martire
Contra i nimici tuoi lieta girasti.
Spezzò il ferro il tuo core e no 'l piegasti
A minaccie o lusinghe, anzi il desire
Corse al suo fin contra i disdegni e l'ire,
Trovando pace in quei fieri contrasti.
L'alma sul divin monte altera siede
U' Dio regge i beati, e 'l mortal velo
Su l'altro ov'ei la legge al popol diede;
Caterina, se in terra il tuo buon zelo
Tanti ne indusse a la verace fede,
Prega ch'io l'abbia viva or che sei in cielo.

84. S1 : 79 (1546), fol. 43r

Se il servo caro, a cui per vivo affetto
Si scopre il mar de la bontà di Dio,
Non avesse per grazia in lungo oblio
Del viver suo sommerso ogni difetto,
Avria con tal ragione odio e dispetto
Al navigar passato obliquo e rio,
Che impedir li porria quel lume pio
Ch'erge e tien saldo al porto il suo intelletto.
Il quale in queste onde tranquille or vuole
Che s'immerga e si sati e non si volga
A mirar le già corse e turbide acque,
Acciò mentre è ancor debil non ritolga
Il pensier da colui ch'accender sòle
La speme, in cui 'l gran padre si compiacque.

85. S1 : 14 (1546), fol. 43v

Veggio di mille ornati veli avolto
Il chiaro e puro vero, e poi con mille
Finte di carità vive faville
Coprir l'amaro petto un dolce volto.

and to make his way straighter, he took it
from another path known only to him
and led it to our own mortal road.[226]

83. S1:122 (1546), fol. 42v

You stilled your foot upon the high eternal wheels,
immortal lady,[227] when with holy passion
you turned with joy the wheel of fate
and martyrdom against your enemies.

With your heart you rent their weapons and you were not
cowed by threats or pleading, but instead your desire
sped to its end, braving scorn and anger
and finding peace in those proud battles.

Your soul sits nobly upon the heavenly mountain
where God rules the blessed,[228] and your mortal veil
upon the other where he gave out his laws to the people;[229]

Catherine, if on earth your great energy
led countless others into the true faith,
pray that I may inherit that living faith now that you are in heaven.[230]

84. S1:79 (1546), fol. 43r

If the beloved servant, to whom with great love
is revealed the ocean of God's bounty,
had not, through grace, in the long oblivion
of his lifetime suppressed every sin,

he would for this reason feel hatred and vexation
at his past navigating through darkness and pain,
which could prevent him from attaining the holy light
that sustains and purifies his intellect in port.[231]

That light[232] now wishes that he immerse himself
and find contentment in these tranquil waves and not turn
to survey the troubled waters that have gone before,[233]

thus, while he is still weak, let him not remove
his thoughts from the one who can set fire to
his hope, in whom our Father was well pleased.

85. S1:14 (1546), fol. 43v

I see the clear and pure truth shrouded
in a thousand ornate veils,[234] and with a thousand
false bright sparks of pity
I see the bitter heart assume a sweet face.

Mille false sirene intorno ascolto,
E so che la lusinga o il ciel sortille
A gradi indegni, ed odo e trombe e squille
Sonar per tal che in vita è già sepolto.
        Secol maligno e maledette arpie,
Ché pur l'occhio ne dà mentre il cor toglie
L'onor, la vita, il tempo e la ricchezza.
        Se Dio con l'arme sempre giuste e pie
Tanti intricati nodi omai non spezza,
La santa mano sua più non li scioglie.

86. S1:81 (1546), fol. 44r
        Fuggendo i re gentili il crudo impero
D'Erode, per divina alta cagione
Fuor de l'umana lor cieca ragione,
Entrar del natio regno al camin vero;
        Così conviene a noi fuggir dal fero
Mondo inimico, e con più forte sprone
Trovar la nostra eterna regione
Per altro più solingo e bel sentiero.
        Altera voglia e rio disubedire
Ne fe' cader dal cielo in questa valle,
U' purga un lungo exilio il grave errore,
        Ma per mercè di Dio può risalire
L'uomo a la patria vera al primo onore,
Per quel de l'umiltà sicuro calle.

87. S1:36 (1546), fol. 44v
        Parea più certa prova al manco lato
Tentar se 'l Signor nostro avea più vita,
Alor che fece al destro ampia ferita
Sul morto corpo in croce il braccio irato.
        Ma perché sempre intero il cor serbato
Esser devea per quei c'han seco unita
L'anima, errò la man cieca e smarrita
Piegandol dal camin de gli altri usato.
        Onde qual Progne i figli entro a suoi nidi,
Tal ei col sangue suo ne ciba sempre
E dal fero angue n'assicura e asconde.

I hear a thousand false sirens calling all around,
and I know that flattery or fate assigns them
to unmerited ranks, and I hear trumpets and bells
sounding out for that which is already buried alive.[235]
    Cursed century and evil harpies,
where honor, life, time, and riches
appear to the eye yet are absent in the heart.
    If God, with his eternally justified and pious arms,
does not now break apart so many complex knots,
his holy hand will never again untie them.[236]

86. S1:81 (1546), fol. 44r
    Fleeing the cruel reign of Herod,
the noble kings, through high divine reason
outside their blind human understanding,
came from their native kingdom onto the true path;[237]
    so too we should flee from the proud
and godless world, and with a stronger spur
seek out our own eternal region
along another more lonely and more lovely way.
    Haughty desires and evil disobedience
caused us to fall from heaven into this vale,
where a long exile purges our terrible sin,[238]
    but through God's mercy man can climb again
back to the true homeland and original honor,
by that secure pathway of humility.[239]

87. S1:36 (1546), fol. 44v
    It seemed more certain proof to test
on the left side of our Lord whether he was still alive,
since that violent hand had cut a deep wound
in the right side of his dead body upon the cross.
    But since all who have joined their souls with him
should try to love him with the whole heart,
that blind, misguided hand fell into error
by straying from the path followed by the others.[240]
    Just as Procne feeds her chicks in the nest,[241]
so too he with his blood nourishes us eternally
and protects and delivers us from the evil serpent.

Oimè! ch'a tal pensier del pianto l'onde
Devriano alzarne fuor de i nostri lidi
Sovra tutte le basse umane tempre.

88. S1:89 (1546), fol. 45r
Dimmi, lume del mondo e chiaro onore
Del ciel, or che 'n te stesso il tuo ben godi,
Qual virtù ti sostenne? o pur quai nodi
T'avinser nudo in croce cotante ore?
Io sol ti scorgo afflitto e dentro e fore
Offeso e grave pender da tre chiodi.
Risponde, "Io legato era in duri modi
Dal mio sempre vèr voi sì dolce amore,
Loqual al morir mio fu schermo degno
Con l'alta obedienza, ma l'ingrato
Spirto d'altrui più che 'l mio mal m'offese.
Ond'io non prendo il cor pentito a sdegno,
Già caldo e molle, ma il freddo indurato
Ch'a tanto foco mio non mai s'accese."

89. S1:26 (1546), fol. 45v
Vede oggi 'l penser mio sotto la mano
Di Battista il figliuol di Dio lavarsi
Al sacro fiume, non già per purgarsi,
Ma lavar seco tutto 'l seme umano
Quanto per sé, ma il nostro folle insano
Voler cerca di novo rimacchiarsi
Nel fango vile, e poi macchiato farsi
Del vivo fonte suo schivo e lontano.
Il gran Padre ad udirlo oggi n'invita,
E 'l divin figlio poi ne dona il pegno
Con la colomba ed ei con l'opra umile.
Ubidir dessi al suon de l'infinita
Virtute, e creder sempre a sì bel segno,
Seguendo poi l'esempio alto e gentile.

90. S1:32 (1546), fol. 46r
Mossi dai grandi effetti, alzaron l'ali
A la prima cagion quei primi ingegni,
Ed a noi tanti e sì possenti segni
De la bontà di Dio son pochi e frali;

Alas! that at this thought the waves of tears
should rise up from our shores
and cover all our lowly mortal traits.[242]

88. S1:89 (1546), fol. 45r

Tell me, light of the world and radiant glory
of the sky,[243] now that you enjoy your bounty within yourself,[244]
what virtue sustained you and what knots
bound your nude body to the cross for so many hours?
I only see you wounded, offended from
within and without, hanging in pain from three nails.
He replies, "I was bound so tightly
by my eternal sweet love for you,
which, with divine obedience, was a worthy shield
at the moment of my death, but the ungrateful
spirit of others hurt me more that the pain I bore.
For I do not scorn the repentant heart,
which is warm and soft, but rather the cold, hard one
that all my fire could not inflame."[245]

89. S1:26 (1546), fol. 45v

Today, in my thoughts, I see beneath the hand
of the Baptist the son of God washing himself
in the sacred river,[246] not in order to cleanse himself,
but to purify the whole race of man
together with his own body, yet our mad and impure
lust compels us to pollute ourselves again
in the vile filth and then, corrupted, distance
ourselves with loathing from his life-giving spring.
Our Holy Father on hearing this calls to us today,[247]
and his divine son offers us his pledge
with a white dove and himself through his humble act.[248]
Therefore let me obey the call of his infinite
virtue and always keep faith in the wondrous sign
and follow his great and perfect example.

90. S1:32 (1546), fol. 46r

Those first spirits,[249] moved by the wondrous effects,
opened their wings in flight towards the first cause,
yet for us so many powerful signs
of God's goodness have proved weak and impotent;

Ma se non può, con gli occhi egri e mortali,
Tanto nostra virtute, almen si degni
Mirar se stessa e converrà si sdegni
Di sentirsi intricata in sì gran mali.

Vedrà quanto il Signor n'aspetta e sempre
Tiene al nostro girar più salda e ferma
La stabil pietra de la sua bontade.

E scorge l'opre nostre con la inferma
Natura inseme e vol che la pietade
Sua dolce il nostro amaro error contempre.

91. S1 : 145 (1546), fol. 46v

Odo ch'avete speso omai gran parte
De' miglior anni dietro al van lavoro
D'aver la pietra che i metalli in oro
Par che converta sol per forza d'arte,

E che 'l vivo mercurio e 'l ferreo marte,
Col vostro falso sol, sono il ristoro
Del già smarrito onor per quel tesoro
Ch'or questo idolo or quel con voi comparte.

Correte a Cristo, la cui vera pietra
Il piombo de l'error nostro converte
Col sol de la sua grazia in oro eterno;

Soffiate al foco suo, che sol ne spetra
Dal duro ghiaccio umano, e per le certe
Ricchezze andate al gran tesor superno.

92. S1 : 33 (1546), fol. 47r

Vedremmo, se piovesse argento ed oro,
Ir con le mani pronte e i grembi aperti
Color che son de l'altra vita incerti,
A raccor lieti il vil breve tesoro;

E sì cieco guadagno e van lavoro
Esser più caro a quei che son più esperti,
Ché le ricchezze danno e non i merti
Oggi le chiare palme e 'l verde alloro.

Ma non si corre a Dio, che dal ciel porta
Dentro la piaga del suo destro lato
D'infinito tesor perpetua pioggia,

but if our virtue, with afflicted mortal eyes,
cannot achieve so much, let it at least
observe itself and admit that it cannot bear
to find itself entrapped in so much sin.
   It will see then how the Lord awaits us
and always maintains the solid rock of his bounty
safe and firm for us to revolve around.[250]
   He sees our deeds united with our sickened
nature and wishes to assuage our bitter
wrongdoings through his sweet mercy.

91. S1:145 (1546), fol. 46v
   I hear that you have by now wasted a great portion
of your best years in the vain task
of seeking that stone, which seems to convert base metal
into gold through the power of art alone,[251]
   and that lively Mercury[252] and iron-willed Mars,[253]
together with your false sun, will restore
your tarnished honor by that treasure
that various false idols share with you.
   Run instead to Christ, whose true stone
converts the lead of our sins,
with the bright sun of his grace, into eternal gold;
   blow upon his fire, which alone can melt
the hard ice of humankind, and with these
certain riches rise to greater treasure in heaven.[254]

92. S1:33 (1546), fol. 47r
   If it should ever rain down gold and silver, we would see,
with their hands held out and their laps opened ready,
those who are doubtful of the other life
going about joyfully collecting up the short-lived treasure;
   we would see that such blind wealth and vain toil
are more beloved of learned men,
for these days riches and not merit
attract the brightest palms and greenest laurel crowns.[255]
   Yet they do not run to God, who from heaven,
within the wound in his right side, brings
an eternal shower of infinite treasure,[256]

E se spirto gentil gli apre la porta
Dicon che inganna il mondo, o ch'è ingannato
Dal suo pensier, che troppo in alto poggia.

93. S1 : 34 (1546), fol. 47v

Parmi veder con la sua face accesa
Ir lo spirto divino, e ovunque trova
Esca l'accende, e già purga e rinova
Del vezzo antico l'alma e vera chiesa.

E i saggi cavalier han or compresa
La lor pace futura; a ciascun giova
Che la guerra cominci e s'arma e prova
Mostrarsi ardito a sì felice impresa.

Già la tromba celeste intorno grida,
E quei che de la gola e de le piume
S'han fatto idolo in terra a morte sfida;

Celar non ponno il vizio a quel gran lume
Che dentro al cor penetra ov'egli annida,
Ma cangiar lor convien vita e costume.

94. S1 : 21 (1546), fol. 48r

Qui non è il loco umil, né l'amorose
Braccia de l'alta madre, né i pastori,
Né del pietoso vecchio i dolci amori,
Né l'angeliche voci alte e gioiose,

Né dei re sapienti le pompose
Offerte fatte con si vivi ardori;
Ma ci sei tu, che te medesmo onori,
Signor, cagion di tutte l'altre cose.

So che quel vero che nascesti Dio
Sei qui, né invidio altrui, ma ben pietate
Ho sol di me non ch'io giungesi tardo,

Non è il tempo infelice, ma son io
Misera che per fede ancor non ardo
Come essi per vederti in quella etate.

95. S1 : 100 (1538), fol. 48v

Vergine pura, che dai raggi ardenti
Del vero sol ti godi eterno giorno,
Il cui bel lume in questo vil soggiorno
Tenne i begli occhi tuoi paghi e contenti;

and if a noble spirit opens the door to him[257]
they claim that he deceives the world or is deceived
by his own mind, which he strives to raise too high.[258]

93. S1:34 (1546), fol. 47v
    It seems to me that I see the Holy Spirit
hovering with face aflame, and wherever it finds
tinder it sets it on fire, and already it purges and renews
the one true church of its ancient vices.
    And the wise warriors have now foreseen
their future peace; they all anticipate the coming
battle and arm themselves and try
to show courage in fighting for this great cause.[259]
    The celestial trumpet is already sounding out,[260]
and those who have made idols of greed and luxury,[261]
it challenges to mortal combat;
    they cannot hide their sin from that great light
that penetrates into every heart that harbors vice,[262]
but they should strive to change their lives and ways.

94. S1:21 (1546), fol. 48r
    This is not the humble dwelling, nor these the loving
arms of the holy mother, nor the shepherds,
nor the sweet affection of that pious old man,
nor the high and joyful angelic voices,
    nor the magnificent gifts of the wise
kings offered with grateful fervor;
yet you are here, you who bring honor upon yourself,
My Lord, creator of all things.[263]
    I know that the truth that you were born a God
is here, and I do not envy others, but I do feel pity
for myself, not because I arrived too late
    or because it is our age that is unhappy, but I
am wretched because I do not yet burn with faith
as they do who saw you in that first state.[264]

95. S1:100 (1538), fol. 48v
    Pure Virgin, you who in the burning rays
of the true sun bask in eternal day,[265]
whose beautiful light, during your toilsome earthly life,
kept your lovely eyes serene and contented;

Uomo il vedesti, e Dio, quando i lucenti
Suoi spirti fer l'albergo umil adorno
Di chiari lumi, e timidi d'intorno
I tuoi ministri al grand'ufficio intenti.
    Immortal Dio nascosto in mortal velo
L'adorasti Signor, figlio il nudristi,
L'amasti sposo et l'onorasti padre;
    Prega lui dunque ch'i miei giorni tristi
Ritorni in lieti, e tu, donna del cielo,
Vogli in questo desio mostrarti madre.

96. S1 : 35 (1546), fol. 49r
    Beata l'alma che le voglie ha schive
Del mondo e del suo vil breve soggiorno;
Misera quella a cui sembra ei sì adorno
Ch'ad uopo suo non l'usa, anzi a lui vive.
    Tutte al padre celeste andremo prive
Del manto che ne copre il vero intorno,
Quel primo amaro o dolce ultimo giorno
Che morte o vita eterna a noi prescrive.
    O quanti piangeran le perdute ore,
Avute in pregio per la breve gioia
Che li lusinga a lor perpetuo danno.
    Poiché il mal per natura non gli annoia,
E del ben per ragion piacer non hanno,
Abbian almen di Dio giusto timore.

97. S1 : 82 (1546), fol. 49v
    Quando il turbato mar s'alza e circonda
Con impeto e furor ben fermo scoglio,
Se saldo il trova, il procelloso orgoglio
Si frange e cade in se medesma l'onda;
    Simil s'incontra a me vien la profonda
Acqua mondana irata, io come soglio
Fermo al ciel gli occhi, e tanto più la spoglio
Del suo vigor, quanto più forte abonda.
    E se talor la barca del desio
Vuol tentar nova guerra, io corro al lido,
E d'un laccio d'amor con fede attorto

you beheld him, both man and God,[266] when his
bright spirits adorned his humble dwelling
with a great light, and your ministers timidly
gathered round intent on their great office.

    Immortal God hidden in a mortal veil,
you worshiped him as Lord, nurtured him as son,
loved him as husband, and honored him as father;[267]

    therefore pray to him now that my sad days
may be transformed to joy, and may you, lady of heaven,
act as a mother to me in this my desire.[268]

96. S1:35 (1546), fol. 49r
    Blessed is the soul that scorns all worldly
desires and this brief, vile stay on earth;
wretched is the soul to which they seem so precious
that it does not merely use them but lives for them alone.[269]

    We will all go to meet our celestial father deprived
of the mantle that now covers our true nature,
on the first bitter day or the last sweet day
on which death or eternal life is granted to us.[270]

    How many then will lament the lost hours,
a high price paid for such brief delight
that entices them to their perpetual damnation.

    Since sinfulness does not offend their nature,
and their reason derives no pleasure from good deeds,
then let them at least justly fear the Lord.[271]

97. S1:82 (1546), fol. 49v
    When the turbulent sea rises up with powerful fury
and engulfs some solid rock,
finding it to be unmoved, its stormy pride
is dashed and the wave falls back upon itself;

    in the same way, if against me the deep seething
waters of life rise up, my habit is to fix
my eyes on heaven, and the more I draw out their force
the more furiously they rage.[272]

    And if sometimes the ship of desire
attempts a renewed attack, I hurry to the shore,
and with the bonds of love made fast by faith,

La lego prima a quella in cui mi fido
Viva pietra, Giesù, sì che quand'io
Voglio posso ad ogni or ritrarla in porto.

98. S1 : 137 (1546), fol. 50r
Diletta una acqua viva a pie' d'un monte
Quando senza arte la bella onda move,
O quando in marmi ed oro imagin nove
Sculte dimostra un ricco ornato fonte,
Ma 'l vostro vago stil fa al mondo conte
Ambe le glorie non vedute altrove:
De la natura l'alte ultime prove
Con la forza de l'arte insieme aggionte,
La qual raccoglie così ben d'intorno
L'acqua e sì pura, che vi lascia intero
De la sua vena il natural onore.
Bembo mio chiaro, or ch'è venuto il giorno
Ch'avete solo a Dio rivolto il core,
Deh! rivolgete ancor la musa al vero.

99. S1 : 141 (1546), fol. 50v
Figlio e signor, se la tua prima e vera
Madre vive prigion, non l'è già tolto
L'anima saggia o 'l chiaro spirto sciolto,
Né di tante virtù l'invitta schiera.
A me, che sembro andar scarca e leggera
E 'n poca terra ho il cor chiuso e sepolto,
Convien ch'abbi talor l'occhio rivolto
Che la seconda tua madre non pera.
Tu per gli aperti spaziosi campi
Del ciel camini, e non più nebbia o pietra
Ritarda o ingombra il tuo spedito corso.
Io, grave d'anni, aghiaccio; or tu ch'avampi
D'alta fiamma celeste, umil m'impetra
Dal comun padre eterno omai soccorso.

100. S1 : 110 (1546), fol. 51r
Eterna luna, alor che fra 'l sol vero
E gli occhi nostri il tuo mortal ponesti,
Lui non macchiasti e specchio a noi porgesti
Da mirar fiso nel suo lume altero.

I first lash my boat to that living rock in which
I trust, Lord Jesus, so that whenever I wish
I can tow it back into his harbor.[273]

98. S1:137 (1546), fol. 50r

The sight of lively waters at the foot of a mountain
enchants us, when a pretty wave moves artlessly,
or when, in marble and gold, new sculpted images
are carved on a rich and ornate fountain,
    but your own lovely style, as no one else's,
demonstrates to the world both these glories:[274]
the high and ultimate proofs of nature
united with the power of art.[275]
    It draws to itself so easily from all around
the purest waters that the natural honor
of inspiration is left to you alone.
    My sweet Bembo, now that the day has come
when you have offered your heart to God alone,[276]
then turn again your muse to its true end.[277]

99. S1:141 (1546), fol. 50v

My son and master,[278] if your first and true
mother abides in prison, yet still her wisdom
is not stolen from her, nor is her noble spirit defeated,
nor are the many virtues take from her unconquered companions.[279]
    To me, who seem to move about unburdened and free
and to keep my heart confined and buried in a small plot,[280]
I pray you turn your eyes from time to time
so that your second mother does not perish.[281]
    You walk upon the open spacious fields
of heaven, and no shadow or rock
can now delay or obstruct your swift progress.
    I, burdened by my years, am frozen here; therefore you
who are aflame with divine fire, pray humbly on my behalf
for help from our common father.

100. S1:110 (1546), fol. 51r

Eternal moon, when you placed your mortal light
between the true sun and our eyes,
you did not blemish him, but offered us a mirror
in which to gaze upon his divine light.[282]

Non l'adombrasti, ma quel denso e nero
Velo del primo error, coi santi onesti
Tuoi prieghi e i vivi suoi raggi, rendesti
D'ombroso e grave candido e leggiero.

Col chiaro che da lui prendi l'oscuro
De le notti ne togli, e la serena
Tua luce il calor suo tempra sovente;

Ché sopra il mondo errante il latte puro
Che qui 'l nudrì, quasi rugiada affrena
De la giusta ira sua l'effetto ardente.

101. S1 : 116 (1546), fol. 51v

Veggo d'alga e di fango omai sì carca,
Pietro, la rete tua, che se qualche onda
Di fuor l'assale o intorno la circonda
Potria spezzarsi e a rischio andar la barca,

La qual, non come suol, leggiera e scarca
Sovra 'l turbato mar corre a seconda,
Ma in poppa e in prora, a l'una e l'altra sponda
È grave sì che a gran periglio varca.

Il tuo buon successor, cui la ragione
Si drittamente elesse, e cor e mano
Move sovente per condurla a porto;

Ma contra 'l voler suo ratto s'oppone
L'altrui malizia, onde ciascun s'è accorto
Ch'egli senza 'l tuo aiuto adopra invano.

102. S1 : 4 (1546), fol. 52r

S'in man prender non soglio unqua la lima
Del buon giudizio, e ricercando intorno
Con l'occhio disdegnoso io non adorno
Né tergo la mia rozza incolta rima,

Nasce perché non è mia cura prima
Procacciar di ciò lode o fuggir scorno,
Né che dopo il mio lieto al ciel ritorno
Viva ella al mondo in più onorata stima;

Ma dal foco divin, che 'l mio intelletto,
Sua mercé, infiamma, convien ch'escan fore
Mal mio grado talor queste faville,

You cast no shadow over him, but that dense black
veil of original sin, through your faithful saintly
prayers and his living rays, you transformed
from dark and heavy to radiant and light.[283]
    With the clarity that you take from him, the darkness
of night is banished, and your calm
light often tempers his heat;
    and moving over the world your pure milk,
which nurtured him on earth, like a dew dampens
the burning fire of his righteous anger.[284]

101. S1:116 (1546), fol. 51v
    I see your net so laden with weeds and mud,
Peter, that if some wave
breaks over it or engulfs it
it may be torn and endanger your boat,[285]
    for it does not, as it should, float easily,
light and unburdened, over the turbulent sea,
but rather, in bow and stern, from one shore to the other,
is so weighed down that it sails in grave danger.
    Your noble successor, elected by
just reason, often turns his heart and his hand
to the task of guiding the boat to port;[286]
    but the wickedness of others
swiftly pits itself against his will, so that all now realize
that without your help he acts in vain.[287]

102. S1:4 (1546), fol. 52r
    If I often fail to take up the file
of good sense[288] and, looking around me
with scornful eyes, refuse to embellish
or erase my rough, uncultivated verses,
    this is because my primary concern is not
to garner praise for it, or avoid contempt,
or that, after my joyful return to heaven,
my poems will live on in the world more highly honored;[289]
    but the divine fire, which through its mercy
inflames my mind, sometimes gives out
these sparks of its own accord,[290]

Et s'alcuna di lor un gentil core
Avien che scaldi, mille volte e mille
Ringraziar debbo il mio felice errore.

103. S1:179 (1546), fol. 52v

Temo che 'l laccio, ov'io molt'anni presi
Tenni li spirti, ordisca or la mia rima
Sol per usanza, e non per quella prima
Cagion d'averli in Dio volti e accesi.

Temo che sian lacciuoli intorno tesi
Di colui ch'opra mal con sorda lima,
E mi faccia parer da falsa stima
Utili i giorni forse indarno spesi.

Di giovar poca, ma di nocer molta
Ragion vi scorgo, ond'io prego 'l mio foco
Ch'entro in silenzio il petto abbracci ed arda.

Interrotto dal duol, dal pianger roco
Esser dee il canto vèr colui ch'ascolta
Dal cielo, e al cor non a lo stil riguarda.

and if one such spark should once warm
some gentle heart, then a thousand times
a thousand thanks I owe to that happy mistake.[291]

103. S1:179 (1546), fol. 52v
 I am afraid that the knot, with which for many years
I have kept my soul bound up, now orders my verses
only through long habit, and not for the primary reason
that they are turned towards God and inflamed by him.[292]
 I am afraid that they are knots tied tightly
by one who works badly with a dull file,[293]
so that, fired with false esteem, I believe
that my days are useful when in fact I waste them.[294]
 I perceive little reason why they should be of use,
but much evidence that they do harm, so I pray that
this internal fire may embrace and scald my heart in silence.
 The song I sing to God, who listens from above,
should be interrupted by pain and hoarse cries,
for he values my heart and not my style.[295]

NOTES

1. The initial number refers to the numbering of the sonnet in Colonna, *Rime,* ed Alan Bullock (Rome: Laterza, 1982). The date is the first date of publication of the sonnet in question. The folio number shows its position within the Vatican manuscript.

2. This is a reference to the poet's earlier amorous sonnets, written in memory of her deceased husband Francesco D'Avalos.

3. The language of this opening sonnet is notably corporeal and rich and in fact might be described as "Michelangelesque" in its affinity to the poetry of Michelangelo himself. This is a striking departure for Colonna, whose verses are generally highly formal and controlled, and it can be thought to signal the new emphasis that this whole manuscript represents, of a sustained interest in evangelical religious questions.

4. In all the published versions of the sonnet, line 8 reads "sì ch'io scriva *per me . . . ,*" "so that I may write down *for myself* all that he suffered." The change to the version in Michelangelo's manuscript reconfirms Colonna's interest in evangelizing a message of reformed spirituality to her friend.

5. Parnassus, a mountain range in Greece, was considered to be sacred to Apollo and the muses and therefore the natural abode of poetry and music. Delos is the island birthplace of Apollo, one of the twelve gods of Olympus. He was seen as the embodiment of the rational and civilized side of man's nature and was therefore lauded as patron of poetry and music. The poet rejects these more traditional locations of poetic inspiration in order to reconfirm her sole interest in seeking out divine poetic expression. Petrarch makes use of a similar conceit in sonnet 166, although instead he bemoans the fact that love has driven him from the path of true poetic inspiration so that he has wandered far from the sacred spring of Parnassus and his verses are no longer fertile.

6. In Mt 16:24, Christ calls upon his followers to take up their crosses with him, a gesture clearly mirrored by the poet here. This second sonnet confirms the manuscript's general Christocentric emphasis. The "narrow path" derives from Mt 7:14: "How narrow is the gate, and strait is the way that leadeth to life: and few there are that find it!"

7.   See Mt 16:13−20, in which Christ asks his disciples to identify him, and Simon Peter alone answers, "Thou art Christ, the Son of the living God." This knowledge, Christ tells Peter, has been granted by heaven, and in reward Peter will be given the keys to the kingdom of heaven, which is thus "opened" for him, as the poet states, along with his eyes.

8.   The reference to the fragility of human hope can be read as a subtle reference to the Protestant doctrine of *sola fide*. Because salvation cannot be earned, the good Christian must let go of the hope of achieving it himself and trust implicitly in the judgment of God, a task that the poet admits to finding difficult to achieve.

9.   The "divine table" derives from Lk 22:29−30: "And I dispose to you, as my father hath disposed to me, a kingdom; That you may eat and drink at my table, in my kingdom: and may sit upon thrones, judging the twelve tribes of Israel." Dante employs the same imagery in *Paradiso* 24.

10.   Jn 6:54: "Then Jesus said to them: Amen, amen, I say unto you: except you eat the flesh of the Son of man and drink his blood, you shall not have life in you."

11.   The union of human and divine manifestations in the person of Christ, known by theologians as the Hypostatic Union, is highlighted most succinctly in the first chapter of John's gospel, for example, in Jn 1:14: "And the Word was made flesh and dwelt among us . . . full of grace and truth." On a general tendency to stress the wonder of the Incarnation in sixteenth-century theology, see John W. O'Malley, *Praise and Blame in Renaissance Rome: Rhetoric, Doctrine, and Reform in the Sacred Orators of the Papal Court, c. 1450−1521* (Durham, NC: Duke University Press, 1979), 138−50. The poet emphasizes the essential duality of Christ's nature through the bipartite structure of her verse, for example, in line 4.

12.   See Mt 11:30: "For my yoke is sweet and my burden light."

13.   The "secret key" is the key to the kingdom of heaven, held by Christ and awarded to Peter for his faith in Mt 16 (see the notes to sonnet 2).

14.   This image is reminiscent of Dante's *Paradiso* 30, in which the poet describes his first vision of the Empyrean, as Beatrice tells him, "We have come forth from the greatest body [the Primum Mobile] to the heaven which is pure light" (lines 38−39).

15.   A reference to the sins of Adam and Eve, recounted in the third chapter of the book of Genesis, which led to their expulsion from the Garden of Eden and the consequent suffering of all humankind.

16.   An echo of the famous words in Ps 22, "The Lord is my shepherd, I shall not want." (In most Protestant versions of the Bible, based on translations from the Hebrew rather than the Vulgate, this is Ps 23, rather than 22. Likewise, most other psalm numbers are at least one digit different from their Roman Catholic equivalents.) See in addition Lk 15:3−7; Jn 10:1−18.

17.   Paul describes knowledge of God as being inscribed, "not with ink, but with the Spirit of the living God; not in tables of stone, but in the fleshly tables of the heart" (2 Cor 3:3). The tone of lines 10−11 is highly evangelical, referring to the notion of incorporation in Christ through faith expressed in such reformist works as the *Beneficio di Cristo* (see Benedetto da Mantova, *Il Beneficio di Cristo con le versioni del secolo XVI: Documenti e testimonianze*, ed. Salvatore Caponetto [Florence: Sansoni, 1972], 26).

18.   The early church fathers sometimes employed the imagery of the church as a ship in which the faithful find safety and are borne to salvation. Thus, by association, the sky that they cross en route becomes an ocean and heaven becomes the celestial shore, as here. Such nautical imagery is frequently used by the poet in this manuscript.

19.   A further reference to the Hypostatic Union of God and man in the person of Christ.

20.   There is a strong echo here of a biblical passage such as 2 Cor 4:6: "For God who commanded the light to shine out of darkness, hath shined in our hearts, to give the light of the knowledge of the glory of God in the face of Christ Jesus."

21.   The references to the lilies and the birds are drawn once again from the New Testament, specifically Mt 6:28–29, "Consider the lilies of the field . . ." (which also occurs in Lk 12:27), and Mt 6:26, "Behold the fowls of the air . . . " (also in Lk 12:24).

22.   The gentle heart, "cor gentil," is frequently evoked in Stilnovist and Petrarchan poetry. Here the poet is clearly revising the tradition by alluding to a heart that loves only Christ, rather than an earthly muse.

23.   In the writings of the Spanish mystic Juan de Valdés, faith is depicted as a fire that gives off heat, the good works that the true Christian will carry out despite himself and without any regard for "earning" salvation. See Juan de Valdés, *Two Catechisms*, 2d ed, trans. William B. and Carol D. Jones. Ed. José C. Nieto (Lawrence, KS: Coronado, 1993), 186–91.

24.   The image of Christ calling down from the cross to his followers is one that is used to great effect in the *Beneficio di Cristo*. In that text, Christ calls out using the words of Mt 11:28, delivered by Christ after the commissioning of the disciples: "Come unto me, all you that labor and are burdened, and I will refresh you." See Mantova, *Il Beneficio di Cristo*, 19 and Abigail Brundin, "Vittoria Colonna and the Poetry of Reform," *Italian Studies* 57 (2002): 61–74, at 64. Such imagery illustrates clearly the reformist notion of a loving and forgiving Christ with whom the Christian can develop an intimate relationship. It seems significant that Michelangelo employs similar imagery in his poetry, for example, in 'Giunto è già 'l corso della vita mia' ('The voyage of my life at last has reached'): 'that divine love/ that opened his arms on the cross to take us in" (Michelangelo Buonarroti, *The Poetry of Michelangelo*, ed. and trans. James M. Saslow [New Haven: Yale University Press, 1991], 476). Juan de Valdés (*Alfabeto cristiano*, ed. Benedetto Croce [Bari: Laterza, 1938], 20) and Bernardino Ochino (cited in Paolo Simoncelli, *Evangelismo italiano del Cinquecento: Questione religiosa e nicodemismo politico* [Rome: Istituto storico italiano per l'età moderna e contemporanea, 1979], 94) both explore the notion of the peace that is conferred upon the human soul by the contemplation of Christ crucified. For a fuller discussion, see Rinaldina Russell, "L'ultima meditazione di Vittoria Colonna e l' '*Ecclesia Viterbiensis*'," *La Parola del Testo: Semestrale di filologia e letteratura italiana e comparata dal medioevo al rinascimento* 4 (2000): 151–66.

25.   The identity of the poet's "angelic escort" is not clarified here. This could perhaps be a sonnet addressed to her spiritual mentor, Reginald Pole, on whom Colonna relied to give her advice about her progress in faith (see the notes to sonnet 99).

26.   There seems to be an echo here of *Inferno* 1.3 in the reference to the "straight path to heaven." Dante loses sight of the straight way in the famous opening of the *Commedia*, "che la diritta via era smarrita," and has to rely on the guidance of his own "angelic escort" in the person of Virgil.

27.   The images in the second quatrain refer to the parable of the wise virgins cited in Mt 25. These prudent women put by enough oil to keep their lamps burning throughout the night as they await the coming of their lord. The foolish virgins, whose lamps have gone out, must go to buy more oil and arrive too late at the wedding, only to find the door closed to them. Colonna's deep identification with this parable is expressed in another way, in a marriage portrait by Sebastiano del Piombo of ca. 1510, believed to be of Colonna in the persona of a wise virgin. See Marjorie Och, "Vittoria Colonna and the Commission for a *Mary Magdalene* by Titian," in *Beyond Isabella: Secular Women Patrons of Art in Renaissance Italy*, ed. Sheryl E. Reiss and David G. Wilkins, 193–223, Sixteenth-Century Essays and Studies, 54 (Kirksville, MO: Truman State University Press, 2001), at 199 and 219.

28.   The reference to Christ as the poet's sun, while by no means unusual in this lyric context, forges an interesting link with Colonna's earlier *rime amorose*, written in memory of her deceased husband D'Avalos, in which the dead soldier is also given the epithet *Sole* ("sun"). This consonance of poetic imagery running through the amorous and spiritual sonnets highlights the poet's uniformity of purpose from her very earliest verses and the subtle yet consistent process of neo-Platonic transformation that she has enacted upon her poetic consort. See Abigail Brundin, "Vittoria Colonna and the Poetry of Reform," 62–63.

29.   The elected souls chosen by God to be saved are described in Mt 24:31: "And he shall send his angels with a trumpet and a great voice, and they shall gather together his elect from the four winds, from the farthest parts of the heavens to the utmost bounds of them." The poet's position here, as in other sonnets, is notably reformist, and the imagery strikingly Dantean in evoking the *Paradiso*.

30.   The metaphors of waves and ocean are frequently employed in the Bible to refer to the immensity of God's might. A potential source here is Ps 41, in which the soul pants after the sustenance of the waters of God, which alone can assuage a spiritual thirst.

31.   Jn 4:13–14: "But he that will drink of the water that I will give him shall not thirst for ever. But the water that I will give him shall become in him a fountain of water, springing up into life everlasting."

32.   In Jn 19:34, blood and water issue from Christ's open wound. Saint Augustine interpreted this to signify the Eucharist and the Baptism, the two main sacraments that issue from the side of Christ at the Crucifixion. Thus, according to Augustine, the church is born from Christ's wound. See, for example, *De genesi contra Manichaeos* 2.34 and *De civitate Dei* 15.26 and 22.17. It seems very significant that, according to the poet, this holy water is not able to cleanse the human soul as it should, so that she seems to be implicitly criticizing the work of the established church, which is failing the individual Christian.

33.   Perhaps the voices of the disciples who worked with Christ to convert men to the true faith and thus bring about the original act of redemption.

34. This poem, in an elaborate initial twist, celebrates the day of the Birth of the Virgin, September 8 according to the Roman Catholic liturgy, yet contrives to laud the birth of Mary as only the initial event that made possible the birth of Christ, so that the second person address is directed, not at Mary, as might first appear, but at Christ. Such convoluted wordplay can be considered to anticipate later mannerist developments within the Petrarchan tradition.

35. Mary is here represented in her traditional role as intercessor with God on behalf of humankind, to whom she is eternally loving and sympathetic (on this and her other roles, see Hilda Graef, *Mary: A History of Doctrine and Devotion,* 2d ed. [London: Sheed and Ward, 1987]; Michael O'Carroll, *Theotokos: A Theological Encyclopedia of the Blessed Virgin Mary* [Wilmington, DE: Michael Glazier, 1983]; Jaroslav Pelikan, *Mary through the Centuries: Her Place in the History of Culture* [New Haven: Yale University Press, 1998]; and Marina Warner, *Alone of All Her Sex: The Myth and Cult of the Virgin Mary* [New York: Vintage Books, 1983]).

36. Colonna's sixteenth-century commentator, Rinaldo Corso, expressed grave doubts, in his analysis of this sonnet, about the propriety of asking God to pray to Mary in this reversal of traditional roles, "because in every other way it would be inappropriate for him to pray to the virgin, over whom he is lord and master, as he is over all creatures, except out of piety and respect for her maternity" (Colonna, *Tutte le Rime della Illustriss. et Eccellentiss. Signora Vittoria Colonna, Marchesana di Pescara. Con l'Espositione del Signor Rinaldo Corso, nuovamente mandate in luce da Girolamo Ruscelli* [Venice: Giovan Battista et Melchior Sessa Fratelli, 1558], 425). The poet's reversal of the traditional celestial hierarchy here could be an indication of her interest, explored in other sonnets as well as in a number of her prose works, in pointing up the autonomy and assertive agency of Mary in her role as intercessor. See Abigail Brundin, "Vittoria Colonna and the Virgin Mary," *Modern Language Review* 96 (2001): 61–81. In addition, as in the previous sonnet, the implicit suggestion is that extra help is needed by the poet (in the form of God's intercession with Mary) in order to gain access to God's grace.

37. As told in Gn 1:27, the image of man reflects that of God: "And God created man to his own image: to the image of God he created him; male and female he created them." The sin that marks all of mankind, however, is not a part of this initial act of creation but was brought by man upon himself through the initial act of disobedience.

38. See the notes to sonnet 2, where the same imagery of miraculous sustenance through Christ is presented.

39. The evangelical emphasis of this statement is notable. The chosen ones are sure of justification, despite their unworthy and sinful state, because they are born with faith, which alone is enough to save them. The poet's individual nuance here is noteworthy, however, the insertion of "quasi," "almost," suggests perhaps her precarious position, poised between reformist *sola fide* and a more orthodox Roman Catholic position. It is interesting that the following two lines, with their bold statement of intent, help to overcome the doubt implicit in "quasi."

40. This is a reference to the Passion, when the violent hand of humankind was turned against Christ, and yet paradoxically the outcome was the opening of the way

to salvation for all. (See also the same paradox encapsulated in the imagery of sonnet 43.) The inevitability of Christ's death upon the cross, and his own awareness of this (inferred in the verb "mostri"), is alluded to in the New Testament, for example, in Jn 16:7: "It is expedient to you that I go. For if I go not, the Paraclete [Comforter] will not come to you; but if I go, I will send him to you."

41.   The reference to the "belted robe" derives from Lk 12:35: "Let your loins be girt and lamps burning in your hands." There are also echoes of Eph 6:14, in which Paul advises his audience to take upon their backs the armor of God and "stand, therefore, having your loins girt about with truth, and having on the breastplate of justice."

42.   This is the second reference to the parable of the wise virgins from Mt 25 (the first being in sonnet 7). Once again, the poet holds aloft her burning lamp or torch and awaits the arrival of the bridegroom. The "bride of Christ" imagery employed here appears to have been interestingly ungendered in its application in sixteenth-century verse, so that Michelangelo felt equally able to use the term "sposa" in relation to his own union with God. See, for example, his poem "Vorrei voler, Signor, quel ch'io non voglio" ('I wish for that, my Lord, which I do not desire'), in Buonarroti, *The Poetry of Michelangelo*, 208) and the poet's reference to his soul as "[la] tuo bella sposa" ('your beautiful bride'). In the *Beneficio di Cristo*, all Christians are categorized as the brides of Christ: "the Church, that is every faithful soul, is the bride of Christ, and Christ is bridegroom of the Church" (Mantova, *Il Beneficio di Cristo*, 27).

43.   In line with her general evangelical tone, the poet once again stresses the loving and forgiving nature of the reformist Christ, who refuses here to expose her weakness as she had feared he might.

44.   The Italian version of this sonnet uses the adjective "tartare," Tartarean, a term deriving from Greek mythology, which refers to the abyss or deep place of punishment in Hades.

45.   This appears to be a reference to the Harrowing of Hell, the period between the Crucifixion and the Resurrection when Christ descended to Hell to release from torment the souls of his ancestors from the Hebrew Bible. Recounted by Dante in *Inferno* 4.52–63 (and alluded to repeatedly in subsequent stages of the protagonist's journey), the Harrowing derives from certain apocryphal gospels, such as *Nicodemus* (post–fifth-century), and from readings of Mt 27 and 1 Pt 3:19, but was firmly embedded in the popular imagination by the Middle Ages. Interestingly, the more common version of Colonna's sonnet has the Lord God *closing*, rather than opening, the infernal gates. See Colonna, *Rime* (1982, 131). (Dante describes the damage done to the gates of Hell during the Harrowing in *Inferno* 8.124–27.)

46.   The closing five lines of this sonnet clearly illustrate the poet's conception of the intimate quality of evangelical faith. She experiences the subtle work of faith within her own soul and implicitly contrasts her own unworthiness with the worthiness of those patriarchs and prophets freed by Christ during the Harrowing of Hell.

47.   The reference is to Lk 19:1–10. Zacchaeus was a rich tax collector who climbed a tree to see Christ enter Jerusalem and then hosted him at a meal in his house. Za-

cchaeus was deemed unworthy of the honor that Christ bestowed upon him, and many complained about this: "And when all saw it, they murmured, saying, that he was gone to be a guest with a man that is a sinner" (Lk 19:7). The poet therefore hopes that her own unworthy status will not prevent her from receiving the benefit of Christ's presence within her heart, where she will "host" him in the same way.

48.   There is a strongly mystical tone to this sonnet, with its repeated imagery of light and fire deriving from such sources as the works of Juan de Valdés and the substance and tone of the *Beneficio di Cristo*. In addition, the progression from rational thought to faith, to light, to hope, and so on, charted in the first tercet, reflects a strongly neo-Platonic conception of the process of ascension towards a pure and loving union with God.

49.   The enemy referred to here is Satan. The armies of Satan (meaning "adversary" in Hebrew) were overcome in battle by the good angels and plunged into Hell. The battle between the angels is derived from the New Testament, primarily Rv 12:7—8 (in which Satan is called "the Dragon"). Satan is personified as an individual adversary for the first time in the New Testament, as for example in Lk 4, when Jesus is tempted by the devil in the wilderness and commands him, "Get thee behind me, Satan."

50.   The angel addressed here is the Archangel Michael, who led the troops of the good angels to victory on God's behalf.

51.   Christ refers to himself as the light of the world in Jn 8:12 and 9:5.

52.   In biblical lore Michael is the greatest of all angels, and verses in Dn 10 and 12 contributed to the late Jewish belief that he was the guardian protector of Israel.

53.   Colonna is using a deliberately paradoxical language here, contrasting wealth and poverty, humility and pride, and so on. As in sonnet 11, this seems to be a way of alluding to the central paradox of the Christian faith, that is, the life through death manifested in the Crucifixion.

54.   This sonnet is a general celebration of the Incarnation of Christ, which brought salvation to humankind.

55.   The flame that sets fire to the earth is Jesus Christ in human form, who descends from heaven to "ignite" faith in humankind. This imagery derives once again from the New Testament, most famously perhaps from Christ's words in Jn 8:12: "Again therefore Jesus spoke to them, saying: I am the light of the world. He that followeth me walketh not in darkness, but shall have the light of life."

56.   The poet's ancient sin is once again, as in sonnet 4, that committed by Adam and Eve in the Garden of Eden, with which all of humankind is tarnished.

57.   The imagery reminds us of the myth of Icarus, who flew too close to the sun so that the wax binding his wings melted and he plunged to his death (Ovid, *Fasti* 4.284).

58.   For the biblical imagery of Christ as the true vine, see Jn 15:1—9.

59.   The statement of salvation by faith alone is unequivocal in this sonnet, as this line makes clear, perhaps more succinctly in the original Italian.

60.   A reference to Christ's famous words in Jn 14:6: "I am the way, and the truth, and the life. No man cometh to the Father, but by me."

61. The parable of the sower and the seed in Mt 13 tells of the stony, the thorny, and the good ground, the latter being the only one in which the seed brings forth fruit: "But he that received the seed upon good ground is he that heareth the word, and understandeth" (Mt 13:23). The poet's reference to her own spiritual fertility in Christ echoes the imagery of a far earlier poem, written in memory of Colonna's husband D'Avalos, in which she indicates that her marriage, while physically sterile, was spiritually rich and fertile. See "Quando Morte fra noi disciolse il nodo" ('When death unbound the knot which joined us'), in Colonna, *Rime* (1982, 18).

62. This is perhaps an allusion to the myth of Danaë, daughter of the King of Argos, who was seduced by Jupiter in the form of a shower of golden rain. As a symbol of chastity and of conception by a virgin through divine intervention, Danaë's myth was interpreted from the Middle Ages as a prefiguration of the Annunciation, thus the reference here links the poet's experience indirectly to that of Mary.

63. The poet's declaration is reminiscent of the lament of David in Ps 21:15: "I am poured out like water, and all my bones are scattered. My heart is become like wax melting in the midst of my bowels." There is also a clear Petrarchan precedent for this imagery, in sonnet 133.

64. The emphasis on the helplessness of the true Christian is once again highly evangelical. Humankind is unable to change its sinful state through the power of its own actions but must await the actions of God's grace (a reference to *sola fide*). Thus, in line 10, the poet's vision comes about not through her own mortal powers but through the illuminating power of God's grace.

65. The tone of this whole sonnet is strikingly sensual and counters the critical judgment of Colonna as a "cold" poet by demonstrating the wide variety of her poetic voices and attitudes.

66. The poet makes mention here, as elsewhere, of the two distinct elements of heat and light, suggesting that even at her most "ardent" (as here), there is always an intellectual quality to her faith (the light).

67. Once again, as in sonnet 3, there is a reference to Christ's words in Mt 11:30: "for my yoke is sweet and my burden light."

68. The extended metaphor of bark and ocean is clearly Petrarchan in its poetic origins (see for example Petrarch's sonnet 189). See the later sonnets 35 and 79, in which this topos is repeated. Also the discussion of this sonnet in the introduction, p. 37.

69. This line is virtually untranslatable. Through the ambiguity of the Italian "lucida," the poet manages to convey both that the light surrounds her and is divine in origin and simultaneously that she is herself "alight." This beautifully subtle and complex wordplay appears to have a reformist message and can be related to the Lutheran premise that faith is intrinsic and not obtainable (you are born saved), and therefore, although the poet struggles continually with this concept, she is already, despite herself, "alight" and therefore saved.

70. The status of humility as the most sacred of virtues is demonstrated in a number of the chapters in Proverbs. See, for example, Prv 11:2, 15:33, 22:4.

71. The enemy of humility is pride.

72.   The general tenor of this sonnet is anti-intellectual: the poet tells us that faith, not knowledge or learning, saves the soul. This attitude is very much in line with the evangelical stance promoted in texts such as the *Beneficio di Cristo*, in which the heart rather than the head is presented as the organ of religion in a highly sensual and emotive language. Such an approach could be considered a reaction against the rational Thomist tradition (reflected in Dante, for example), which saw the process of reasoned meditation on the wonders of the universe as the first step in a spiritual ascent towards God. See Etienne Gilson, *Thomism: The Philosophy of Thomas Aquinas* (Toronto: Pontifical Institute of Medieval Studies, 2002).

73.   This sonnet is addressed to Mary Magdalene, who in popular mythology was believed to have spent time after the death of Christ in a self-imposed exile in a grotto in Sainte-Baume in France (a myth originating in eleventh-century France and recounted in Jacobus de Voragine's *Golden Legend*). Petrarch also composed a poem to Mary Magdalene, in the 1330s, when he undertook a pilgrimage to her shrine at Sainte-Baume (a journey that Colonna also wished to make; see sonnet 63). For a translation of the poem, see Francesco Petrarca, *Letters of Old Age: Rerum senilium libri I–XVIII*, 2 vols., trans. A. S. Bernardo, S. Levin, and R. A. Bernardo (Baltimore: Johns Hopkins University Press, 1992), 597; and Och, "Vittoria Colonna and the Commission for a *Mary Magdalene* by Titian," 203–4.

74.   Mary Magdalene is considered to be the first bride of Christ in her role as a devoted disciple who was granted the special privilege of being the first to witness the Resurrection and thus became the *apostola apostolorum*, spreading the news to the other disciples. The poet seeks to follow in her footsteps, using her example in order to become herself a bride of Christ (as she also states in sonnet 12, with its reference to the parable of the wise virgins), as well as a proselytizer for Christ, in her role as poet.

75.   The rock to which the poet refers is presumably the rocky island of Ischia off the coast of Naples, where she spent a large part of her early married life, as well as returning there frequently in later years. There are references to the same rock in a number of other early sonnets (see for example Colonna, *Rime* [1982, 62, 63]). Some critics believe that this sonnet was inspired by a sermon on the subject of Mary Magdalene given in Naples by the evangelical preacher Bernardino Ochino (see Domenico Tordi, *Il codice delle Rime di Vittoria Colonna, Marchesa di Pescara, appartenuto a Margherita d'Angoulême, Regina di Navarra* [Pistoia: Flori, 1900]). Certainly the reference to Ischia suggests that the poem was first composed in the early Neapolitan period of the poet's life.

76.   The image of Mary Magdalene kneeling at Christ's feet derives from the account of the woman washing his feet with her hair in Lk 7, 36–50. On the confusion between the various Marys in the Bible, which led to this cross-association, see Susan Haskins, *Mary Magdalene: Myth and Metaphor* (London: Harper Collins, 1993). The chains referred to in line 14 can be linked to the long blond tresses with which she entwines Christ's feet, as depicted, for example, in a painting such as Titian's Pitti *Magdalene*, probably commissioned by Colonna (see Och, "Vittoria Colonna and the Commission for a *Mary Magdalene* by Titian").

77.   There are numerous references in the Old Testament to a promised land flowing with milk and honey, such as, for example, the one promised to the Jews coming out of Egypt in Ex 3:8, 17; and 13:5.

78.   The use of the bee metaphor in poetic texts has a long and distinguished history, to which the poet is here no doubt referring. Most famously, Virgil in *Georgics* 4 explores in detail the concept of the altruism of the industry of bees, their hardworking and disciplined communities (mistakenly believed to be governed by a king bee, rather than a queen), and their status as celibate and infertile, therefore symbolic of purity and virginity (*Georgics* 4, 197–202). He also alludes to their divinity and supernatural aspects (219–27), a notion that derives from Aristotle (*On the Generation of Animals* 3.10). In *Aeneid* 6, the souls of the dead crowding towards Lethe in the hope of a new incarnation are compared with bees busy around a flower in high summer (707–9). (For general information on these classical sources, see Francesco della Corte, ed., *Enciclopedia Virgiliana*. Vol. 1. [Rome: Istituto della Enciclopedia Italiana, 1984], 211–16.) In this sonnet, Colonna appears to combine such classical notions of the divinity of bees with the long tradition of poetic imitation referring to bees (who gather the nectar from the most beautiful flowers just as the poet selects the most beautiful from nature to make up his art), found, for example, in Seneca and Petrarch.

79.   The sense seems to be that Christ will himself feed humankind with his own milk in his role as the good shepherd of men. Such "maternal" imagery in relation to Christ also has biblical precedents, as in, for example, Mt 23:37.

80.   The famous Ps 22 tells us of the Lord's role as the shepherd of men. Here, as in the previous sonnet, it is Christ who adopts the role in relation to humankind.

81.   See the notes to sonnet 8.

82.   There are a number of biblical precedents for such imagery, among them Ps 67:3: "as wax melteth before the fire, so let the wicked perish at the presence of God." Again, Petrarch's sonnet 133 is a clear poetic precedent here.

83.   As man is made in the image of God, so our sins defile that image.

84.   Mt 6, 19–20: "Lay not up to yourselves treasures on earth [. . .] but lay up to yourselves treasures in heaven."

85.   Jove is another name for Jupiter, son of Saturn (whom he overthrew) and king of the Roman gods; here his name is used to denote the Christian God. The version of this sonnet cited in Bullock's edition (Colonna, *Rime*, 1982, 96) omits the reference to Jove altogether, perhaps because the poet later decided that a strictly Christian terminology was more appropriate. Significantly, Erasmus, in the *Dialogus Ciceronianus* (1528), criticizes precisely the Italian humanistic habit of employing pagan terminology of this kind in Christian writings.

86.   A parallel can be seen with the biblical Song of Solomon, in which the coming of the lover heralds fresh growth and new life in a similar way. In both cases, the tone is rhapsodic and the language somewhat sexualized in the references to fertility and fecundity.

87.   This sonnet celebrates the feast day of the birth of Christ, December 25. Although not directly named in the poem, Mary is also implicated as being responsible for this "divinely elected birth."

88.   John O'Malley uses the term "incarnational theology" to define the early modern tendency to identify the Redemption with the Incarnation rather than with the Crucifixion, that is, to hold that the redemption of humankind was already accomplished at the moment of Christ's conception in Mary's womb (O'Malley, *Praise and*

Blame in Renaissance Rome, 138–59). According to such a theology, Mary's body becomes the locus for the salvation of humankind and she is thus afforded a great share in the responsibility for the event. A sonnet such as this one celebrating the birth of Christ seems in accordance with such a theology, although it is by no means the only attitude adopted by the poet, who expresses a more pessimistic and Passion-oriented spirituality in other sonnets.

89.   The most perfect angel is Gabriel, who announced the birth of Christ to Mary on earth.

90.   In Rv 14, the song of the redeemed is heard sounding out from heaven, and in Rv 15, seven angels can be heard "singing the canticle of Moses" (Rv 15:3).

91.   The poet wonders in this sonnet at the power of the call to heaven, which, although heard so weakly on earth, is enough to fill the heart with hope and determination and in heaven will overwhelm the soul with its potency.

92.   Christ is the captain of the army of Christians. Such military imagery is employed in the *Beneficio di Cristo* in references to the arms that the Christian must take up in spiritual combat, such as prayer and frequent communion (see Mantova, *Il Beneficio di Cristo*, ch. 6).

93.   Saint Francis of Assisi (ca. 1182–1226), founder of the Franciscan Order, rejected worldly goods in order to follow Christ, taking vows of poverty, chastity, and obedience. He lived in such close imitation of Christ that followers came to refer to him as the *Alter Christus*, or second Christ.

94.   The poet refers to the five marks of the stigmata, which appeared on Francis's hands, feet, and side, corresponding with Christ's wounds. Legend tells us that Francis received the stigmata in 1224 while at prayer and that they remained on his body until his death when they were discovered by his followers. The five wounds were frequently used to distinguish Francis in art of the period (see James Hall, *Dictionary of Subjects and Symbols in Art*, rev. ed. [London: John Murray, 1984], 131–33).

95.   The reference to Saint Francis as the *Alter Christus* is made even more explicit in this sonnet.

96.   According to Saint Bonaventure, when Francis traveled to Rome to seek papal sanction for the Franciscan order, the pope had a dream in which he saw the Lateran Church about to topple and Francis propping it up. A common representation in early modern art shows the saint holding up the Lateran Church (Hall, *Dictionary of Subjects and Symbols in Art*, 132). Thus here the temple referred to is presumably the Lateran Church; the throne is the Godhead, represented by the altar (in Byzantine Christian art a throne is often used as a symbol of God—see Hall, *Dictionary of Subjects and Symbols in Art*, 303); the emblem is the Holy Cross used to represent the church.

97.   The feminine form throughout the tercets continues to refer to "la sposa," "the wife" that is the Franciscan order and, by association with Francis, the Lateran Church. Francis's poverty and humility are contrasted with the greed and pride that the poet feels are now dominant within the church.

98.   The poet here describes her own lowly position and contrasts it with that of the elected souls, who feel the fire of faith within them. This self-denigration is in contradiction to her self-depiction in sonnets such as 11 and 13, for example, in which

she counts herself among their number, reflecting no doubt the poet's insecurity and changing states of mind.

99.   The ancient enemy is sin, or perhaps worldly temptation. The "final battle" may allude to the divine Day of Judgment when the present world will end. Although its roots derive from the Hebrew Bible (e.g., Jl 3, Is 2), by the sixteenth century a different emphasis was well established, confirmed by the Apostles' and Nicene Creeds, which identified Christ as the agent of God who comes to judge the living and the dead. This emphasis is particularly prevalent in the Pauline literature. See, for example, 1 Cor 3:13 and 5:5; 2 Cor 1:14; and Rm 2:16. It is clearly reflected in art of the Renaissance period, as, for example, in Michelangelo's depiction of the Last Judgment in the Sistine Chapel in Rome.

100.   The language of struggle and combat in this sonnet mirrors the tone of the *Beneficio*, in which the Christian is also called upon to arm himself with the true faith and to follow Christ, the Captain, into battle. See also sonnet 32. Notably, the subject is persistently feminine until the final line of this sonnet ("il cor"), suggesting perhaps that women are equally implicated with men in the spiritual process being described.

101.   Gal 3:9: "Therefore, they that are of faith shall be blessed with faithful Abraham."

102.   Once again, as in sonnet 22, the Petrarchan metaphor of the boat is employed. Here Christ is represented by the port in which the poet's soul will find respite from the storms of life.

103.   As in the previous sonnet, the poet once again counts herself apart from the saved and the blessed and envies their true and unwavering faith, which she is struggling to achieve. By contrast, as she makes explicit in the final two lines, the blessed themselves are not afflicted by jealousy, despite the hierarchical structure of Paradise. This is a point made clearly by Dante in *Paradiso* 6.

104.   The story of the building of Noah's ark and the coming of the flood is related in Gn 6–8. The ark here can also be considered to represent the church (the ship), which carries the faithful to heaven.

105.   The story of Moses leading the Israelites across the Red Sea is told in Ex 14: 19–31.

106.   This story is recounted in Mt 14:22–33: Peter walks across the water towards Christ but begins to sink as he is beset by doubts, until Christ reaches out to help him and raises him above the waves.

107.   The implication of this final tercet is that it is the poet's own humble and lowly state that precludes her from receiving such benefits.

108.   Noah's sanctity is confirmed in Gn 6:9: "Noe was a just and perfect man in his generations, he walked with God."

109.   All Saints Day, commemorated by this sonnet, is celebrated in the Western church on November 1.

110.   The fountain pouring from Christ's side is the blood from the wound in his side at the Crucifixion, which becomes a "holy treasure" in its status as a Christian symbol of life and of man's redemption through the shedding of Christ's blood. This

salutary quality is foregrounded by Christ at the Last Supper when he offers the wine to his disciples as his blood (see Mt 26:27–29).

111.   Acts 20:35: "It is a more blessed thing to give, rather than to receive." The argument is extremely pertinent in the context of this manuscript gift for Michelangelo, offered by Colonna to her friend as a personal spiritual gift with strong evangelical overtones. See Michelangelo's letter to Colonna, in which he struggles not to resist the obligation of the gift, cited in the volume editor's introduction, p. 32. See also Alexander Nagel, "Gifts for Michelangelo and Vittoria Colonna," Art Bulletin 79 (1997): 647–68.

112.   The status of God as lover of the true church is expressed with great sensuality in the biblical Song of Solomon.

113.   The notion of gift giving is central to sixteenth-century reformist theology, as reflected here. The poet describes her belief in sola fide in terms of her gratitude to God for his gift of grace coupled with her certainty of guaranteed salvation. Colonna's reformist tone is at its most explicit in sonnets such as this one.

114.   See Acts 22:11, in which Saul is blinded by the light of Christ and led forward by his companions.

115.   The first martyr was Stephen, stoned to death as a result of a sermon that aroused the wrath of the Jewish authorities in Jerusalem. See Acts 7:2–56.

116.   Acts 7:55–56: "But he, being full of the Holy Ghost, looking up steadfastly to heaven, saw the glory of God and Jesus standing on the right hand of God. And he said: Behold, I see the heavens opened and the Son of man standing on the right hand of God."

117.   The reference here is to Christ informing John of his imminent death at the Last Supper. That the "dearly beloved disciple" is John is clarified through the reference to his head upon Christ's breast, deriving from Jn 13:23: "Now there was leaning on Jesus' bosom one of his disciples, whom Jesus loved." This is traditionally read as a reference to John, who is often depicted in this posture at the Last Supper in Renaissance art. (See, for example, Giotto's depiction of the scene in the Scrovegni Chapel in Padua.)

118.   Together with two other disciples, John slept during Christ's agony in the garden of Gethsemane. See Mt 26:37, in which John is referred to as one of the sons of Zebedee.

119.   John the Evangelist is associated with the eagle; the source for this is found in Ez 1:5–14, and it is reiterated in Rv 4 and 3. Medieval commentators explained the association by the fact that the eagle, of all birds, flies closest to heaven, and John's vision of God was most pure and closest to the truth.

120.   This sonnet deals with Virgin's conflicting states of mind at moment of Christ's death, her mother's grief and her simultaneous thanksgiving at the salvation of humankind that he has enacted. This is a subject explored in some detail in other works by Colonna, most notably in her prose meditation, the Pianto della Marchesa di Pescara sopra la passione di Cristo. It is also a conflict reflected powerfully in Michelangelo's gift drawing of the Pietà made for Colonna at around the same time as this manuscript gift, in 1540. See Nagel, "Gifts for Michelangelo and Vittoria Colonna"; and Brun-

din, "Vittoria Colonna and the Virgin Mary." It is interesting to note that the sonnet closes with the insistence upon Mary's humanity (line 12), rather than her divinity, in line with reformist rethinking of the role of the mother of Christ.

121.   As in the previous sonnet, the paradox of joy in grief is laid bare, here emphasized by the juxtaposition of the two verbs "open" and "close" in line 9, which drives home their painful yet necessary interrelation.

122.   The reference to a "mortal blow" derives from Simeon's words to Mary in the temple where Christ is brought to be blessed after the Nativity, Lk 2 : 35: "And thy own soul a sword shall pierce, that, out of many hearts thoughts may be revealed." In the Christian church Candlemas is celebrated on February 2, commemorating through the words of the *Nunc Dimittis* Simeon's acknowledgment of Christ as the light of the world. Simeon's prediction of Mary's grief at this time has established Candlemas as a pivot in the church year, looking backwards to the Nativity and simultaneously forwards to the events of the Passion and Christ's suffering, death, and Resurrection. Here, of course, Mary's faith in Christ is sufficient to protect her from the sword.

123.   Mary is well established in the traditions of Renaissance Roman Catholic Mariology as the Mediatrix between humankind and Christ, begging for clemency on behalf of all sinners. The original Italian version of this sonnet sets up an echo between the "mortal colpo" of line 13 and the "colpa antica" of line 11: Mary is thus reconfirmed as the "second Eve" (or second mother) of Gn 3 : 15, who cancels the sin of the first Eve through her coming. For the history of debate surrounding the interpretation of this much-disputed passage from Genesis, see Graef, *Mary: A History of Doctrine and Devotion*, 1–3; Constance Jordan, *Renaissance Feminism: Literary Texts and Political Models* (Ithaca, NY: Cornell University Press, 1990), 21–24, 88–89.

124.   Mary's status as one of the disciples who follows Christ and learns from his teachings is not one that is alluded to in the New Testament gospels. Colonna seems determined in much of her poetry and many prose works, however, to establish a more active role for Mary during her lifetime. See Brundin, "Vittoria Colonna and the Virgin Mary."

125.   The "greater bonds" that reinforce Mary's love for Christ presumably refer to the Coronation of the Virgin in heaven after her Assumption, where she is enthroned at Christ's right hand to coreign with him as the *Regina Coeli*, Queen of Heaven. Such imagery derives most directly from Gothic art of the thirteenth century (Hall, *Dictionary of Subjects and Symbols in Art*, 323–25).

126.   The reference to Christ's three distinct roles in relation to Mary, as father, son, and husband, mirrors the four roles she is able to play towards him cited in lines 10–11. The breadth and variety of Mary's roles are significant and are a theme reiterated elsewhere in Colonna's poetry (see for example sonnet 95). As with the mention in the first quatrain of her work as a disciple of Christ, the inference is that the poet is seeking ways in which to underline Mary's multifaceted and complex manifestations.

127.   The reward granted to Mary is probably an allusion to the Assumption, when tradition maintains that she was lifted by angels into heaven (unlike Christ who ascended unaided).

128.   The sonnet refers to one of the two Saint Luke Madonnas in Rome, paintings of the Madonna attributed to the disciple Luke. The poet does not make it clear whether she is referring to the painting housed in Santa Maria del Popolo or that in Santa Maria Maggiore, but she could well have been familiar with both.

129.   Although initially the poet wonders whether the divinity of his subject has overwhelmed Luke and blocked his artistry, she here decides that he has rather turned away from overly sophisticated methods in favor of a simple yet heartfelt rendering of his subject. A parallel comes to mind with a passage from Castiglione's dedicatory letter to the *Book of the Courtier* (1528), in which he excuses his "portrait" of the court of Urbino for its crude lack of sophistication: "not by the hand of Raphael or Michelangelo, but by a lowly painter who only knows how to sketch in the main outlines, and who cannot adorn the truth with beautiful colours or through the art of perspective make it seem that which it is not" (Baldassare Castiglione, *Il libro del cortegiano*, ed. Ettore Bonora [Milan: Mursia, 1988], 25). Although the author's tone is self-effacing, the inference is that such artistic "progress," while attractive, is also inherently dangerous and misleading. See, on the reformist tendency to search for earlier, less sophisticated models as a way back to a more untrammeled faith, Alexander Nagel, *Michelangelo and the Reform of Art* (Cambridge: Cambridge University Press, 2000), 1–22.

130.   This sonnet refers to the legend of Saint Ursula, which existed in several versions in the Middle Ages, including in the *Golden Legend*, although its origins cannot be traced. Ursula, the daughter of a king of Brittany, died together with eleven thousand virgin companions in a massacre at Cologne on their return from a pilgrimage to Rome. Saint Ursula's saint's day is celebrated on October 21, perhaps the reason for the composition of this sonnet. In addition, the poet could be alluding to the work of the Company of Saint Ursula, founded in Brescia in 1535 by Angela Merici as a group of laywomen dedicated to serving the poor and the sick (see Weisner, *Women and Gender in Early Modern Europe* (Cambridge: Cambridge University Press, 1993), 196. The poet is clearly envisioning Saint Ursula and her companions through a process of meditative contemplation, as the juxtaposition of "eye" in line 1 with "mind" in line 5 makes clear. Here the poet imagines angels descending from heaven with the palms and crowns of Christian martyrdom, which they will present to the eleven thousand virgins, their "prey."

131.   The organization of this final tercet is tripartite: the virgins have earned high praise, the angels still rejoice in their accomplishment, and God alone bears the responsibility for all events. The virgins are "wise" (line 11) because they recognize, as the final tercet asserts, that they are only instruments of God's will.

132.   1 Cor 13:12: "We see now through a glass in a dark manner: but then face to face."

133.   According to Greek myth, Delos is the island where Apollo was born. Here Apollo, the Sun God, is allied with the sun, which represents Jesus Christ, and Delos becomes the humble cattle shed where the Nativity took place.

134.   This sonnet presents the idea that the elected souls have existed in Paradise from the beginning of creation and could therefore look down upon the earth at the

time of Christ's birth, as recounted here. Dante, in *Paradiso* 30, describes these elect as existing in the Empyrean in the form of white roses, which are "pollinated" by angels flying between them and God. While in sonnet 34 the poet imagines the troops of the elect gathering for battle, here, employing the same militaristic imagery, she envisions that battle won at the moment of the Nativity, when salvation was guaranteed. The stress seems to be on the same incarnational theology outlined in the notes to sonnet 30.

135.   Andrew was a Galilean fisherman and brother to Peter. He was the first to follow Christ. See Jn 1 : 40 – 41.

136.   Andrew's recognition of the potency and sweetness of the Crucifixion is significant. According to the apocryphal third-century "Acts of Andrew," retold in the *Golden Legend*, he too was crucified, by Egeas, the Roman governor of Patras in the Peloponnese, although he was bound to the cross with rope rather than fixed with nails.

137.   Mt 2 tells of the star that guides the wise men from the East to the manger where the infant Christ lies.

138.   The manner in which the poet encourages her reader to concentrate upon the details of Christ's lowly birthplace is in line with the practice of empathic meditation, laid down most succinctly in a text such as the anonymous thirteenth-century *Meditationes vitae Christi* (attributed to Saint Bonaventure), which advises the faithful to concentrate in particular upon the most pathetic elements of Christ's life cycle, in order to be moved more easily to pity and understanding. See David Freedberg, *The Power of Images. Studies in the History and Theory of Response* (Chicago: University of Chicago Press, 1989), on Renaissance practices of empathic meditation; see also Brundin, "Vittoria Colonna and the Virgin Mary," 68.

139.   Christ, although still a tiny child, is here depicted as the brave leader of these other innocent children. The flight from Bethlehem into Egypt, when Joseph learns in a dream of Herod's plan to destroy Christ, is recounted in Mt 2 : 13 – 14.

140.   This sonnet commemorates the Massacre of the Innocents from Mt 2 : 16. These Holy Innocents were venerated as the first martyrs from early in the Christian era (see Hall, *Dictionary of Subjects and Symbols in Art*, 204 – 5).

141.   The infants are "faithless" because they were murdered before Baptism, although this does not detract from their venerated position as Holy Innocents, often included in depictions of the Virgin and Child with saints in early modern Italian art.

142.   The Italian word "amori," used here for the babies, in combination with the image of sprouting wings, is very evocative of classical *putti* or *amorini*, cherubs. This seems to be another instance, as found in numerous of Colonna's sonnets, in which the poetic imagery is clearly informed by the visual arts.

143.   In a letter to her cousin Costanza D'Avalos Piccolomini (first published in Venice in 1544), Colonna explores the same theme of the wondrous nature of the Virgin's maternal duties. See Brundin, "Vittoria Colonna and the Virgin Mary," 78 – 79.

144.   The poet maintains here that her previous questions are inappropriate for one whose instructions come directly from God. The mysteries of faith are not intended

to be understood by the mortal man, who should not presume to seek clarification (O'Malley, *Praise and Blame in Renaissance Rome,* 49).

145.   A reference once again to the wonder of the Hypostasis.

146.   Referring to the Assumption of the Virgin, which saw her raised to heaven to sit beside Christ as his bride. While there is no biblical precedent for this belief, it was established early in the apocryphal gospels and popular practice of the church. Mary's Assumption was finally declared an article of faith by Pius XII in 1950.

147.   Here, as in so many of her sonnets addressed to the Virgin, the poet clearly holds her up as a role model for imitation by others, in her unwavering devotion, faith, and strength of purpose. In particular, in the penultimate tercet, the poet implies that she herself wavers in her faith because of the relentless demands of reason.

148.   The Virgin is often traditionally referred to as *Stella Maris,* or star of the sea, deriving from the meaning of the Hebrew form of her name, Miriam. Thus she comes also to represent the protectress of seamen and sailors, who associate her with the north or morning star. "Our sea" is the sea of life over which man must journey. See the notes to sonnet 22.

149.   These are references to Mary's maternal duties on earth, when she nurtured Christ (the sun) in human form.

150.   The ancient enemy is Satan, who attempts to lead humankind into sin.

151.   As Mary is identified with the *Stella Maris,* so too Christ is traditionally identified with the "bright and morning star" of Rv 22 : 16. Such associations derive from the ancient Greek and Roman practice of identifying the stars with various of the gods.

152.   The sonnet addresses the army of angels led by the Archangel Michael, who fought Satan and the other rebel angels in heaven and cast them out. For a more detailed explanation, see note 1 to sonnet 16.

153.   Once again the poet seems to be referring to the practice of empathic meditation on the holy stories, in this case, through gazing at a crucifix. Initially, her concentration on Christ's terrible suffering at the Passion leads to horror and pity, but in accordance with the instructions laid down in works such as the *Meditationes vitae Christi,* this pity then cleanses the soul and gives rise to purer faith and hope.

154.   The poet instructs her heart to rejoice at the Crucifixion, rather than to weep and grieve. Such an approach is absolutely in line with reformist attitudes to the Passion. In her prose meditation, *Pianto [. . .] sopra la passione di Cristo,* Colonna takes the opposite approach and shows Mary mourning at the Crucifixion. Contemporary sources state that this work drew criticism from other reformists for its lack of the appropriate joy and thanksgiving (see Simoncelli, *Evangelismo italiano del Cinquecento,* 216–17; see also Brundin, "Vittoria Colonna and the Virgin Mary," 68–76).

155.   While the Roman Catholic faith offers prayer and other penance as means of cleansing the mortal soul of sin, the reformist attitude, reflected here, maintains that we are all irrevocably sinful, a state we cannot hope or work to change, but those of us born with faith will be saved nonetheless.

156.   There is a strong neo-Platonic flavor to the image of the wings of holy love that the Christian must carry upon his back. Plato, in *Phaedrus 7,* describes the mortal soul using the figure of two winged horses driven by a charioteer and recounts the

myth of the ascent of the soul to a realm outside the cosmos where "True Being" dwells.

157.   The images in the second quatrain refer to Christ's sermon on the mount, Mt 7:24–27. The solid rock is faith in God, which should, as Christ preaches, form the firm foundations of all our lives.

158.   The sign that the proud fear and the faithful yearn for is death and by association perhaps the trumpet call at the Day of Judgment, which will call all the elect to heaven, as illustrated in Mt 24:31.

159.   The last line is a reference to Christ's death upon the cross, which has paved the way for humankind to find salvation.

160.   The "happy day" is Good Friday, on which Christ offered his body upon the cross in sacrifice for the sins of humankind. Here again, as in sonnet 55, the poet expresses joy at the scene of the Crucifixion in line with reformist practice.

161.   As elsewhere (see, for example, sonnet 2), the poet refers to the imagery deriving from Christ's words in Jn 6:35: "I am the bread of life." In addition, this is an allusion to the Last Supper, recounted in Mt 26, which takes place shortly before Christ is betrayed by Judas and condemned to death.

162.   The poet refers in the final tercets to the state of mind needed by the faithful in order to accept the immensity of Christ's gift of salvation. Once again, the stress is on the reformist notion of the impossibility of reciprocation (see also the notes to sonnet 39). The proud feel horror because they recognize the enormous disparity between the wealth of Christ's gift and their own spiritual poverty; the meek, on the other hand, rejoice in this disparity.

163.   There is an allusion here, as in sonnet 14, to the story of Zacchaeus, which is recounted in Lk 19. Once again the poet gives thanks for the honor Christ does her in entering her home, here not her physical dwelling, but her heart.

164.   Juxtapositions of contrasting images are a frequent element of Colonna's poetry, deriving in the main from her primary poetic model Petrarch. Here the imagery of fire and ice, and the notion of being simultaneously urged on and held back, can be seen to have their most direct literary roots in sonnet 178, "Amor mi sprona in un tempo et affrena" ('Love at once urges me on and holds me back'). Dante employs similar "fire and ice" imagery in *Paradiso* 33, in which the sun melts the snow as understanding floods the poet's heart. This entire sonnet rests on the sustained use of such contrasting imagery.

165.   The manner in which the poet's faith is personified and presented here is interesting, reflecting as it does a reformist belief in the working of faith outside the control of the individual, who responds to its call but cannot hope to supplement or improve it through good works.

166.   The poet's excuse for daring to write of heavenly things, when, as she has clearly stated in previous sonnets, her mortal intellect is insufficient, is that such matters are the only fitting topic for poetry. See in addition sonnet 98, addressed to Pietro Bembo, in which Colonna urges him to turn his poetic muse to spiritual matters.

167.   The imagery of knots and bonds, frequent in Colonna's verse, derives from Petrarch, who also commonly refers to the knots and ties of love, which bind both

his tongue and his heart. See for example sonnets 59, 71, 73, 119, 175, and 197 of his *Canzoniere*. There is also a biblical precedent for such imagery in Mk 7:35, when a man who was deaf and had a stammer is cured by Christ so that the bonds fall from his tongue. Here the poet employs the imagery to assert that her poetry is God-given (he "moves her thoughts" and thus dictates her writing) and therefore intimately linked to her faith. Significantly, such avoidance of responsibility for the act of writing is a useful literary ploy for the woman writer seeking a public reputation for humility, and there is a clear religious precedent for this in the role of Mary as the scribe of the *Magnificat*, taking dictation from a divine source.

168.   2 Cor 3:16: "But when they shall be converted to the Lord, the veil shall be taken away."

169.   In Gal 3:27, Paul presents the image of the Christian clothed in faith in Christ, an image that is often employed in the evangelical literature of the Renaissance period and that Colonna re-evokes on occasion in her poetry, as here.

170.   In his *Canzoniere*, Petrarch uses the imagery of the "fuggitivo raggio," the fugitive ray that shines from Laura and that he cannot capture or pin down (see sonnet 23); likewise, Laura holds the key to his heart and mind (see, for example, sonnet 143). This Petrarchan imagery is redeployed by Colonna in the service of her new, entirely spiritual subject matter.

171.   The serpent is the creature that tempted Eve in the Garden of Eden and thus brought about the Fall of man, made good through Christ's sacrifice upon the cross.

172.   Once again, as in sonnet 24, the poet stresses that humility is the primary Christian virtue, the adversary of which is pride.

173.   The notion of the perfume of Christ derives from Paul's words in 2 Cor 2:14–16, in which he describes the faith carried within each Christian as the "good odor of Christ."

174.   Once again the sensuality of this opening quatrain is notable, reflecting the particular reformist inflection of the poet's relationship with Christ.

175.   God's brave warrior is Christ, who faces the crucifix alone and unarmed. The militaristic imagery can once again be seen to have a reformist precedent in works such as the *Beneficio di Cristo*.

176.   This is probably a reference to Colonna's plan, never realized, to travel to the Holy Land on a personal pilgrimage to Christ's birthplace. (She hoped also to pass via the site of the Magdalene's retreat in the south of France.) See the letter from Pope Paul III granting permission for Colonna's pilgrimage, in Colonna, *Carteggio*, 2d ed., ed. Ermanno Ferrero and Giuseppe Müller, supplemented by Domenico Tordi (Turin: Ermanno Loescher, 1892), 131–32; also Peter Armour, "Michelangelo's Two Sisters: Contemplative Life and Active Life in the Final Version of the Monument to Julius II," in *Sguardi sull'Italia. Miscellanea dedicata a Francesco Villari dalla Society for Italian Studies*, ed. Gino Bedani et al., 55–83 (Exeter: Society for Italian Studies, 1997).

177.   These "gente intrepida" of whom the poet has heard talk are perhaps missionaries working in the service of Christ in the recently discovered New World. If so, the poet views their mission as entirely laudable (although arguments over the ugly practices taking place in the colonies were already raging in this period). Her

idealism reflects her view of a vast evangelical project, advancing and confirming on a worldwide scale the more circumscribed activities of her own group of evangelical "missionaries" in Italy, the *spirituali*, who also endured "suffering and death" in later years at the hands of the Inquisition. Alternatively, she could be referring to the Protestant martyrs who were spearheading the wave of reformist feeling sweeping northern Europe in this period, although such an overt allusion to the Reformation in this context might seem surprising.

178.   A reference to the proselytizing work of Christ's twelve disciples.

179.   Addressed to Gabriel, who took the message of the birth of Christ to Mary, although in fact the sonnet treats, once again, the poet's desire to learn from the example of the Virgin. Lady Day, celebrating the Annunciation to the Virgin, is celebrated in the Roman Catholic calendar on March 25.

180.   The language here is strongly reminiscent of Mary's opening words in the *Magnificat* (Lk 1:46–55).

181.   As in sonnet 4, there is an echo of Saint Paul in 2 Cor 3:3. Once again, the poet's desire to witness the particularities of a holy scene, down to its tiniest details, recalls the intimate practice of empathic meditation.

182.   This sonnet describes the experience of Saint Ignatius of Antioch, also called "Theophorus" (the God-bearer—see 2 Cor 6:16), who was martyred in ca. 107 A.D. Bishop of Antioch in Syria for forty years, Ignatius was taken to Rome under the Emperor Trajan and thrown to wild beasts in the amphitheater during the public games. En route to Rome he wrote seven letters concerning the faith, which are still extant and have caused a great deal of controversy among theologians (see William Schoedel, *Ignatius of Antioch: A Commentary on the Letters of Ignatius of Antioch*, ed. Helmut Koester [Philadelphia: Fortress Press, 1985]). Ignatius used for the first time the term "the Catholic Church" to designate all Christians and explored notions of the church as divinely established—a factor that caused Calvin, among other reformers, to dismiss the letters as misguided and probably fake (see *Institutes* 1–3). Colonna may perhaps have composed this sonnet on his saint's day, February 1.

183.   The shield mentioned here is the shield of faith.

184.   See Jn 1:9, on the Light of Christ, which John was sent by God to bear witness: "That was the true Light, which enlighteneth every man that cometh into this world."

185.   Plato uses the Allegory of the Cave, in *Republic* 7, to describe the limited perspective of humankind, dwelling underground and taking shadows on the wall to be reality.

186.   The poet emphasizes in this quatrain the infirmity of the human will, which causes our actions to fail to reflect our desires. Her interpretation differs here from that of Michelangelo, who, in a poem such as "Vorrei voler, Signor, quel ch'io non voglio" ('I wish I wanted, Lord, what I don't want'; Buonarroti, *The Poetry of Michelangelo*, 208), pinpoints instead the inaction of a divided will that is at war with itself (a concept he adopts from Petrarch). See Thomas E. Mussio,"The Augustinian Conflict in the Lyrics of Michelangelo: Michelangelo Reading Petrarch," *Italica* 74 (1997): 339–59 at 340–42.

187. Mt 3:3: "Prepare ye the way of the Lord, make straight his paths" (also in Mk 1:3 and Lk 3:4).

188. There seems to be an echo here of the famous Psalm 22, especially of verse 4, "For though I should walk in the midst of the shadow of death."

189. Acts 26:13: "At midday, O king, I saw in the way a light from heaven, above the brightness of the sun, shining round about me and them that were in company with me."

190. The imagery is reminiscent of Paul's words to Elymas the sorcerer in Acts 13:11: "And now behold, the hand of the Lord is upon thee: and thou shalt be blind, not seeing the sun for a time. And immediately there fell a mist and darkness upon him: and going about, he sought some one to lead him by the hand."

191. The poet introduces a neo-Platonic belief in the possibility of ascension from the imperfect mirror of light found in the stars to the perfect light of the sun. In the same way, in the development of her verses from amorous to spiritual, the poet's early love for her husband, the mortal mirror, leads her gradually to a spiritual love for Christ, which aspires to be perfect and complete. Michelangelo's manuscript, of course, lacks any of the earlier *rime amorose* and presents the reader only with the image of the poet's loving bond with Christ, but it is a bond that, in its intimacy, recalls the mortal love for her husband that has inspired it.

192. At the scene of the Crucifixion, at the moment of Christ's death the earth shook and the rocks were rent wide. This event is described in Mt 27:51; Mk 15:38; and Lk 23:45. The "figures" cited here could be constellations, shaking as the earth is rent, or alternatively the meaning could be more allusive, perhaps figurative writings that have until this time been unintelligible to man (and this reading is reinforced by line 8). The imagery used by the poet in this opening quatrain is close to that of a late sonnet by Michelangelo, in which the physical effects of the Crucifixion are described. See Buonarroti, *The Poetry of Michelangelo*, 494.

193. Evangelical texts such as the *Beneficio di Cristo* placed a special emphasis on a God of love, not fear, a notion derived from the teachings of Saint Paul (see, for example, 1 Tm 1 and Mantova, *Il Beneficio di Cristo*, 77–78). The Old Testament abject fear of the Lord is replaced by a more intimate relationship with a sweet and loving Christ, a change clearly reflected in Colonna's intimate attitude towards Christ in her verses as has been alluded to elsewhere.

194. See Paul's advice in Eph 6:11: "Put you on the armor of God, that you may be able to stand against the deceits of the devil."

195. God, the Cosmic Mind, is represented in Aristotelian and Platonic thought as a sphere containing the whole universe including spirit, mind, and matter in descending concentric circles. (See, for example, Aristotle, *Metaphysics* 8.12) The imagery used here by the poet is also strongly Dantean, evoking Dante's journey in the *Paradiso* through the celestial spheres and into Empyrean.

196. An apostle, although not one of the original twelve, first mentioned in the New Testament at the stoning of Stephen (see sonnet 40), Paul was converted on the road to Damascus (Acts 9:1–9) and thereafter devoted himself to converting the gentiles, as his Epistles document. Of special relevance for Lutherans and other re-

formists, Paul is cited as the source for the controversial doctrine of *sola fide* to which Colonna was strongly attached (see Rm 3:28).

197.   Dionysius the Areopagite was converted by Paul (Acts 17:34) and may have become the first bishop of Athens. He is often conflated with Dionysius of Paris, third-century bishop and martyr and patron saint of France (Saint Denis).

198.   The imagery is reminiscent of Ps 35:10: "For with thee is the fountain of life: in thy light we shall see light."

199.   Once again, as in sonnet 66, the poet seems to be referring to the shadows of Socrates' Allegory of the Cave in Plato's *Republic*.

200.   The references to sparks and chains could both have a possible neo-Platonic resonance. In the *De vita coelitus comperanda* (1489), Ficino refers to the concept of the *archon*, when light joins matter and is transformed, creating sparks of life specific to each individual being. The chains of love in line 3 evoke the neo-Platonic *vinculum animae* or chain of the soul, which binds mortals to God. See D. P. Walker, *Spiritual and Demonic Magic: From Ficino to Campanella* (London: Sutton Publishing, 2000), 96–106. Dante's *Paradiso* has many flying sparks. See, for example, *Paradiso* 28.88–93.

201.   The term to describe the contrasting of light and shade in art to give a sculptural and three-dimensional quality, an effect used particularly in the Baroque period in the work of a painter such as Caravaggio. Colonna is clearly drawing on pictorial qualities in order to represent the difficult concept (also treated by Dante in, for example, *Paradiso* 30) of pure light, shadowless yet still able to produce difference.

202.   The reference is to the Virgin Mary, who stands second to Christ in the celestial hierarchy.

203.   The impossibility of representing with any accuracy the beauty and holiness of Mary is alluded to here. The same theme is explored in the context of the visual arts in sonnet 45, on the Saint Luke Madonna.

204.   Once again, as in sonnet 69, God is represented as a celestial sphere, surrounded here by the stars that are the angels who accompany him in the heavens. In the *Paradiso*, Dante describes the presence of God in a similar way, as a shining circle of light reflected on the surface of the Primum Mobile (see *Paradiso* 30.100–8).

205.   The poet alludes to her incapacity to express the divine concepts and images that she sees in her mind's eye, a continuation of the notion expressed in the previous sonnet of the impossibility of representation.

206.   There is a definite reformist character to the idea expressed here that the Christian is ultimately helpless without the guidance and preferment of God. The doctrine of *sola fide* essentially deprives the faithful of the power to act in any way to change their preordained fate. See also sonnet 21.

207.   The apostle Thomas or Didymus (twin), popularly called "Doubting Thomas," was absent at the moment of Christ's Resurrection and refused to believe the news until Christ placed his fingers in the wounds in his hands and side. See Jn 20:19–29.

208.   Thomas expresses here, no doubt on behalf of the poet, the reformist certainty of salvation through faith in Christ.

209.   Christ's words here are a paraphrase of his message in Jn 20:29: "blessed are they that have not seen and have believed." He implicitly criticizes Thomas for re-

quiring proof of the Resurrection instead of having faith in that which he was asked to believe. So too, the poet implicitly alludes to herself and her own difficulty in overcoming the actions of her reason.

210.   The poet once again employs the close juxtaposition of opposites in order to reinforce the paradox of salvation through death. See also sonnets 43 and 58 for striking examples of this technique.

211.   The poet chooses a very practical and familiar image here, in a Dantesque vein, in order to reinforce the reader's engagement with the spiritual attitude she then goes on to advocate, of seeking in every possible way to shore up faith (the fire) against the assaults of worldly experience (the cruel wind).

212.   In line with the practice of empathic meditation, the poet once again focuses on the most pitiful aspects of Christ's state at the Passion in order to evoke in herself the necessary level of pity and repentance. And again she highlights the paradox of Christ's victory won through humility and defeat, as in sonnet 61.

213.   Once again the poet alludes to our inability to understand the wonders of God's actions, which we must simply accept with gratitude. See also sonnets 72 and 73.

214.   Another subtle reference to the reformist doctrine of *sola fide.*

215.   Again the poet expresses the essential anti-intellectualism of the reformist position. It is not knowledge gained from books, but faith, which is God-given, that assures salvation. See also sonnet 25.

216.   The imagery is strongly reminiscent of the verse from Sg 8:6: "Put me as a seal upon thy heart." See also 2 Cor 1:22, which depicts a similar image.

217.   This sonnet is addressed to Christ, the poet's "dolce conforto," but was written for Michelangelo in response to a poem from him. See the introduction, p. 29, for a fuller discussion.

218.   As in sonnets 22 and 35, the poet makes use of the Petrarchan conceit of the bark cast out to sea to describe the state of her soul.

219.   God the Father is often represented as an eye in early art, sometimes framed in a triangle to symbolize the Holy Trinity. The eye represents his all-seeing power and is referred to in Ps 33:16 and Prv 15:3. A Renaissance example of such imagery is the depiction of the *Supper at Emmaus* by Jacopo Pontormo (1525, in the Uffizi, Florence), in which a triangle framing an eye dominates the picturescape above Christ's head (see Peter Murray and Linda Murray, *The Oxford Companion to Christian Art and Architecture* [Oxford: Oxford University Press, 1996], 177).

220.   Adam blamed Eve in Genesis for leading him into disobeying God. Now that Christ has redeemed their sin through his sacrifice, the poet maintains that humankind can no longer excuse its sinful state but must openly declare it to God (as, according to the doctrine of *sola fide,* it will not in any case impede its access to grace).

221.   This reference to music picks up on the earlier mention of the celestial choirs in sonnet 31. In the *Paradiso,* Dante describes the music that emanates from the "living lights" shining in the heavens and the sound of flutes and angelic chimes that reach his ears. Like the poet in sonnet 73, Dante too finds himself unable to commit the wonder of all that he witnesses in heaven to memory and the songs he hears cannot later be recalled. See *Paradiso* 20.10—21.

222. The composer of the celestial music is of course God, who controls its beats and harmonies as the poet describes. In the story of the Nativity, a heavenly choir descends to earth to announce the birth of Christ to a group of humble shepherds (Lk 2 : 13–14). The poet's allusion to the beauty of variety in lines 12–13 perhaps reflects this, in indicating that God's music extends to all of humankind regardless of status or situation, just as all Christians, regardless of their station, must act as evangelists of the message of Christ (Mt 28 : 18–20).

223. The lines refer to the Immaculate Conception, that is, the fact that Mary was conceived without a trace of original sin and therefore set apart from the rest of humankind by the grace of God. Although exempt from sin, however, she was not exempted from the temporal penalties incurred by Adam and Eve, that is, sorrow, infirmity, and death. The scriptural "proof" for this much-debated concept (which was only made dogma by Pius IX in 1854) is found in Gn 3 : 15. As the new Eve to Christ's new Adam, Mary is restored to the state of sinlessness that Eve enjoyed before the Fall. See also Lk 1 : 28 and Sg 4 : 7.

224. The universal knot of sin binds all of humankind, made in Adam's image from birth and despite ourselves. Mary was never unbound because she was never bound, having been born immaculate.

225. In Rv 21 : 11, the heavenly city of Jerusalem is described as emitting a light "clear as crystal." Jerusalem has been taken to symbolize the bride of Christ, or the true church, both also manifestations of Mary, thus the link made by the poet here between the Virgin and the crystal.

226. The reference is once again to the straight and narrow path to heaven from Mt 7 : 14.

227. Addressed to Catherine of Alexandria, who was famously tied to a spiked wheel to be martyred for refusing the advances of the Emperor Maxentius, but who was saved when God smote the wheel with a heavenly thunderbolt and released her. She was later executed by the Emperor and came to be venerated as the patron saint of education and eloquence, students, noblewomen, and spinsters (see Hall, *Dictionary of Subjects and Symbols in Art,* 58–59). Catherine's Feast Day is celebrated on November 25.

228. The heavenly mountain where God resides is referred to in Rv 21 : 10.

229. Catherine's body was, according to legend, carried to Mount Sinai by angels for burial. This is also the place where Moses received the tablets of stone upon which were written the ten commandments; Ex 19–20.

230. In a published letter to her cousin, Costanza D'Avalos Piccolomini, Colonna explored the potential of Catherine of Alexandria and of Mary Magdalene as role models, whose examples were more attainable for the mortal woman than that of the most perfect Virgin Mary. See Brundin, "Vittoria Colonna and the Virgin Mary," 79–80.

231. The nautical imagery of sea and boats once again has a strong Petrarchan resonance to it, reminiscent in particular of sonnet 189. See also his sonnets 34 and 345.

232. The "holy light" of line 7, referred to again here, is the light of Christ, who guides the servant to calmer waters.

233.   The concept being outlined here has a notably reformist slant to it. The poet suggests that we are not on earth to atone for our sins, as Roman Catholic orthodoxy dictates. Thus the faithful need not remain continually in penance for past sins but can look forward optimistically to their guaranteed salvation. This wholly positive stance essentially frees the Christian from guilt for all past wrongdoings.

234.   These "ornate veils" are the trappings and luxuries of a worldly existence, which distract man from the true worth of the spiritual life.

235.   That which is buried alive is presumably faith, in an age in which, as the poet here laments, so much status is ascribed to the meaningless things of this world.

236.   This sonnet is rather obscure, yet its sense of crisis is notable. The poet seems to be calling for some sign from God or some radical action to restore true virtue to humans before it is too late. The definition of her own age as a "cursed century" arises perhaps from her sense of anxiety about the crisis in which the Roman Catholic Church now finds itself.

237.   The reference is to the three kings who came to worship the Christ child. See Mt 2. After they have visited the baby in Bethlehem (guided there by the star), the kings learn in a dream of Herod's evil intentions towards Christ and return home via another route in order to evade him. The "true path" cited by the poet in line 4 is of course figurative, signifying the path of faith.

238.   Once again this is a reference to the sin of Adam and Eve, which led to the Fall in the Book of Genesis.

239.   As in sonnet 24, the emphasis is again on humility as the primary virtue.

240.   This is another reference to Doubting Thomas, who was not able to believe in the Resurrection until he had placed his hand in Christ's wound. Lines 7–8 point to Thomas's error in failing to believe the word of the other disciples and seeking proof.

241.   In Greek mythology, Procne was the wife of Tereus, who raped her sister Philomela. She retaliated by killing their son Itys and feeding him to his father and was turned into a swallow. Philomela became a nightingale. The, perhaps rather surprising, link here is via the notion of feeding upon blood, in Procne's case the blood of her son Itys, but here it is the blood of Christ, which is wholly good and nourishing. Christ is also referred to as a bird feeding his chicks in Mt 23:37.

242.   This appears to be a wholly orthodox response to the events of the Passion, which inspire waves of weeping and shame in those who contemplate them. Such a response is in stark contrast to the joyful celebration of the Passion advocated in reformist circles.

243.   Christ as the light of the world is cited in Jn 8:12 and 9:5.

244.   Presumably a reference to Christ's state of grace after the Ascension.

245.   The poet's conversation with Christ is highly personal, indicating once again her intimate and loving relationship with him. Here Christ expresses his hurt at the ungratefulness of humankind for his act of sacrifice.

246.   John the Baptist baptized Christ in the river Jordan during a general baptism of the people. At the moment when Christ rose out of the water, the heavens opened and the Holy Spirit descended in the form of a dove (referred to in line 11 of the

sonnet). See Mt 3:13–17; Mk 1:9–11; Lk 3:21–22; and Jn 1:29–34. Once again the poet is enacting a process of visualization and meditation as she composes this sonnet.

247.   Saint John's Day is celebrated on June 24. It is interesting that a number of the sonnets in this manuscript refer to specific dates and religious celebrations. Colonna, like Petrarch, appears to be highly influenced by the liturgical timetable, although her sonnet sequence in this manuscript does not follow a chronological sequence as Petrarch's does.

248.   The pledge or promise of salvation is offered at the moment of Baptism when the dove descends. It is fulfilled at the Crucifixion.

249.   The first spirits are probably the disciples of Christ, who witnessed his wondrous acts first hand and were therefore not slow to offer their souls to God in faith. The poet is aware of how frail and weak in comparison seems to be her own response and that of her contemporaries to the same call to faith.

250.   The rock can symbolize God, Christ, the church, or else, more generally, Christian steadfastness. See, for example, Ps 17:3; Mt 7:42 and 16:18; and 1 Cor 10:4.

251.   Addressed to a group evidently involved with the black art of alchemy, which the church made various attempts through the ages to condemn along with other magical practices. Alchemy was discussed and condemned by Petrarch in *De remediis utriusque fortunae* (1358), and Marsilio Ficino translated the *Corpus Hermeticum* into Latin in 1463 (a collection of the central texts of the tradition of Hellenistic Gnosticism attributed to the mythical Hermes Trismegistus, which allowed many to argue for the importance of magical practices in the Christian church). In Colonna's own period, Henricus Cornelius Agrippa published three books of *Occult Philosophy* in 1531, and an Italian vernacular treatise on alchemy by Vannoccio Biringuccio, *De la Pirotecnia*, was published in 1540. See Gareth Roberts, *The Mirror of Alchemy: Alchemical Ideas and Images in Manuscripts and Books from Antiquity to the Seventeenth Century* (Toronto: University of Toronto Press, 1995).

252.   The messenger of the gods on Olympus. More significantly in this context, Mercury is also the god of commerce, sometimes depicted with a money purse.

253.   Mars is the god of war and one of the twelve Olympians. He was known to be brutal and aggressive to the extent that even his parents, Jupiter and Juno, hated him. According to ancient alchemical texts, the five base metals to be used in the process were Mercury, Mars, Jupiter, Venus, and Saturn.

254.   The clever use of the alchemy metaphor allows the poet to reject earthly gold in favor of spiritual treasure created by Christ, the only true alchemist.

255.   The poet remains within the general theme explored in the previous sonnet, of man's material greed at the expense of his spiritual wealth. Here she expresses bitterness about the state of her contemporary society, which rewards material status over true moral worth.

256.   This image of a shower of treasure raining from Christ's wound is employed by the poet elsewhere, as in sonnet 38, for example. In addition to the reference to Mt 26, there are possible prefigurations in the imagery of Dt 28:12 and 32:2. This

form of imagery is also common in evangelical literature of the period. See Brundin, "Vittoria Colonna and the Poetry of Reform," 64–65.

257.   The most striking biblical precedent for this image is Rv 3:20: "Behold, I stand at the gate and knock. If any man shall hear my voice and open to me the door, I will come in to him and will sup with him: and he with me."

258.   The final tercet seems to be a reference to the disbelief and persecution faced by those who openly embrace a Christian faith, which is valued so little by the greedy world. The poet may have in mind the particular problems faced by her own group of reform-minded friends, perhaps even a specific individual such as her mentor Reginald Pole, who was criticized for his open-minded response to various reformist doctrines by more strictly orthodox members of the papal court. See Dermot Fenlon, *Heresy and Obedience in Tridentine Italy: Cardinal Pole and the Counter Reformation* (Cambridge: Cambridge University Press, 1972); Massimo Firpo, "Vittoria Colonna, Giovanni Morone e gli 'spirituali,'" *Rivista di storia e letteratura religiosa* 24 (1988): 211–61; Thomas F. Mayer, *Reginald Pole: Prince and Prophet* (Cambridge: Cambridge University Press, 2000).

259.   The atmosphere in this poem is of contained excitement and building tension before the great battle of faith (fought by the reformists) will begin. Once again the militaristic flavor is reminiscent of evangelical texts such as the *Beneficio di Cristo.*

260.   The call to arms of the trumpet bringing the faithful to battle has biblical precedents in the Old Testament. See, for example, Neh 4:20 and Is 18:3. In Mt 24:31 (cited in the notes to sonnet 8), the trumpet call is used to summon God's elect who have found salvation through faith.

261.   There are strong Petrarchan echoes to this line in the original Italian. See Petrarch's sonnet 7, line 1.

262.   1 Cor 4:5: "Therefore judge not before the time, until the Lord come, who both will bring to light the hidden things of darkness and will make manifest the counsels of the hearts. And then shall every man have praise from God." Similar imagery is explored in sonnet 5 and in 2 Cor 4:6.

263.   This detailed evocation of the Nativity scene is once more in line with the rules for successful empathic meditation on biblical events. See also sonnets 49, 55, and 64.

264.   In her meditative prose work, the *Pianto [. . .] sopra la passione di Cristo,* Colonna explores a similar theme to this one, expressing pity for and anger at all those who should have witnessed the Crucifixion, but who failed to attend and offer the Virgin their support. (She cites such figures as Martha, Lazarus, and various of the disciples, as well as more minor characters who had encountered Christ such as the Samaritan woman at the well from Jn 4.) See Brundin, "Vittoria Colonna and the Virgin Mary," 69. In this sonnet, the pity and anger are turned against herself, however, as she clearly feels that her meditation on events is not sufficient to evoke them as vividly as she wishes.

265.   The poet adopts the format of Petrarch's famous culminating *canzone* to the Virgin in the *Canzoniere,* "Vergine bella, che di sol vestita" (Beautiful Virgin, clothed in the sun, poem 366). The importance of Colonna's sonnet is testified to by the fact that it is the opening poem in the other gift manuscript assembled by the poet in

around 1540, which was offered as a gift to Marguerite de Navarre. See Brundin, "Vittoria Colonna and the Virgin Mary," 63–65.

266.   Once again the poet refers to the wonder of the Hypostasis. See, in addition, sonnets 3, 5, and 51.

267.   As in the earlier sonnet 44, emphasis is placed on Mary's ability to play a variety of roles in relation to Christ, which is viewed as a wholly affirmative quality.

268.   Stress is placed here on Mary's role as mediatrix and her infinite maternal pity for humankind, which causes her to intercede with Christ on our behalf.

269.   Christ warns against the evils of worldly greed in his sermon on the mount in Mt 6.

270.   This is of course another reference to the Day of Judgment, already cited in sonnets 34 and 56.

271.   The note of warning sounded here is quite at odds, in its pessimistic and morbid overtones, with the optimism and confidence displayed in a highly evangelical sonnet such as 68, which encourages humankind to cast off fear of the Lord in favor of a more intimate bond. Perhaps, as she nears the end of her sonnet cycle, the poet begins to suspect that her optimism has been misplaced (and see also the doubts expressed concerning the value of her lyric enterprise in the closing sonnet 103).

272.   Clearly drawing once more on the Petrarchan motif of the storm-tossed craft as a metaphor for the chaotic experience of life, the poet again overlays the image with strong Christian connotations. The imagery has a further personal association with Colonna, as her emblem, devised by Paolo Giovio, represents an unyielding rock battered by stormy waters, bearing the device *Conantia frangere frangunt* ('They break themselves in the attempt to break me'). Giovio interprets the rock as the representation of Colonna's unassailable virtue, which withstands any assault. See Paolo Giovio, *Dialogo dell'imprese militari e amorose*, ed. Maria Luisa Doglio (Rome: Bulzoni, 1978), 110–11.

273.   This sonnet is reminiscent of earlier poems composed on the island of Ischia and dedicated to the poet's deceased husband D'Avalos, in which the sea that surrounds the island is a negative and destructive force that assaults the vulnerable poet, abandoned by the death of her consort. (See, for example, "Provo tra duri scogli e fiero vento" ('Amid the hard rocks and the fierce winds I face'; *Rime*, 1982, 29.) Here her state has changed markedly, however, as she is no longer alone but anchored firmly to the rock of faith. Her personal and positive appropriation of the reformist message of *sola fide* in this sonnet reinforces the poet's authority, establishing her once again as among the group of the elect who will be granted salvation.

274.   The sonnet is addressed to the scholar and poet Pietro Bembo, undisputed grand master of the Petrarchan style in the period and Colonna's own poetic mentor for much of her life.

275.   In contrast to the attitude expressed in sonnet 45, on the Saint Luke Madonna, in which the poet praises the painter's lack of artistry, here she finds Bembo's ability to combine nature and art particularly laudable. Perhaps she is making a distinction between the genres of painting and poetry, in particular, the Petrarchan lyric, which she believed to require a greater level of control and artfulness than the painted image. The "paragone" debate on the relative merits of painting and poetry (as well as of painting and sculpture) was a popular forum for erudite discussion in the sixteenth

century. See Michael Baxandall, *Giotto and the Orators: Humanist Observers of Painting in Italy and the Discovery of Pictorial Composition* (Oxford: Clarendon, 1986).

276. Bembo was elected to the College of Cardinals in 1539, with the public backing of Colonna. He wrote to her after the event to thank her for her support, which he believed had greatly influenced the pope's decision (Colonna, *Carteggio,* 171–72). His new spiritual involvement after this point links him closely to the poet, in her own choice of a new spiritual direction expressed in the opening sonnet of this manuscript.

277. The poet pleads with Bembo not to abandon his poetic vocation but rather to turn it, as she has done, to the service of his new life. This plea underlines her conviction, expressed throughout this manuscript cycle, of the importance of poetry as a vehicle for exploring faith and as central to the internal spiritual development of the enlightened.

278. This sonnet is addressed to Cardinal Reginald Pole. Pole here embodies a dual role for the poet, as a son requiring her nurturing and protection and as, in turn, her own soul's protector from the doubts and fears that beset her as she searches for divine understanding. The reference to Pole here, and to Bembo in the previous sonnet, helps to link the sonnet cycle firmly to the poet's own contemporary Roman context (which was also, it should be remembered, that of her manuscript's recipient), and points out more clearly its reformist leanings.

279. Pole's mother Margaret was imprisoned by Henry VIII in 1539 and executed in 1541, essentially martyred for her son's failure to endorse the king's divorce and his subsequent move over to Rome.

280. The small plot is the grave of her husband D'Avalos, whom the poet has mourned in her verses for many years.

281. By referring to herself as the Cardinal's "second mother," the poet establishes a significant link with the role of the Virgin Mary, second mother after Eve according to Gn 3:15. The careful employment of such Marian terminology in order to legitimate public participation in literary activities is discussed in Brundin, "Vittoria Colonna and the Virgin Mary," 66–67.

282. The moon here acts as mediatrix between the sun and the earth, thus symbolizing the Virgin's role as mediatrix between humankind and God. Greek Christians considered the moon to be a mother, giving birth to each new morning, and thus made the connection between the harmony of the sun and moon and the ideal of the Church's relations with Christ (see Warner, *Alone of All Her Sex,* 257–58). Classical associations link the moon with Diana, virgin goddess and also goddess of the hunt, which emphasizes her strength and autonomy.

283. The darkness of original sin is rendered "radiant" by the moon's intercession, just as Mary is the second Eve whose coming serves to cancel the former's sin and curse according to interpretations of Gn 3.

284. The reference to milk and nurturing underlines the connection between the moon and the Virgin Mary. Here the Virgin's milk dampens the fire of God's anger as she acts as intercessor, moved always by her deep pity and understanding of humankind's plight.

285. The Apostle Peter left his boat and nets on the Sea of Galilee to follow Christ and become the leader of the other disciples. He was later made first bishop of Rome.

Mt 16:18–19 recounts Christ's metaphorical handing over of the keys of authority to Peter, a subject often depicted in Renaissance art. Peter's overloaded net here symbolizes the dire state of the Roman Catholic Church, which is burdened with corruption and vice and, in the poet's opinion, in desperate need of reform.

286. The successor of Peter as Bishop of Rome is in this period Pope Paul III, who in 1540 was still seeking a compromise with the reformers from Northern Europe and endeavoring to cleanse the church from within. One of Paul III's ill-fated attempts at this was the convening of a reforming council, which included Reginald Pole among its numbers, in Rome in 1536. The council produced a frank document, the *Consilium de emendanda ecclesia* (Advice on the Reform of the Church) but ultimately failed to make any noticeable move towards reform. See G. R. Elton, *Reformation Europe 1517–1559*, 2d ed. (Oxford: Blackwell, 1999), 130–32.

287. The poet calls upon Peter to help Pope Paul in his attempt to effect the changes so direly needed. The poet seems aware that thus far his efforts have been in vain and some form of divine intervention is now required. Once again, as in sonnets 98 and 99, the poet's reader is firmly positioned in the context of contemporary Rome, with the tense expectation of religious renewal that the poet describes.

288. The poet, significantly, borrows the tool of a sculptor in this poem, the file with which he would polish and smooth the marble.

289. The poet's self-effacing denouncement of her work in the quatrains reads as a standard literary ploy to establish modesty and humility, especially when read alongside the statements that follow.

290. Once again, as in sonnet 6, the poet seems to be referring to the notion expressed in Valdés's *Catechisms* of faith as a divine fire burning within the chosen ones. Despite themselves, it will emit heat and light, the good works that all true Christians automatically carry out in imitation of Christ. Thus once again the poet succeeds, despite her apparent modesty in the sonnet's opening, in situating herself within the body of the preordained. In addition, the reference allies her with a great tradition of writers, notably Cicero and Petrarch, who claimed that poetry was born of divinely conferred inspiration and could not be achieved through mere toil. See, for example, Petrarch's oration on the capitol of 1341, cited in David Summers, *Michelangelo and the Language of Art* (Princeton: Princeton University Press, 1981), 33–35.

291. The poet highlights the circularity of her sonnet sequence in this manuscript by returning to the notion, cited in sonnet 1, of her altruistic intentions in writing for the benefit of others. The manuscript gift for Michelangelo is firmly established as divinely inspired and conferred, and thus the poet's authority is also subtly reconfirmed.

292. The poet's fear that she has lost touch with the original necessity of her faith reminds us once again of the sonnet in praise of the Saint Luke Madonna (sonnet 45), with its impulse towards earlier and purer, less "artful" modes of worship.

293. Counteracting the conviction expressed in the previous sonnet, here the poet expresses the fear that her verses are not in fact divinely inspired, but only feeble and pointless expressions of her weak, earthbound intellect. There is a sense, however, reflected in the neat binary arrangement of the verbs in the two quatrains, that the poet is only paying lip service to the notion of such a fear.

294.   Petrarchan echoes of sonnet 62, "Padre del ciel, dopo i perduti giorni" ('Eternal father, after the lost days'), in fact serve, despite the poet's lament, to reinforce the subtle affirmation of her supreme poetic skill. The reader infers that her verses are so polished that the spirit invested in them may not always be apparent, almost that she writes perfect poetry *despite* herself.

295.   God is the only true judge of such spiritual poetry. Thus the sonnet can be seen to constitute a bold and final shaking off of the ties of earthly status and the judgment of her fellows. Before God, the poet appears supremely confident that her verses will be understood.

SERIES EDITORS'
BIBLIOGRAPHY

PRIMARY SOURCES

Alberti, Leon Battista (1404–72). *The Family in Renaissance Florence.* Translated by Renée Neu Watkins. Columbia: University of South Carolina Press, 1969.

Arenal, Electa and Stacey Schlau, eds. *Untold Sisters: Hispanic Nuns in Their Own Works.* Translated by Amanda Powell. Albuquerque: University of New Mexico Press, 1989.

Astell, Mary (1666–1731). *The First English Feminist: Reflections on Marriage and Other Writings.* Edited and introduction by Bridget Hill. New York: St. Martin's Press, 1986.

Atherton, Margaret, ed. *Women Philosophers of the Early Modern Period.* Indianapolis, IN: Hackett, 1994.

Aughterson, Kate, ed. *Renaissance Woman: Constructions of Femininity in England: A Source Book.* London: Routledge, 1995.

Barbaro, Francesco (1390–1454). *On Wifely Duties* (preface and book 2). Translated by Benjamin Kohl in Kohl and R. G. Witt, eds., *The Earthly Republic.* Philadelphia: University of Pennsylvania Press, 1978, 179–228.

Behn, Aphra. *The Works of Aphra Behn.* 7 vols. Edited by Janet Todd. Columbus: Ohio State University Press, 1992–96.

Boccaccio, Giovanni (1313–75). *Famous Women.* Edited and translated by Virginia Brown. The I Tatti Renaissance Library. Cambridge, MA: Harvard University Press, 2001.

———. *Corbaccio or the Labyrinth of Love.* Translated by Anthony K. Cassell. 2nd rev. ed. Binghamton, NY: Medieval and Renaissance Texts and Studies, 1993.

Brown, Sylvia. *Women's Writing in Stuart England: The Mother's Legacies of Dorothy Leigh, Elizabeth Joscelin and Elizabeth Richardson.* Thrupp, Stroud, Gloucestershire: Sutton, 1999.

Bruni, Leonardo (1370–1444). "On the Study of Literature (1405) to Lady Battista Malatesta of Moltefeltro." In *The Humanism of Leonardo Bruni: Selected Texts.* Translated and introduction by Gordon Griffiths, James Hankins, and David Thompson. Binghamton, NY: Medieval and Renaissance Studies and Texts, 1987, 240–51.

Castiglione, Baldassare (1478–1529). *The Book of the Courtier.* Translated by George Bull. New York: Penguin, 1967. *The Book of the Courtier.* Edited by Daniel Javitch. New York: W. W. Norton, 2002.

Christine de Pizan (1365–1431). *The Book of the City of Ladies.* Translated by Earl Jeffrey
Richards. Foreword by Marina Warner. New York: Persea, 1982.
———. *The Treasure of the City of Ladies.* Translated by Sarah Lawson. New York:
Viking Penguin, 1985. Also translated and introduction by Charity Cannon
Willard. Edited and introduction by Madeleine P. Cosman. New York: Persea,
1989.

Clarke, Danielle, ed. *Isabella Whitney, Mary Sidney and Aemilia Lanyer: Renaissance Women
Poets.* New York: Penguin, 2000.

Crawford, Patricia, and Laura Gowing, eds. *Women's Worlds in Seventeenth-Century En-
gland: A Source Book.* London: Routledge, 2000.

Daybell, James, ed. *Early Modern Women's Letter Writing, 1450–1700.* Houndmills, En-
gland: Palgrave, 2001.

Elizabeth I: Collected Works. Edited by Leah S. Marcus, Janel Mueller, and Mary Beth
Rose. Chicago: University of Chicago Press, 2000.

Elyot, Thomas (1490–1546). *Defence of Good Women: The Feminist Controversy of the Re-
naissance.* Facsimile Reproductions. Edited by Diane Bornstein. New York: Del-
mar, 1980.

Erasmus, Desiderius (1467–1536). *Erasmus on Women.* Edited by Erika Rummel. To-
ronto: University of Toronto Press, 1996.

Female and Male Voices in Early Modern England: An Anthology of Renaissance Writing. Edited
by Betty S. Travitsky and Anne Lake Prescott. New York: Columbia University
Press, 2000.

Ferguson, Moira, ed. *First Feminists: British Women Writers 1578–1799.* Bloomington: In-
diana University Press, 1985.

Galilei, Maria Celeste. *Sister Maria Celeste's Letters to Her Father, Galileo.* Edited by and
Translated by Rinaldina Russell. Lincoln, NE: Writers Club Press of Universe
.com, 2000. Also published as *To Father: The Letters of Sister Maria Celeste to Galileo,
1623–1633.* Translated by Dava Sobel. London: Fourth Estate, 2001.

Gethner, Perry, ed. *The Lunatic Lover and Other Plays by French Women of the 17th and
18th Centuries.* Portsmouth, NH: Heinemann, 1994.

Glückel of Hameln (1646–1724). *The Memoirs of Glückel of Hameln.* Translated by
Marvin Lowenthal. New introduction by Robert Rosen. New York: Schocken
Books, 1977.

Henderson, Katherine Usher, and Barbara F. McManus, eds. *Half Humankind: Contexts
and Texts of the Controversy about Women in England, 1540–1640.* Urbana: Illinois Uni-
versity Press, 1985.

Hoby, Margaret. *The Private Life of an Elizabethan Lady: The Diary of Lady Margaret Hoby
1599–1605.* Thrupp, Stroud, Gloucestershire: Sutton, 1998.

Humanist Educational Treatises. Edited and translated by Craig W. Kallendorf. The I Tatti
Renaissance Library. Cambridge, MA: Harvard University Press, 2002.

Joscelin, Elizabeth. *The Mothers Legacy to Her Unborn Childe.* Edited by Jean leDrew Met-
calfe. Toronto: University of Toronto Press, 2000.

Kaminsky, Amy Katz, ed. *Water Lilies, Flores del agua: An Anthology of Spanish Women Writ-
ers from the Fifteenth Through the Nineteenth Century.* Minneapolis: University of Minne-
sota Press, 1996.

Kempe, Margery (1373–1439). *The Book of Margery Kempe.* Translated by and edited
by Lynn Staley. A Norton Critical Edition. New York: W. W. Norton, 2001.

King, Margaret L., and Albert Rabil, Jr., eds. *Her Immaculate Hand: Selected Works by and about the Women Humanists of Quattrocento Italy.* Binghamton, NY: Medieval and Renaissance Texts and Studies, 1983; second revised paperback edition, 1991.

Klein, Joan Larsen, ed. *Daughters, Wives, and Widows: Writings by Men about Women and Marriage in England, 1500–1640.* Urbana: University of Illinois Press, 1992.

Knox, John (1505–72). *The Political Writings of John Knox: The First Blast of the Trumpet against the Monstrous Regiment of Women and Other Selected Works.* Edited by Marvin A. Breslow. Washington, DC: Folger Shakespeare Library, 1985.

Kors, Alan C., and Edward Peters, eds. *Witchcraft in Europe, 400–1700: A Documentary History.* Philadelphia: University of Pennsylvania Press, 2000.

Krämer, Heinrich, and Jacob Sprenger. *Malleus Maleficarum* (ca. 1487). Translated by Montague Summers. London: Pushkin Press, 1928. Reprint, New York: Dover, 1971.

Larsen, Anne R., and Colette H. Winn, eds. *Writings by Pre-Revolutionary French Women: From Marie de France to Elizabeth Vigée-Le Brun.* New York: Garland, 2000.

de Lorris, William, and Jean de Meun. *The Romance of the Rose.* Translated by Charles Dahlbert. Princeton, NJ: Princeton University Press, 1971. Reprint, University Press of New England, 1983.

Marguerite d'Angoulême, Queen of Navarre (1492–1549). *The Heptameron.* Translated by P. A. Chilton. New York: Viking Penguin, 1984.

Mary of Agreda. *The Divine Life of the Most Holy Virgin.* Abridgment of *The Mystical City of God.* Abridged by Fr. Bonaventure Amedeo de Caesarea, M.C. Translated from the French by Abbé Joseph A. Boullan. Rockford, IL: Tan Books, 1997.

Myers, Kathleen A., and Amanda Powell, eds. *A Wild Country Out in the Garden: The Spiritual Journals of a Colonial Mexican Nun.* Bloomington: Indiana University Press, 1999.

Russell, Rinaldina, ed. *Sister Maria Celeste's Letters to Her Father, Galileo.* San Jose: Writers Club Press, 2000.

Teresa of Avila, Saint (1515–82). *The Life of Saint Teresa of Avila by Herself.* Translated by J. M. Cohen. New York: Viking Penguin, 1957.

Weyer, Johann (1515–88). *Witches, Devils, and Doctors in the Renaissance: Johann Weyer, De praestigiis daemonum.* Edited by George Mora with Benjamin G. Kohl, Erik Midelfort, and Helen Bacon. Translated by John Shea. Binghamton, NY: Medieval and Renaissance Texts and Studies, 1991.

Wilson, Katharina M., ed. *Medieval Women Writers.* Athens: University of Georgia Press, 1984.

———, ed. *Women Writers of the Renaissance and Reformation.* Athens: University of Georgia Press, 1987.

Wilson, Katharina M., and Frank J. Warnke, eds. *Women Writers of the Seventeenth Century.* Athens: University of Georgia Press, 1989.

Wollstonecraft, Mary. *A Vindication of the Rights of Men and a Vindication of the Rights of Women.* Edited by Sylvana Tomaselli. Cambridge: Cambridge University Press, 1995. Also *The Vindications of the Rights of Men, The Rights of Women.* Edited by D. L. Macdonald and Kathleen Scherf. Peterborough, Ontario, Canada: Broadview Press, 1997.

Women Critics 1660–1820: An Anthology. Edited by the Folger Collective on Early Women Critics. Bloomington: Indiana University Press, 1995.

Women Writers in English, 1350–1850. 15 vols. published through 1999 (projected 30-volume series suspended). Oxford University Press.

Wroth, Lady Mary. *The Countess of Montgomery's Urania.* 2 parts. Edited by Josephine A. Roberts. Tempe, AZ: MRTS, 1995, 1999.

———. *Lady Mary Wroth's "Love's Victory": The Penshurst Manuscript.* Edited by Michael G. Brennan. London: The Roxburghe Club, 1988.

———. *The Poems of Lady Mary Wroth.* Edited by Josephine A. Roberts. Baton Rouge: Louisiana State University Press, 1983.

de Zayas, Maria. *The Disenchantments of Love.* Translated by H. Patsy Boyer. Albany: State University of New York Press, 1997.

———. *The Enchantments of Love: Amorous and Exemplary Novels.* Translated by H. Patsy Boyer. Berkeley and Los Angeles: University of California Press, 1990.

SECONDARY SOURCES

Ahlgren, Gillian. *Teresa of Avila and the Politics of Sanctity.* Ithaca, NY: Cornell University Press, 1996.

Akkerman, Tjitske, and Siep Sturman, eds. *Feminist Thought in European History, 1400–2000.* London: Routledge, 1997.

Allen, Sister Prudence, R.S.M. *The Concept of Woman: The Aristotelian Revolution, 750 B.C.–A.D. 1250.* Grand Rapids, MI: William B. Eerdmans, 1997.

———. *The Concept of Woman.* Vol. 2, *The Early Humanist Reformation, 1250–1500.* Grand Rapids, MI: William B. Eerdmans, 2002.

Andreadis, Harriette. *Sappho in Early Modern England: Female Same-Sex Literary Erotics 1550–1714.* Chicago: University of Chicago Press, 2001.

Armon, Shifra. *Picking Wedlock: Women and the Courtship Novel in Spain.* New York: Rowman & Littlefield Publishers, Inc., 2002.

Backer, Anne Liot Backer. *Precious Women.* New York: Basic Books, 1974.

Ballaster, Ros. *Seductive Forms.* New York: Oxford University Press, 1992.

Barash, Carol. *English Women's Poetry, 1649–1714: Politics, Community, and Linguistic Authority.* New York: Oxford University Press, 1996.

Battigelli, Anna. *Margaret Cavendish and the Exiles of the Mind.* Lexington, KY: University of Kentucky Press, 1998.

Beasley, Faith. *Revising Memory: Women's Fiction and Memoirs in Seventeenth-Century France.* New Brunswick: Rutgers University Press, 1990.

Beilin, Elaine V. *Redeeming Eve: Women Writers of the English Renaissance.* Princeton, NJ: Princeton University Press, 1987.

Benson, Pamela Joseph. *The Invention of Renaissance Woman: The Challenge of Female Independence in the Literature and Thought of Italy and England.* University Park, PA: Pennsylvania State University Press, 1992.

Benson, Pamela Joseph, and Victoria Kirkham, eds. *Strong Voices, Weak History? Medieval and Renaissance Women in their Literary Canons: England, France, Italy.* Ann Arbor: University of Michigan Press, 2003.

Bilinkoff, Jodi. *The Avila of Saint Teresa: Religious Reform in a Sixteenth-Century City.* Ithaca: Cornell University Press, 1989.

Bissell, R. Ward. *Artemisia Gentileschi and the Authority of Art.* University Park: Pennsylvania State University Press, 2000.

Blain, Virginia, Isobel Grundy, AND Patricia Clements, eds. *The Feminist Companion to Literature in English: Women Writers from the Middle Ages to the Present.* New Haven, CT: Yale University Press, 1990.

Bloch, R. Howard. *Medieval Misogyny and the Invention of Western Romantic Love.* Chicago: University of Chicago Press, 1991.

Bornstein, Daniel and Roberto Rusconi, eds. *Women and Religion in Medieval and Renaissance Italy.* Translated by Margery J. Schneider. Chicago: University of Chicago Press, 1996.

Brant, Clare, and Diane Purkiss, eds. *Women, Texts and Histories, 1575–1760.* London: Routledge, 1992.

Briggs, Robin. *Witches and Neighbours: The Social and Cultural Context of European Witchcraft.* New York: HarperCollins, 1995; Viking Penguin, 1996.

Brink, Jean R., ed. *Female Scholars: A Tradition of Learned Women before 1800.* Montréal: Eden Press Women's Publications, 1980.

Broude, Norma, and Mary D. Garrard, eds. *The Expanding Discourse: Feminism and Art History.* New York: HarperCollins, 1992.

Brown, Judith C. *Immodest Acts: The Life of a Lesbian Nun in Renaissance Italy.* New York: Oxford University Press, 1986.

Brown, Judith C. , and Robert C. Davis, eds. *Gender and Society in Renaissance Italy.* London: Addison Wesley Longman, 1998.

Bynum, Carolyn Walker. *Fragmentation and Redemption: Essays on Gender and the Human Body in Medieval Religion.* New York: Zone Books, 1992.

———. *Holy Feast and Holy Fast: The Religious Significance of Food to Medieval Women.* Berkeley: University of California Press, 1987.

Cambridge Guide to Women's Writing in English. Edited by Lorna Sage. Cambridge: University Press, 1999.

Cavanagh, Sheila T. *Cherished Torment: The Emotional Geography of Lady Mary Wroth's Urania.* Pittsburgh: Duquesne University Press, 2001.

Cerasano, S. P. and Marion Wynne-Davies, eds. *Readings in Renaissance Women's Drama: Criticism, History, and Performance 1594–1998.* London: Routledge, 1998.

Cervigni, Dino S., ed. *Women Mystic Writers. Annali d'Italianistica* 13 (1995) (entire issue).

Cervigni, Dino S., and Rebecca West, eds. *Women's Voices in Italian Literature. Annali d'Italianistica* 7 (1989) (entire issue).

Charlton, Kenneth. *Women, Religion and Education in Early Modern England.* London: Routledge, 1999.

Chojnacka, Monica. *Working Women in Early Modern Venice.* Baltimore: Johns Hopkins University Press, 2001.

Chojnacki, Stanley. *Women and Men in Renaissance Venice: Twelve Essays on Patrician Society.* Baltimore: Johns Hopkins University Press, 2000.

Cholakian, Patricia Francis. *Rape and Writing in the "Heptameron" of Marguerite de Navarre.* Carbondale: Southern Illinois University Press, 1991.

———. *Women and the Politics of Self-Representation in Seventeenth-Century France.* Newark: University of Delaware Press, 2000.

Christine de Pizan: A Casebook. Edited by Barbara K. Altmann and Deborah L. McGrady. New York: Routledge, 2003.

Clogan, Paul Maruice, ed. *Medievali et Humanistica: Literacy and the Lay Reader.* Lanham, MD: Rowman & Littlefield, 2000.

Clubb, Louise George (1989). *Italian Drama in Shakespeare's Time*. New Haven, CT: Yale University Press.

Conley, John J., S.J. *The Suspicion of Virtue: Women Philosophers in Neoclassical France*. Ithaca, NY: Cornell University Press, 2002.

Crabb, Ann. *The Strozzi of Florence: Widowhood and Family Solidarity in the Renaissance*. Ann Arbor: University of Michigan Press, 2000.

Cruz, Anne J., and Mary Elizabeth Perry, eds. *Culture and Control in Counter-Reformation Spain*. Minneapolis: University of Minnesota Press, 1992.

Davis, Natalie Zemon. *Society and Culture in Early Modern France*. Stanford: Stanford University Press, 1975. Especially chapters 3 and 5.

———. *Women on the Margins: Three Seventeenth-Century Lives*. Cambridge, MA: Harvard University Press, 1995.

DeJean, Joan. *Ancients Against Moderns: Culture Wars and the Making of a Fin de Siècle*. Chicago: University of Chicago Press, 1997.

———. *Fictions of Sappho, 1546–1937*. Chicago: University of Chicago Press, 1989.

———. *The Reinvention of Obscenity: Sex, Lies, and Tabloids in Early Modern France*. Chicago: University of Chicago Press, 2002.

———. *Tender Geographies: Women and the Origins of the Novel in France*. New York: Columbia University Press, 1991.

Dictionary of Russian Women Writers. Edited by Marina Ledkovsky, Charlotte Rosenthal, and Mary Zirin. Westport, CT: Greenwood Press, 1994.

Dixon, Laurinda S. *Perilous Chastity: Women and Illness in Pre-Enlightenment Art and Medicine*. Ithaca: Cornell Universitiy Press, 1995.

Dolan, Frances, E. *Whores of Babylon: Catholicism, Gender and Seventeenth-Century Print Culture*. Ithaca: Cornell University Press, 1999.

Donovan, Josephine. *Women and the Rise of the Novel, 1405–1726*. New York: St. Martin's Press, 1999.

De Erauso, Catalina. *Lieutenant Nun: Memoir of a Basque Transvestite in the New World*. Translated by Michele Ttepto and Gabriel Stepto; foreword by Marjorie Garber. Boston: Beacon Press, 1995.

Encyclopedia of Continental Women Writers. 2 vols. Edited by Katharina Wilson. New York: Garland, 1991.

Erdmann, Axel. *My Gracious Silence: Women in the Mirror of Sixteenth-Century Printing in Western Europe*. Luzern: Gilhofer and Rauschberg, 1999.

Erickson, Amy Louise. *Women and Property in Early Modern England*. London: Routledge, 1993.

Ezell, Margaret J. M. *The Patriarch's Wife: Literary Evidence and the History of the Family*. Chapel Hill: University of North Carolina Press, 1987.

———. *Social Authorship and the Advent of Print*. Baltimore: Johns Hopkins University Press, 1999.

———. *Writing Women's Literary History*. Baltimore: Johns Hopkins University Press, 1993.

Farrell, Michèle Longino. *Performing Motherhood: The Sévigné Correspondence*. Hanover, NH: University Press of New England, 1991.

The Feminist Companion to Literature in English: Women Writers from the Middle Ages to the Present. Edited by Virginia Blain, Isobel Grundy, and Patricia Clements. New Haven, CT: Yale University Press, 1990.

The Feminist Encyclopedia of German Literature. Edited by Friederike Eigler and Susanne Kord. Westport, CT: Greenwood Press, 1997.

Feminist Encyclopedia of Italian Literature. Edited by Rinaldina Russell. Westport, CT: Greenwood Press, 1997.

Ferguson, Margaret W. *Dido's Daughters: Literacy, Gender, and Empire in Early Modern England and France.* Chicago: University of Chicago Press, 2003.

Ferguson, Margaret W., Maureen Quilligan, and Nancy J. Vickers, eds. *Rewriting the Renaissance: The Discourses of Sexual Difference in Early Modern Europe.* Chicago: University of Chicago Press, 1987.

Ferraro, Joanne M. *Marriage Wars in Late Renaissance Venice.* Oxford: Oxford University Press, 2001.

Fletcher, Anthony. *Gender, Sex and Subordination in England 1500–1800.* New Haven, CT: Yale University Press, 1995.

French Women Writers: A Bio-Bibliographical Source Book. Edited by Eva Martin Sartori and Dorothy Wynne Zimmerman. Westport, CT: Greenwood Press, 1991.

Frye, Susan and Karen Robertson, eds. *Maids and Mistresses, Cousins and Queens: Women's Alliances in Early Modern England.* Oxford: Oxford University Press, 1999.

Gallagher, Catherine. *Nobody's Story: The Vanishing Acts of Women Writers in the Marketplace, 1670–1820.* Berkeley: University of California Press, 1994.

Garrard, Mary D. *Artemisia Gentileschi: The Image of the Female Hero in Italian Baroque Art.* Princeton, NJ: Princeton University Press, 1989.

Gelbart, Nina Rattner. *The King's Midwife: A History and Mystery of Madame du Coudray.* Berkeley: University of California Press, 1998.

Glenn, Cheryl. *Rhetoric Retold: Regendering the Tradition from Antiquity through the Renaissance.* Carbondale: Southern Illinois University Press, 1997.

Goffen, Rona. *Titian's Women.* New Haven, CT: Yale University Press, 1997.

Goldberg, Jonathan. *Desiring Women Writing: English Renaissance Examples.* Stanford: Stanford University Press, 1997.

Goldsmith, Elizabeth C. *Exclusive Conversations: The Art of Interaction in Seventeenth-Century France.* Philadelphia: University of Pennsylvania Press, 1988.

———, ed. *Writing the Female Voice.* Boston: Northeastern University Press, 1989.

Goldsmith, Elizabeth C., and Dena Goodman, eds. *Going Public: Women and Publishing in Early Modern France.* Ithaca: Cornell University Press, 1995.

Grafton, Anthony, and Lisa Jardine. *From Humanism to the Humanities: Education and the Liberal Arts in Fifteenth-and Sixteenth-Century Europe.* London: Duckworth, 1986.

Greer, Margaret Rich. *Maria de Zayas Tells Baroque Tales of Love and the Cruelty of Men.* University Park: Pennsylvania State University Press, 2000.

Hackett, Helen. *Women and Romance Fiction in the English Renaissance.* Cambridge: Cambridge University Press, 2000.

Hall, Kim F. *Things of Darkness: Economies of Race and Gender in Early Modern England.* Ithaca, NY: Cornell University Press, 1995.

Hampton, Timothy. *Literature and the Nation in the Sixteenth Century: Inventing Renaissance France.* Ithaca, NY: Cornell University Press, 2001.

Hannay, Margaret, ed. *Silent But for the Word.* Kent, OH: Kent State University Press, 1985.

Hardwick, Julie. *The Practice of Patriarchy: Gender and the Politics of Household Authority in Early Modern France.* University Park: Pennsylvania State University Press, 1998.

Harris, Barbara J. *English Aristocratic Women, 1450–1550: Marriage and Family, Property and Careers.* New York: Oxford University Press, 2002.

Harth, Erica. *Ideology and Culture in Seventeenth-Century France.* Ithaca: Cornell University Press, 1983.

——. *Cartesian Women: Versions and Subversions of Rational Discourse in the Old Regime.* Ithaca: Cornell University Press, 1992.

Harvey, Elizabeth D. *Ventriloquized Voices: Feminist Theory and English Renaissance Texts.* London: Routledge, 1992.

Haselkorn, Anne M., and Betty Travitsky, eds. *The Renaissance Englishwoman in Print: Counterbalancing the Canon.* Amherst: University of Massachusetts Press, 1990.

Herlihy, David. "Did Women Have a Renaissance? A Reconsideration." *Medievalia et Humanistica,* NS 13 (1985): 1–22.

Hill, Bridget. *The Republican Virago: The Life and Times of Catharine Macaulay, Historian.* New York: Oxford University Press, 1992.

A History of Central European Women's Writing. Edited by Celia Hawkesworth. New York: Palgrave Press, 2001.

A History of Women in the West.
  Volume 1: *From Ancient Goddesses to Christian Saints.* Edited by Pauline Schmitt Pantel. Cambridge, MA: Harvard University Press, 1992.
  Volume 2: *Silences of the Middle Ages.* Edited by Christiane Klapisch-Zuber. Cambridge, MA: Harvard University Press, 1992.
  Volume 3: *Renaissance and Enlightenment Paradoxes.* Edited by Natalie Zemon Davis and Arlette Farge. Cambridge, MA: Harvard University Press, 1993.

A History of Women Philosophers. Edited by Mary Ellen Waithe. 3 vols. Dordrecht: Martinus Nijhoff, 1987.

A History of Women's Writing in France. Edited by Sonya Stephens. Cambridge: Cambridge University Press, 2000.

A History of Women's Writing in Germany, Austria and Switzerland. Edited by Jo Catling. Cambridge: Cambridge University Press, 2000.

A History of Women's Writing in Italy. Edited by Letizia Panizza and Sharon Wood. Cambridge: University Press, 2000.

A History of Women's Writing in Russia. Edited by Alele Marie Barker and Jehanne M. Gheith. Cambridge: Cambridge University Press, 2002.

Hobby, Elaine. *Virtue of Necessity: English Women's Writing 1646–1688.* London: Virago Press, 1988.

Horowitz, Maryanne Cline. "Aristotle and Women." *Journal of the History of Biology* 9 (1976): 183–213.

Howell, Martha. *The Marriage Exchange: Property, Social Place, and Gender in Cities of the Low Countries, 1300–1550.* Chicago: University of Chicago Press, 1998.

Hufton, Olwen H. *The Prospect Before Her: A History of Women in Western Europe, 1: 1500–1800.* New York: HarperCollins, 1996.

Hull, Suzanne W. *Chaste, Silent, and Obedient: English Books for Women, 1475–1640.* San Marino, CA: The Huntington Library, 1982.

Hunt, Lynn, ed. *The Invention of Pornography: Obscenity and the Origins of Modernity, 1500–1800.* New York: Zone Books, 1996.

Hutner, Heidi, ed. *Rereading Aphra Behn: History, Theory, and Criticism.* Charlottesville: University Press of Virginia, 1993.

Hutson, Lorna, ed. *Feminism and Renaissance Studies.* New York: Oxford University Press, 1999.

Italian Women Writers: A Bio-Bibliographical Sourcebook. Edited by Rinaldina Russell. West-port, CT: Greenwood Press, 1994.

Jaffe, Irma B., with Gernando Colombardo. *Shining Eyes, Cruel Fortune: The Lives and Loves of Italian Renaissance Women Poets.* New York: Fordham University Press, 2002.

James, Susan E. *Kateryn Parr: The Making of a Queen.* Aldershot: Ashgate, 1999.

Jankowski, Theodora A. *Women in Power in the Early Modern Drama.* Urbana: University of Illinois Press, 1992.

Jansen, Katherine Ludwig. *The Making of the Magdalen: Preaching and Popular Devotion in the Later Middle Ages.* Princeton, NJ: Princeton University Press, 2000.

Jed, Stephanie H. *Chaste Thinking: The Rape of Lucretia and the Birth of Humanism.* Bloo-mington: Indiana University Press, 1989.

Jordan, Constance. *Renaissance Feminism: Literary Texts and Political Models.* Ithaca: Cor-nell University Press, 1990.

Kagan, Richard L. *Lucrecia's Dreams: Politics and Prophecy in Sixteenth-Century Spain.* Berke-ley: University of California Press, 1990.

Kehler, Dorothea and Laurel Amtower, eds. *The Single Woman in Medieval and Early Mod-ern England: Her Life and Representation.* Tempe, AZ: MRTS, 2002.

Kelly, Joan. "Did Women Have a Renaissance?" In her *Women, History, and Theory.* Chicago: University of Chicago Press, 1984. Also in Renate Bridenthal, Claudia Koonz, and Susan M. Stuard, eds., *Becoming Visible: Women in European History.* 3rd ed. Boston: Houghton Mifflin, 1998.

————. "Early Feminist Theory and the *Querelle des Femmes.*" In *Women, History, and Theory.*

Kelso, Ruth. *Doctrine for the Lady of the Renaissance.* Foreword by Katharine M. Rogers. Urbana: University of Illinois Press, 1956, 1978.

King, Catherine E. *Renaissance Women Patrons: Wives and Widows in Italy, c. 1300–1550.* Manchester: Manchester University Press (distributed in the U.S. by St. Martin's Press), 1998.

King, Margaret L. *Women of the Renaissance.* Foreword by Catharine R. Stimpson. Chi-cago: University of Chicago Press, 1991.

Krontiris, Tina. *Oppositional Voices: Women as Writers and Translators of Literature in the En-glish Renaissance.* London: Routledge, 1992.

Kuehn, Thomas. *Law, Family, and Women: Toward a Legal Anthropology of Renaissance Italy.* Chicago: University of Chicago Press, 1991.

Kunze, Bonnelyn Young. *Margaret Fell and the Rise of Quakerism.* Stanford: Stanford Uni-versity Press, 1994.

Labalme, Patricia A., ed. *Beyond Their Sex: Learned Women of the European Past.* New York: New York University Press, 1980.

Laqueur, Thomas. *Making Sex: Body and Gender from the Greeks to Freud.* Cambridge, MA: Harvard University Press, 1990.

Larsen, Anne R. and Colette H. Winn, eds. *Renaissance Women Writers: French Texts/Amer-ican Contexts.* Detroit, MI: Wayne State University Press, 1994.

Lerner, Gerda. *The Creation of Patriarchy* and *Creation of Feminist Consciousness, 1000–1870.* 2 vols. New York: Oxford University Press, 1986, 1994.

Levin, Carole, and Jeanie Watson, eds. *Ambiguous Realities: Women in the Middle Ages and Renaissance.* Detroit: Wayne State University Press, 1987.

Levin, Carole, et al. *Extraordinary Women of the Medieval and Renaissance World: A Biographical Dictionary.* Westport, CT: Greenwood Press, 2000.

Lewalsky, Barbara Kiefer. *Writing Women in Jacobean England.* Cambridge, MA: Harvard University Press, 1993.

Lewis, Jayne Elizabeth. *Mary Queen of Scots: Romance and Nation.* London: Routledge, 1998.

Lindsey, Karen. *Divorced Beheaded Survived: A Feminist Reinterpretation of the Wives of Henry VIII.* Reading, MA: Addison-Wesley, 1995.

Lochrie, Karma. *Margery Kempe and Translations of the Flesh.* Philadelphia: University of Pennsylvania Press, 1992.

Lougee, Carolyn C. *Le Paradis des Femmes: Women, Salons, and Social Stratification in Seventeenth-Century France.* Princeton, NJ: Princeton University Press, 1976.

Love, Harold. *The Culture and Commerce of Texts: Scribal Publication in Seventeenth-Century England.* Amherst: University of Massachusetts Press, 1993.

MacCarthy, Bridget G. *The Female Pen: Women Writers and Novelists, 1621–1818.* Preface by Janet Todd. New York: New York University Press, 1994. Originally published 1946–47 by Cork University Press.

Maclean, Ian. *Woman Triumphant: Feminism in French Literature, 1610–1652.* Oxford: Clarendon Press, 1977.

———. *The Renaissance Notion of Woman: A Study of the Fortunes of Scholasticism and Medical Science in European Intellectual Life.* Cambridge: Cambridge University Press, 1980.

MacNeil, Anne. *Music and Women of the Commedia dell'Arte in the Late Sixteenth Century.* New York: Oxford University Press, 2003.

Maggi, Armando. *Uttering the Word: The Mystical Performances of Maria Maddalena de' Pazzi, a Renaissance Visionary.* Albany: State University of New York Press, 1998.

Marshall, Sherrin. *Women in Reformation and Counter-Reformation Europe: Public and Private Worlds.* Bloomington: Indiana University Press, 1989.

Masten, Jeffrey. *Textual Intercourse: Collaboration, Authorship, and Sexualities in Renaissance Drama.* Cambridge: Cambridge University Press, 1997.

Matter, E. Ann, and John Coakley, eds. *Creative Women in Medieval and Early Modern Italy.* Philadelphia: University of Pennsylvania Press, 1994. (Sequel to the Monson collection, below.)

McLeod, Glenda. *Virtue and Venom: Catalogs of Women from Antiquity to the Renaissance.* Ann Arbor: University of Michigan Press, 1991.

Medwick, Cathleen. *Teresa of Avila: The Progress of a Soul.* New York: Knopf, 2000.

Meek, Christine, ed. *Women in Renaissance and Early Modern Europe.* Dublin-Portland: Four Courts Press, 2000.

Mendelson, Sara and Patricia Crawford. *Women in Early Modern England, 1550–1720.* Oxford: Clarendon Press, 1998.

Merchant, Carolyn. *The Death of Nature: Women, Ecology, and the Scientific Revolution.* New York: HarperCollins, 1980.

Merrim, Stephanie. *Early Modern Women's Writing and Sor Juana Inés de la Cruz.* Nashville, TN: Vanderbilt University Press, 1999.

Messbarger, Rebecca. *The Century of Women: The Representations of Women in Eighteenth-Century Italian Public Discourse.* Toronto: University of Toronto Press, 2002.

Miller, Nancy K. *The Heroine's Text: Readings in the French and English Novel, 1722–1782.* New York: Columbia University Press, 1980.

Miller, Naomi J. *Changing the Subject: Mary Wroth and Figurations of Gender in Early Modern England*. Lexington: University Press of Kentucky, 1996.

Miller, Naomi J., and Gary Waller, eds. *Reading Mary Wroth: Representing Alternatives in Early Modern England*. Knoxville: University of Tennessee Press, 1991.

Monson, Craig A., ed. *The Crannied Wall: Women, Religion, and the Arts in Early Modern Europe*. Ann Arbor: University of Michigan Press, 1992.

Musacchio, Jacqueline Marie. *The Art and Ritual of Childbirth in Renaissance Italy*. New Haven, CT: Yale University Press, 1999.

Newman, Barbara. *God and the Goddesses: Vision, Poetry, and Belief in the Middle Ages*. Philadelphia: University of Pennsylvania Press, 2003.

Newman, Karen. *Fashioning Femininity and English Renaissance Drama*. Chicago: University of Chicago Press, 1991.

Okin, Susan Moller. *Women in Western Political Thought*. Princeton, NJ: Princeton University Press, 1979.

Ozment, Steven. *The Bürgermeister's Daughter: Scandal in a Sixteenth-Century German Town*. New York: St. Martin's Press, 1995.

Pacheco, Anita, ed. *Early [English] Women Writers: 1600–1720*. New York: Longman, 1998.

Pagels, Elaine. *Adam, Eve, and the Serpent*. New York: HarperCollins, 1988.

Panizza, Letizia, ed. *Women in Italian Renaissance Culture and Society*. Oxford: European Humanities Research Centre, 2000.

Parker, Patricia. *Literary Fat Ladies: Rhetoric, Gender, and Property*. London: Methuen, 1987.

Pernoud, Regine, and Marie-Veronique Clin. *Joan of Arc: Her Story*. Revised and translated by Jeremy DuQuesnay Adams. New York: St. Martin's Press, 1998 (French original, 1986).

Perry, Mary Elizabeth. *Crime and Society in Early Modern Seville*. Hanover, NH: University Press of New England, 1980.

———. *Gender and Disorder in Early Modern Seville*. Princeton, NJ: Princeton University Press, 1990.

Perry, Ruth. *The Celebrated Mary Astell: An Early English Feminist*. Chicago: University of Chicago Press, 1986.

Petroff, Elizabeth Alvilda, ed. *Medieval Women's Visionary Literature*. New York: Oxford University Press, 1986.

Rabil, Albert. *Laura Cereta: Quattrocento Humanist*. Binghamton, NY: MRTS, 1981.

Ranft, Patricia. *Women in Western Intellectual Culture, 600–1500*. New York: Palgrave, 2002.

Rapley, Elizabeth. *A Social History of the Cloister: Daily Life in the Teaching Monasteries of the Old Regime*. Montreal: McGill-Queen's University Press, 2001.

Raven, James, Helen Small, and Naomi Tadmor, eds. *The Practice and Representation of Reading in England*. Cambridge: University Press, 1996.

Reardon, Colleen. *Holy Concord within Sacred Walls: Nuns and Music in Siena, 1575–1700*. Oxford: Oxford University Press, 2001.

Reiss, Sheryl E., and David G. Wilkins, ed. *Beyond Isabella: Secular Women Patrons of Art in Renaissance Italy*. Kirksville, MO: Truman State University Press, 2001.

Rheubottom, David. *Age, Marriage, and Politics in Fifteenth-Century Ragusa*. Oxford: Oxford University Press, 2000.

Richardson, Brian. *Printing, Writers and Readers in Renaissance Italy.* Cambridge: University Press, 1999.

Riddle, John M. *Contraception and Abortion from the Ancient World to the Renaissance.* Cambridge, MA: Harvard University Press, 1992.

——. *Eve's Herbs: A History of Contraception and Abortion in the West.* Cambridge, MA: Harvard University Press, 1997.

Rose, Mary Beth. *The Expense of Spirit: Love and Sexuality in English Renaissance Drama.* Ithaca, NY: Cornell University Press, 1988.

——. *Gender and Heroism in Early Modern English Literature.* Chicago: University of Chicago Press, 2002.

——, ed. *Women in the Middle Ages and the Renaissance: Literary and Historical Perspectives.* Syracuse: Syracuse University Press, 1986.

Rosenthal, Margaret F. *The Honest Courtesan: Veronica Franco, Citizen and Writer in Sixteenth-Century Venice.* Foreword by Catharine R. Stimpson. Chicago: University of Chicago Press, 1992.

Sackville-West, Vita. *Daughter of France: The Life of La Grande Mademoiselle.* Garden City, NY: Doubleday, 1959.

Sánchez, Magdalena S. *The Empress, the Queen, and the Nun: Women and Power at the Court of Philip III of Spain.* Baltimore: Johns Hopkins University Press, 1998.

Schiebinger, Londa. *The Mind Has No Sex? Women in the Origins of Modern Science.* Cambridge, MA: Harvard University Press, 1991.

——. *Nature's Body: Gender in the Making of Modern Science.* Boston: Beacon Press, 1993.

Schutte, Anne Jacobson, Thomas Kuehn, and Silvana Seidel Menchi, eds. *Time, Space, and Women's Lives in Early Modern Europe.* Kirksville, MO: Truman State University Press, 2001.

Schofield, Mary Anne, and Cecilia Macheski, eds. *Fetter'd or Free? British Women Novelists, 1670–1815.* Athens: Ohio University Press, 1986.

Shannon, Laurie. *Sovereign Amity: Figures of Friendship in Shakespearean Contexts.* Chicago: University of Chicago Press, 2002.

Shemek, Deanna. *Ladies Errant: Wayward Women and Social Order in Early Modern Italy.* Durham, NC: Duke University Press, 1998.

Smith, Hilda L. *Reason's Disciples: Seventeenth-Century English Feminists.* Urbana: University of Illinois Press, 1982.

——. *Women Writers and the Early Modern British Political Tradition.* Cambridge: Cambridge University Press, 1998.

Sobel, Dava. *Galileo's Daughter: A Historical Memoir of Science, Faith, and Love.* New York: Penguin, 2000.

Sommerville, Margaret R. *Sex and Subjection: Attitudes to Women in Early-Modern Society.* London: Arnold, 1995.

Soufas, Teresa Scott. *Dramas of Distinction: A Study of Plays by Golden Age Women.* Lexington: The University Press of Kentucky, 1997.

Spencer, Jane. *The Rise of the Woman Novelist: From Aphra Behn to Jane Austen.* Oxford: Basil Blackwell, 1986.

Spender, Dale. *Mothers of the Novel: 100 Good Women Writers Before Jane Austen.* London: Routledge, 1986.

Sperling, Jutta Gisela. *Convents and the Body Politic in Late Renaissance Venice.* Foreword by Catharine R. Stimpson. Chicago: University of Chicago Press, 1999.

Steinbrügge, Lieselotte. *The Moral Sex: Woman's Nature in the French Enlightenment.* Translated by Pamela E. Selwyn. New York: Oxford University Press, 1995.

Stocker, Margarita. *Judith, Sexual Warrior: Women and Power in Western Culture.* New Haven, CT: Yale University Press, 1998.

Stretton, Timothy. *Women Waging Law in Elizabethan England.* Cambridge: Cambridge University Press, 1998.

Stuard, Susan M. "The Dominion of Gender: Women's Fortunes in the High Middle Ages." In *Becoming Visible: Women in European History,* edited by Renate Bridenthal, Claudia Koonz, and Susan M. Stuard. 3rd ed. Boston: Houghton Mifflin, 1998.

Summit, Jennifer. *Lost Property: The Woman Writer and English Literary History, 1380–1589.* Chicago: University of Chicago Press, 2000.

Surtz, Ronald E. *The Guitar of God: Gender, Power, and Authority in the Visionary World of Mother Juana de la Cruz (1481–1534).* Philadelphia: University of Pennsylvania Press, 1991.

———. *Writing Women in Late Medieval and Early Modern Spain: The Mothers of Saint Teresa of Avila.* Philadelphia: University of Pennsylvania Press, 1995.

Teague, Frances. *Bathsua Makin, Woman of Learning.* Lewisburg, PA: Bucknell University Press, 1999.

Tinagli, Paola. *Women in Italian Renaissance Art: Gender, Representation, Identity.* Manchester: Manchester University Press, 1997.

Todd, Janet. *The Secret Life of Aphra Behn.* London: Pandora, 2000.

———. *The Sign of Angelica: Women, Writing and Fiction, 1660–1800.* New York: Columbia University Press, 1989.

Valenze, Deborah. *The First Industrial Woman.* New York: Oxford University Press, 1995.

Van Dijk, Susan, Lia van Gemert, and Sheila Ottway, eds. *Writing the History of Women's Writing: Toward an International Approach.* Proceedings of the Colloquium, Amsterdam, 9–11 September. Amsterdam: Royal Netherlands Academy of Arts and Sciences, 2001.

Vickery, Amanda. *The Gentleman's Daughter: Women's Lives in Georgian England.* New Haven, CT: Yale University Press, 1998.

Vollendorf, Lisa, ed. *Recovering Spain's Feminist Tradition.* New York: MLA, 2001.

Walker, Claire. *Gender and Politics in Early Modern Europe: English Convents in France and the Low Countries.* New York: Palgrave, 2003.

Wall, Wendy. *The Imprint of Gender: Authorship and Publication in the English Renaissance.* Ithaca, NY: Cornell University Press, 1993.

Walsh, William T. *St. Teresa of Avila: A Biography.* Rockford, IL: TAN, 1987.

Warner, Marina. *Alone of All Her Sex: The Myth and Cult of the Virgin Mary.* New York: Knopf, 1976.

Warnicke, Retha M. *The Marrying of Anne of Cleves: Royal Protocol in Tudor England.* Cambridge: Cambridge University Press, 2000.

Watt, Diane. *Secretaries of God: Women Prophets in Late Medieval and Early Modern England.* Cambridge: D. S. Brewer, 1997.

Weber, Alison. *Teresa of Avila and the Rhetoric of Femininity.* Princeton, NJ: Princeton University Press, 1990.

Welles, Marcia L. *Persephone's Girdle: Narratives of Rape in Seventeenth-Century Spanish Literature.* Nashville: Vanderbilt University Press, 2000.

Whitehead, Barbara J., ed. *Women's Education in Early Modern Europe: A History, 1500–1800.* New York: Garland, 1999.

Wiesner, Merry E. *Women and Gender in Early Modern Europe.* Cambridge: Cambridge University Press, 1993.

———. *Working Women in Renaissance Germany.* New Brunswick, NJ: Rutgers University Press, 1986.

Willard, Charity Cannon. *Christine de Pizan: Her Life and Works.* New York: Persea Books, 1984.

Winn, Colette and Donna Kuizenga, eds. *Women Writers in Pre-Revolutionary France.* New York: Garland, 1997.

Woodbridge, Linda. *Women and the English Renaissance: Literature and the Nature of Womankind, 1540–1620.* Urbana: University of Illinois Press, 1984.

Woods, Susanne. *Lanyer: A Renaissance Woman Poet.* New York: Oxford University Press, 1999.

Woods, Susanne, and Margaret P. Hannay, eds. *Teaching Tudor and Stuart Women Writers.* New York: MLA, 2000.

INDEX OF FIRST LINES

GENERAL INDEX

Accademia Pontaniana, 15
Adam: and Eve, 121, 142n15, 147n56,
    164n223, 165n238; sin of, 59,
    164n224, 163n220. *See also* Eve
Agrippa, Henricus Cornelius, 166n251
alchemy, 129, 166n251, 166n253–
    54
Andreini (or Adreini), Isabella, 2n7, 5
Andrew, Saint, 95, 156n135–36
Apollo, 93, 141n5, 155n133
Ariosto, Ludovico, 11; *Orlando furioso,*
    ˋ 1–2, 19
Aristotle: misogyny of, 4; *Metaphysics,*
    161n195; *On the Generation of Animals,*
    150n78
Ascension of Christ, 165n244
Asolani, Gli (Bembo), 40
Augustine, Saint, 14, 15, 144n32

Baptism of Christ, 127, 144n32,
    156n141, 165n246, 166n248.
    See also John the Baptist, Saint
Battiferri Ammannati, Laura, 3n7
bees, 77, 150n78
Bembo, Pietro: as Colonna's mentor, 8,
    11, 12, 19n61; in Colonna's son-
    nets, 37, 135, 168–69nn274–78;
    critical commentary on, 22n71; as
    linguist, 3, 19, 40; works of (*see un-
    der individual works*)
Beneficio di Cristo, Il (Mantova): anti-
    intellectualism in, 149n72; bride of

Christ imagery in, 146n42; and the
    ecclesia viterbiensis, 16–17l; military
    imagery in, 30, 151n92, 152n100,
    159n175; poetic language of, 21,
    147n48; representation of Christ
    in, 29, 31, 142n17, 143n24,
    161n193
blood of Christ: cleansing qualities
    of, 63, 144n32; as food, 142n10,
    153n110, 165n241; as fountain, 79,
    87, 113, 129, 152n110; as gift to
    God, 31; as ink, 23, 35, 57; as ru-
    bies, 87
Boccaccio, Giovanni, 29n93
Bonaventure, Saint, 151n96; *Meditatio-
    nes vitae Christi,* 156n138, 157n153.
    See also empathic meditation
Bullock, Allan, viii, 1n2, 38n123, 39–
    40, 150n85
Buonarroti, Michelangelo: artworks by,
    xxxii, 30, 153n120; Colonna's man-
    uscript for, 15, 18, 33–39; friend-
    ship with Colonna, 12, 26–29;
    poetic language, 142n3, 143n24,
    146n42; religious thought of, 30–
    31

Calvin, Jean, 12: imported works by,
    16; *Institutes,* 31, 160n182; on pre-
    destination, 15
Campiglia, Maddalena, 5
Candlemas, 154n122

Made in the USA
San Bernardino, CA
29 June 2014